AN INTRODUCTION TO
WOLFRAM'S 'PARZIVAL'

wie Herzeloyden kint den grâl
erwarp, als im daz gordent was.
                    Parzival 827, 6 f.

AN
INTRODUCTION TO
WOLFRAM'S
'PARZIVAL'

BY

HUGH SACKER

Lecturer in German in
University College London

CAMBRIDGE
AT THE UNIVERSITY PRESS
1963

PUBLISHED BY
THE SYNDICS OF THE CAMBRIDGE UNIVERSITY PRESS
Bentley House, 200 Euston Road, London, N.W.1
American Branch: 32 East 57th Street, New York 22, N.Y.
West African Office: P.O. Box 33, Ibadan, Nigeria

©

CAMBRIDGE UNIVERSITY PRESS
1963

Printed in Great Britain by
Spottiswoode, Ballantyne & Co. Ltd., London and Colchester

For Liza

CONTENTS

PREFACE

Wolfram von Eschenbach's *Parzival*, which dates from the first decade of the thirteenth century and is written in medieval German, is proved to have enjoyed considerable success in its own day by the large number of manuscripts which have survived in whole or part, and by the influence it had on later writers. Since it was first rediscovered by Bodmer in the mid eighteenth century[1] and published in a scholarly edition by Lachmann in 1833, it has been studied and admired by scholars of medieval German almost more than any other work. Both its medieval and its modern popularity are paralleled by those of other works of its time; but, in spite of fierce arguments which suggest the contrary, it seems to me that scholars have made more progress with *Parzival* than with other great medieval German works, and are in general more agreed about its interpretation. In writing this book I have therefore set out to introduce new students to the work as it has appeared to leading scholars in the first half of this century. I do this not because I think that future students should feel bound by the work of their predecessors—indeed, the weakness of the most recent *Parzival* scholarship lies precisely in its failure to break new ground successfully—but because they can hardly start at all without a clear impression of prevailing positions.

Wolfram's story is complicated, and his language tortuous. Accordingly beginners find *Parzival* difficult to read—and are not helped by the total lack of an extensive introductory work in any language. Dr M. F. Richey has helped English readers by her studies and translations,[2] but she has not attempted a full introduction; and the one possible German candidate, Benedikt Mockenhaupt's doctoral thesis, *Die Frömmigkeit im Parzival Wolframs von Eschenbach*,[3] has very disappointingly not

---

[1] See Paul Merker,'J. J. Bodmers Parzivalbearbeitung' in *Vom Werden des deutschen Geistes. Festgabe Gustav Ehrismann* (Berlin and Leipzig, 1925).

[2] See especially *Studies of Wolfram von Eschenbach* (Edinburgh and London, 1957).   [3] Bonn, 1942.

been reprinted since its stocks were destroyed in the last war. I hope the present book will fill this gap, at least for English-speaking undergraduates. After reading it, they should be equipped both to explore *Parzival* for themselves and to understand the arguments which pervade the literature about it. They should not, however, consider this book as more than introductory.

On occasion I have thought it worth while to dispute the opinions of other critics or to refer to other medieval works besides *Parzival*; in general, however, my limits are those of the single work under study. The justification of this limitation lies in the twin belief that Wolfram's *Parzival* is a successful work of art, and that any successful work of art is to a considerable degree autonomous. Works of art arise out of a particular background, the background of their creator and his world, and of the artistic tradition to which they adhere—and a knowledge of this background will facilitate access to them. Too great an insistence on it will nevertheless obscure the independent originality, the created uniqueness, of the particular work, and will distract attention from the very factors which have made it live on when its creator, his world, and much of the literature he knew, have died. In particular, the world of the medieval German chivalrous romance has been represented on occasion as more remote from us than it seems to me. Certainly its conventions are different from ours, but on the one hand they are not so very different, and on the other we can with a little imagination feel ourselves into any set of conventions which are so fully presented as are those of *Parzival*, and can appreciate their advantages and limitations. (The conventions of Arthurian romance never existed in real life anyway, but were from the first a literary fiction.)

As for the much proclaimed fundamental otherness of the whole Middle Ages from modern times in the matter of religion —the world of medieval man is supposed to have been religiously informed in a way which is barely conceivable today—to some extent I would claim this as a Romantic delusion, to some extent deny its relevance to the problem of understanding a particular work: a work of art establishes its own world within its own limits, and need only be understood in its own terms—not in terms of modern generalities about the times in which it was composed. Nor, may I add, does it seem certain to me that a story with similar conventions and a similar religiosity to *Parzival* could not be written today: it is of course more characteristic of its own time, but it is not inconceivable in ours. Such basic Wolframesque concepts as inherited potentialities (*art*), the values of social uprightness and success (*werdekeit*)— and the limitation of such values (*got*)—are all immediately accessible to us; moreover, their exact significance in *Parzival* is not to be determined from generalities about medieval man, but only from a close reading of a unique work.

Wolfram's *Parzival* contains the stories of three men: the titular hero, his father and his friend. The story of his father, Gahmuret, precedes that of the other two, and is known to German critics as the 'Vorgeschichte'; Parzival's and Gawan's stories are intertwined. All three men are knights, and the work is primarily concerned with the possibilities of life open to a knight; other professions play little part in the story, though hermits are of some importance, since a knight—or lady—can forsake the social position to which he was born, and devote himself to God. None of the three men ever consciously betrays the code of chivalry; they always do their best, and the trials which come their way are not those which beset a man who deliberately turns to evil, but those which overtake the best-intentioned of men. The three are distinguished from each other according to their potentialities and their fate: Gahmuret is an independent adventurer, who can never resist the call of battle or of love, and dies young, leaving two broken-hearted wives and two sons behind him; Gawan is a leading member of society, a knight of the Round Table who is both sensible and valiant and who, after resolving a number of his society's vexed questions, marries and may be presumed to settle down; Parzival inherits his father's reckless drive, early acquires membership of the Round Table and the happiness of a perfect marriage—and then discovers to his dismay that for him this is not enough. He is ignorant that through his mother's family he is called to higher things—in which for obscure reasons of inheritance and upbringing he fails—and is cursed in public by a messenger from the mysterious Grail. There follow four and a half years of misery and isolation, then an investigation of spiritual truth and of the values and constitution of the Grail— to which he is eventually called with his wife and one son, when he is fit to be its king. The work as a whole is thus not simply concerned with an exceptional man, though it does present his problems with subtlety, insight and conviction, but also with his relationship to other types of men and to society in general. Those who concentrate, as many have done, on the story of the main hero, miss this wider significance.

It is not my belief that in this book I have adequately interpreted Wolfram's work. Nobody will ever do that, because the only (relatively concise) way of stating the problem is the way Wolfram took: a successful work of art is by definition the shortest method of making a particular statement. I have not even endeavoured to be especially profound. What I have tried to do is to introduce undergraduates to the original text, to give them some idea of how scholars who have studied this text in detail regard it; and above all, by means of ample quotation and argued interpretation, to encourage them to develop their own view of it. No attempt has been made to indicate all the points at which individual scholars diverge from the views expressed here. What has been done is to indicate where further literature can be found—so that readers who wish can follow up the various points for themselves.

The quotations are not usually translated; that tends to be tedious, and also distracts from the original version. I have, however, tried to arrange the text so that it can be understood without the quotations—so that beginners need not be unduly put off. The purpose of the quotations is to support my statements, and also to invite readers to think for themselves. Where

I am particularly aware of failing is in the task of presenting the complex simply, but without over-simplification. Wolfram's story has too much in it, and the interrelationships are too involved, for the task to be easy; I hope that at least my version is easier to follow than the original. (In the chapter on Gahmuret I have simplified most, since for more detailed information readers can consult Dr Richey's book.[1] At the other extreme I have gone into unusual detail about Gawan, since his story has been much neglected and yet is quite complex. But even in my version its later stages are rather summarily treated.)

The order of my chapters reflects to some extent the order of events in the work, chapter I dealing with the first two books, and so on. This arrangement is possible because on the whole the work presents its various problems in sequence, one after the other. Nevertheless I have occasionally deviated from the order of the original. Thus chapters III and IV both discuss the whole of Books III to VI, but from different points of view; chapter VII tries to assemble information about the Grail scattered in various parts of the work; and chapters VIII and IX both treat Books XIV and XV, where the stories of Gawan and Parzival overlap. Lastly, even in those chapters which concentrate on a particular stretch of the story, I have of course felt free to assemble information from elsewhere when it seemed appropriate.

Occasionally I refer to Wolfram's public as 'the reader', although of course in his day most of his public was illiterate, and would have listened while the work was read aloud. Those who think the nature of the contemporary audience vital to the interpretation of any work may regret my practice—which was simply adopted for brevity.

I have tried to introduce the beginner to generally held views about *Parzival* without distracting his attention by constant reference to the scholarship of others. This may give offence, but I am not claiming great originality for what I say. In general my interpretation is dependent on the work of Gustav Ehrismann

[1] *Gahmuret Anschevin* (Oxford, 1923).

and Julius Schwietering, the two greatest Wolfram scholars of this century—though of course I have deviated from their views where I thought fit, and may on occasion have failed to understand them correctly. On many points I am indebted to Dr Richey, and occasionally I pay tribute to others. Of those with whom I disagree, I have only alluded at all frequently to Gottfried Weber.[1] Some may think that I give him more attention than he merits, but his book is challenging, and fairly recent; moreover, Schwietering has publicly supported it.[2] Weber makes sweeping statements about the twelfth and thirteenth centuries, and tries to show how *Parzival* illustrates them. At several points I have argued against his interpretation in detail; an objection of principle could, however, be made to his whole procedure. It is based upon the fallacy, common enough in this country but even more deeply entrenched in Germany, that a work of art has a 'meaning', which can be stated in some other terms. This is not so; a work of art cannot be paraphrased. All that can be done is to make statements in other terms which either draw attention to some features of the original work, or which themselves possess a structure in some way parallel to the original work. Weber may have found in other medieval phenomena similar structures to that found in *Parzival*, but only by excessive abstraction can the similarity be seen as dominant. An unbiased eye can see that the differences between the phenomena Weber compares are enormous; and of course these differences are just as important to *Parzival* as are the similarities.

The knights who wrote the great medieval German works around 1200 appear to have been for the most part very humble members of their class; like most of them, Wolfram von

---

[1] *Parzival: Ringen und Vollendung* (Oberursel, 1948). Note that I do not always give detailed references to Weber, any more than I do to Ehrismann or Schwietering. This did not seem to me to be called for in a general introduction.

[2] *Anzeiger für deutsches Altertum*, vol. 64 (1948–50). Ludwig Wolff puts the case against Weber in 'Die höfisch-ritterliche Welt und der Gral in Wolframs Parzival', *Beiträge zur Geschichte der deutschen Sprache und Literatur*, vol. 77 (Tübingen, 1955).

Preface

Eschenbach is mentioned in no historical document of any sort, and all we can reconstruct about his life derives from statements in his own works and a few references to him in works by other poets.[1] Fortunately he himself makes an unusually large number of allusions to persons, places and events of his time, from which we can with reasonable assurance date his writings and determine the area in which he lived: the upper Main valley. Several Eschenbachs exist in this area, but there is fairly conclusive evidence for supposing that he came from the village near Ansbach (south-west of Nuremberg), which was renamed 'Wolframseschenbach' in 1918. He seems associated with various courts in central Germany, and jokes somewhat bitterly about the poverty of his own home (*Parzival*, 184, 27 ff.): presumably he was dependent for his living on patronage, and the patronage was uncertain and not over-generous. Since he wrote two long works (the second is *Willehalm*, an unusually humane crusading epic of considerable interest, based on the French *chanson de geste*, *Aliscans*), a few—perhaps over-rated—lyrics, and two fragments of a lyrical epic known as *Titurel*, it is probable that he was a professional poet. He himself, however, denies this vehemently, proclaiming that he can neither read nor write and that his profession is that of a knight (i.e. soldiering; cf. *Parzival*, 114, 5–116, 4). Scholars have been willing to admit that he may have known no Latin and that his French was faulty; but few now believe that he could have translated and composed so effectively while being quite illiterate.[2] One may assume that he was presenting a poetic *persona* in the allusions he makes to himself in the work— an assumption supported by the fact that he presents the whole work as a service offered to a lady (*Parzival*, 827, 25 ff.). The general impression he conveys is that of a proud, gifted and

[1] A sensible short reconstruction of Wolfram's life is found in Marta Marti's introduction to her revision of the edition of *Parzival* and *Titurel* by Karl Bartsch (Leipzig, 1927), a longer more naïve one in Albert Schreiber's book *Neue Bausteine zu einer Lebensgeschichte Wolframs von Eschenbach* (Frankfurt am Main, 1922).

[2] See, however, Blanka Horacek, 'Ichne kan deheinen buochstap', in *Festschrift für Dietrich Kralik* (Horn, 1954).

wilful man, who despised bookishness, insisted on his own inspiration, and maintained his equality with the best. He may have been married and have had children, but this is no more certain than that he wrote *Parzival* for a lady: the distinction between fact and fiction cannot be drawn with certainty.

It is partly for this reason that I have tried to distinguish in this study between 'the poet'—Wolfram von Eschenbach— who is external to and responsible for the whole work, and 'the narrator' who exists only inside the work and passes comment on the action and the characters. The creator is different from his creation, and much confusion has been caused by not recognising this, confusion both about the person of the poet and the nature of his work. The narrator's comments in *Parzival* seem usually to accord with the implicit significance of the action; they do not, however, exhaust this significance—and even their accord with it need not be taken for granted. Such accord is not found in the works of Hartmann von Aue or in the *Nibelungenlied*, and future scholarship may find it profitable to question it for Wolfram.

Parzival is written, like most German works of the time, in short rhyming couplets of remarkable flexibility; in all there are over 12,000 of them, which have been divided into 30-line sections by modern editors. (References are to these sections, and to the line within them. Thus 59, 4 refers to section 59, line 4.) The manuscripts suggest that these sections, which are often marked by capital letters and sometimes coincide with sense divisions, may derive from Wolfram's original manuscript (which is not extant); possibly the columns of the page he used were 30 lines long. The division of the work into 16 books is also the result of editorial decision, which again was based both on the manuscripts, where illuminated initials occur occasionally, and on the sense; like the sections, the books may derive from the author but need not.[1]

---

[1] The literature on both the 30-line sections and on the book divisions is reviewed in an excursus to the dissertation by Werner Jäger, *Strukturprobleme im 'Parzival' Wolframs von Eschenbach* (Tübingen, 1959).

Preface

As in the twelfth and thirteenth centuries France led the rest
of Europe, and especially Germany, in most fields, so she did
in literature: many medieval German epics are loose translations—or at best creative adaptations—of French originals.
Nor is Wolfram's *Parzival* any exception, depending as it does
for the most part upon *li contes del graal* of Chrestien de
Troyes.[1] But Chrestien's Grail epic is unfinished, and in this
and other respects differs considerably from Wolfram's adapta-
tion—so considerably indeed that Wolfram himself claims
another source, the untraceable poet Kyot, in whose existence
earlier scholars were more inclined to believe than modern ones.
The problem of the source is touched on elsewhere in this study,[2]
but will probably never be finally solved, and is in any case not
really relevant here. Our concern is not with where Wolfram
got his story from, nor with how much he himself added to it,
but with what he made of the story—and this can be discovered
quite adequately by examining his own version.

I am not sure whether it is appropriate to include here some
comments on present (and possible future) developments in
Parzival scholarship. If I do so, it is on the assumption that
everyone will realise that my opinions on these points are more
than usually liable to error.

Source studies have been very common in the past, but are
now relatively rare: with few exceptions, they have served very
little to illuminate *Parzival*—presumably Wolfram's work is
too creative, too independent to be bound by its sources. The
belief of many students of 'Geistesgeschichte', that works of art
reflect their age in essence (not merely in incidentals) and can
only be understood in the light of contemporary phenomena,
especially of contemporary thought, has contributed considerably

[1] A straightforward comparison of Wolfram with Chrestien is given by
Otto Springer in *Arthurian Literature in the Middle Ages*, edited by R. S.
Loomis (Oxford, 1959), more ambitious ones by Jean Fourquet in *Wolfram
d'Eschenbach et le conte del Graal* (Paris, 1938), and by Bodo Mergell in
Wolfram von Eschenbach und seine französischen Quellen, Part II, *Wolframs
Parzival* (Münster in Westfalen, 1943).

[2] See below, p. 112 f.

Preface

to the criticism of Ehrismann and Schwietering, but seems now to be leading to innumerable mutually contradictory claims (particularly as to which medieval stream of thought most influenced Wolfram), without casting any further light on *Parzival* itself. The medieval background could in my opinion for a time be best forgotten, and attention concentrated on the individual work. (The excellence of the terms used for interpreting a work of art is never proved by their contemporaneity, but only by the extent to which they illuminate the work—and any terms, even modern ones, which do this, are to that extent acceptable.)

In general the philosophy of *Parzival* has been better investigated than its form. Wolfram's ethical terms have, for instance, been thoroughly and convincingly interpreted, but comments on his style and on the structure of his work are almost always amateurish and subjective. If future students would pay more attention to the systematic study of the form of *Parzival*, in the conviction that this must in a very real sense determine the meaning, then they may reveal much that is so far hidden. In particular I suggest that it is those aspects of the structure and those implications of the story on which the narrator and characters do not comment—and of which the author was very likely unaware—that would now best reward imaginative but disciplined investigation. And because of this belief in the need for formal studies in the future, I include a final chapter introducing students to the study of the style and structure of *Parzival*—even if only in a short and rather sketchy manner.

A number of people have helped and encouraged me with this book. I am grateful to them all, and shall not forget my debt. But above all I am grateful to the officers and staff of the Cambridge University Press, and to the printers, for an unfailing diligence, courtesy and forbearance which have not only been most pleasant to meet, but have greatly improved my work.

H. D. S.

April 1963

GENEALOGICAL TABLE

(Note that only an outline is given here, and that brothers and sisters are not necessarily listed in age order.)

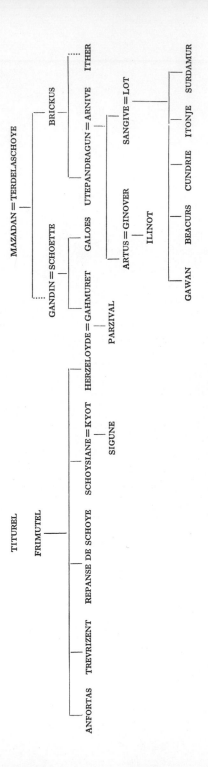

I

THE PROLOGUE

diz vliegende bîspel
ist tumben liuten gar ze snel.[1]

It is doubtful whether any part of *Parzival* has been so much
written about as the Prologue (1, 1–4, 26).[2] The chief reason
for this is its exceptional obscurity: few pieces of Middle High
German are so linguistically difficult, and the relevance of no
other part of *Parzival* to the main story is so elusive. Fortunately an introductory study like the present can be content with
introducing, and need not attempt to solve, the problems involved; even to do this, however, it will be necessary to say a few
words about the principles underlying the relationship of any
prologue to the story which follows it, and also to discuss at
least the first fourteen lines at some length. The main body of
the Prologue need not detain us very long since its general importance for the work is highly problematic; and the final sections
in which the narrator leads into the story itself (4, 9–26) need no
discussion.

If a story is preceded by a series of general reflections, then it
should be plain both that the reflections are separate from the
story, and that reflections and story are part of the total work.
Each forms a unit of its own, but the two are joined in a greater
unit; the interpreter should therefore bear in mind both the
distinction between them and their close relationship. In any
particular case it is of course possible that the reflections have
been attached to the story for purely external reasons, and that
no meaningful relationship can be found between the two; then
the reflections need not be considered in discussing the work. It

[1] 1, 15 f.
[2] The recent literature on the Prologue is listed by Heinz Rupp in his
sensible article 'Wolframs Parzival-Prolog', *Beiträge zur Geschichte der
deutschen Sprache und Literatur*, vol. 82, *Sonderband* (*Festschrift für Elisabeth
Karg-Gasterstädt*, Halle, 1961).

is also possible that the reflections summarise the implicit meaning of the story so perfectly that little is left to the reader's deduction; then the story adds nothing to the reflections and can itself be dismissed. Normally, however—and ideally—the two will be meaningfully related, but the relationship will not be absolutely simple; then there will be a tension between the two which should stimulate the reader and add to the stature of the work.

In *Parzival* the relevance of the opening reflections to the story is so obscure that some critics have denied it altogether. It has been claimed that the first fourteen lines contain irrelevant general reflections, inspired by the Prologue to *Gregorius*, the work of Wolfram's predecessor Hartmann von Aue,[1] and that the rest contains an irrelevant attack on a rival, Gottfried von Strassburg, the author of *Tristan*.[2] In my opinion the possibility of the influence of *Gregorius* and of an attack on *Tristan* can neither be proved nor disproved, for the simple reason that relationships can be found between Wolfram's remarks and the works of Hartmann and of Gottfried, but that these relationships are not overwhelmingly strong. I shall not therefore go into them at length here, for even if they exist, they contribute little to our understanding of the *Parzival* story, and moreover their existence would not of itself disprove the existence of an internal relevance. A passage can fit into several contexts; one context of Wolfram's Prologue is the other works of the time, another—and much more immediate—context is this particular work. It is with the relevance of this internal context that I shall primarily be concerned here[3]; first, however, I must examine in some detail at least the beginning of the Prologue.

All critics concede a break after line 14, though while some

---

[1] See Hermann Schneider, *Parzival-Studien* (*Sitzungsberichte der bayrischen Akademie der Wissenschaften. Philosophisch-historische Klasse*, 1944–6. Munich, 1947), section I.

[2] See Heinrich Hempel, 'Der Eingang von Wolframs Parzival', *Zeitschrift für deutsches Altertum*, vol. 83 (1951–2); and F. Norman, 'The Enmity of Wolfram and Gotfried', *German Life and Letters*, vol. 15 (1961).

[3] See Walter Johannes Schröder, 'Der Prolog von Wolframs Parzival', *Zeitschrift für deutsches Altertum*, vol. 83 (1951–2).

consider it total, others consider it only relative. Whichever view one accepts, it seems to me that the first fourteen lines are far more important for the body of the work than is the rest of the Prologue, and so I shall consider them at greater length:

> Ist zwîvel herzen nâchgebûr,
> daz muoz der sêle werden sûr.
> gesmæhet unde gezieret
> ist, swâ sich parrieret
> unverzaget mannes muot,
> als agelstern varwe tuot.
> der mac dennoch wesen geil:
> wand an im sint beidiu teil,
> des himels und der helle.
> der unstæte geselle
> hât die swarzen varwe gar,
> und wirt och nâch der vinster var:
> sô habet sich an die blanken
> der mit stæten gedanken.   (1, 1–14)

The sequence of thought is roughly this:

A doubting heart is bitter to the soul. Undaunted manliness, coloured like a magpie, has a share in both heaven and hell. The companion of inconstancy is all black; whoever has constant thoughts, cleaves to white.

Two things are clear: the passage is religious, and in isolation it has no precise meaning. Various interpretations are possible of the significance and interrelationship of its component parts, and only with reference to something else (the *Gregorius* Prologue, or the *Parzival* story) can one of them be preferred to others. For instance: how close is *zwîvel* to *unstæte*? Different words are used, but their meanings can be identical. Thus in the *Gregorius* Prologue *zwîvel* is 'despair' and is represented as the unforgivable sin; 'muoz der sêle werden sûr' might then be taken as 'must damn the soul'—and *zwîvel* would appear as quite hellish like *unstæte*. On the other hand the first couplet may only mean that uncertainty is distressing—and the very fact that this interpretation of *zwîvel* is possible may be considered as proof of a contrast with the unambiguous *unstæte*.

3

zwîvel, one might say, may be as bad as *unstæte*, but is not certainly so. All will then depend on the wider context: seen against the *Gregorius* Prologue, *zwîvel* is wholly bad; what is it when seen against the story of *Parzival*?[1]

This question cannot be investigated without first discussing the relationship of *zwîvel* to *unverzaget mannes muot*. The difficulty here is that the second sentence can be interpreted in at least two ways. Does the magpie image refer to *unverzaget mannes muot* alone? (Courage is two-coloured, divine and diabolic.) Or does it refer to the combination of doubt and courage? (The one is black, the other white, and there is hope where they are found together.) The verb *sich parrieren* (to 'slash' clothes—so as to show the colour underneath) has been shown to fit either construction; and although no grammatical relationship is indicated between the two sentences, they *are* contiguous. As with *zwîvel*, so with *unverzaget mannes muot*: there is an ambiguity which could only be resolved by reference to a wider context.

What then do we find in the context provided for these lines by their author, in the story of *Parzival*? The chief discovery is that there is nowhere a conclusive combination of both verbal and sense resemblance: where the same words recur, the sense appears on the whole to diverge; and where an appropriate sense could be found, there is seldom any support from the words. For instance, the magpie image is used in the story—but not of Parzival, the main hero; it is used, twice, of his half-brother Feirefiz who, born of a black mother and a white father, is himself coloured like a magpie (57, 27; 748, 7). And even if Feirefiz's development could be described in terms of the opening lines, it is very unimportant for the work, and is portrayed as rather shallow!

---

[1] *zwîvel* has been much discussed; see, for instance, Helen Adolf, 'The theological and feudal background of Wolfram's *zwîvel*', *Journal of English and Germanic Philology*, vol. 49 (1950); Heinrich Hempel, 'Der *zwîvel* bei Wolfram und anderweit' in *Erbe der Vergangenheit. Festgabe für Karl Helm* (Tübingen, 1951); Peter Wapnewski, *Wolframs Parzival* (Heidelberg, 1955), ch. I.

Then the word *zwîvel* occurs a number of times in passages clearly unrelated to the Prologue—and twice in passages which may be related. One of these concerns not Parzival, but his friend Gawan, and is more concerned with his honour than his religion (cf. below, p. 74). Nevertheless, doubt is resolved by trust in God, and some sort of test seems to be implied—though of a not very profound nature, and concerning a secondary hero. The second occurrence of *zwîvel* which is at all relevant is more promising. When Parzival's mother first tells her son about God, she warns him to avoid *zwîvel*, and refers to the lord of hell as black (cf. below, p. 48). Here the connection with the opening lines is unmistakable, and the reader feels that Parzival's story will probably develop from this point. Opinions are, however, divided on whether it does or not—and no further guidance is provided. The common interpretation of Parzival's abandonment of his allegiance to God (his 'Gotteshass') as *zwîvel* will never be certain, for the simple reason that the word itself is never used in this connection.

Lastly, there is *unverzaget mannes muot*. Few readers have doubted that Parzival possesses this quality, but there is doubt whether it is entirely positive ('white') or capable of being used for good or ill ('pied'). Moreover, it is also a quality of other characters in the work; and the phrase itself recurs nowhere. Thus does Wolfram tantalise us (cf. below, pp. 63 and 162).

Can it be maintained then that the opening lines are irrelevant to the course of the story? Although many distinguished scholars have believed this, it is in my opinion not wholly defensible. One cannot deny that both Prologue and story are religious, that undaunted manliness is prominent in both, and that in both the main character—if one can speak of a 'character' in the Prologue—is made up of both divine and diabolic constituents. There is thus a relationship between the two— and the fact that both are joined in one 'work' invites consideration of this relationship. Easy solutions are, however, not available. The effect of the Prologue is to compel us to consider the story in its terms; the terms, if not immediately obvious, are

5

certainly suggestive; in introducing them the poet has added to the dimensions of his work.

By contrast the relevance of the rest of the Prologue to the central problems of the story is in my opinion quite uncertain; since, moreover, its obscurity and ambiguity are quite as great as those of the opening lines, I intend to spend little time on it. According to the features on which one concentrates, it can be divided up in various ways; attempts to prove certain of these right and others wrong are usually misguided, since they ignore its essential ambiguity. There seems to me little doubt that Wolfram combines here defence of his work and of its style—perhaps against Gottfried's attack—with addresses to his audience and comments on men and women of a fairly conventional nature; he possibly also elaborates some of the thought of the first fourteen lines and touches on some issues of importance to his story. The total impression, however, is one of deliberate mystification and irrelevant over-complexity; and if this impression is correct, then it would be a pity for beginners to be diverted from the main story by this obscure and relatively unimportant introduction.

The last lines of the Prologue, as has already been said, lead in to the story itself.

II

GAHMURET

strît und minne was sîn ger.[1]

The first two books of Wolfram's *Parzival* describe the life and death of the hero's father, Gahmuret. No such account is found in the *Contes del Graal* of Chrestien de Troyes, which provided Wolfram's chief source; nor is there any evidence that Gahmuret's story had ever been told before. On the contrary, a detailed investigation has suggested that Wolfram himself invented Gahmuret, drawing freely on contemporary French literature for particular motifs.[2]

The narrator indicates briefly the purpose of the addition at the end of Book II, when shortly after the death of Gahmuret his son Parzival is born:

> sîns vater freude und des nôt,
> beidiu sîn leben und sîn tôt,
> des habt ir wol ein teil vernomn.
> nu wizzet wâ von iu sî komn
> diss mæres sachewalte,
> und wie man den behalte.
> man barg in vor ritterschaft,
> ê er kœme an sîner witze kraft. (112, 13–20)

In order to understand the character and life of the main hero of the work it is necessary, the narrator implies, to know his background, to know in particular what manner of man his father was. And this is especially necessary in Parzival's case, because his early conditioning—he is brought up by his mother Herzeloyde on an isolated farmstead, remote from and ignorant

---

[1] 35, 25.
[2] See Friedrich Panzer, *Gahmuret: Quellenstudien zu Wolframs 'Parzival'* (*Sitzungsberichte der Heidelberger Akademie der Wissenschaften. Philosophisch-historische Klasse*, 1939–40).

of the courtly world—represents a reaction against the chivalrous life typified by Gahmuret. Chivalry appears, upon Gahmuret's death in battle, to lead inevitably to death and sorrow, and so is rejected outright by his widow upon whom, at the end of this second book, the reader's attention is concentrated.

The main story of *Parzival* must be interpreted against this background. Not only are both the hero's character and many of the events of his life determined in part by his paternal heritage—so that to understand Parzival one must continually refer back to his father—but also the incomplete and problematic chivalry of the opening books anticipates the more perfect and satisfactory chivalry embodied in the twin figures of Gawan and Parzival at the end of the work. The Gahmuret type of chivalry is not ultimately rejected—Herzeloyde's attempt in this direction proves a failure—but is illuminated and given a deeper meaning in the light of the Grail: the mysterious stone which links the courtly world to God. The Grail's influence is not felt in the opening books, but Parzival inherits through his mother a special relationship to it. That the reader learns nothing of this relationship in the first two books is part of the structural design of the work: one aspect of Parzival's heritage is fully displayed at the beginning, the other is only revealed gradually as the story unfolds.

Gahmuret's life has been interpreted at length and in detail by Margaret F. Richey; her book remains to this day the best on the subject. My interpretation depends largely on hers, though my intention is different: namely to stress, not the 'intrinsic literary value of these opening books' but 'the position they occupy as prelude to the more famous story of Parzival and the Grail'.[1] Those who want a fuller account of Gahmuret I refer to Dr Richey; here I propose first briefly to outline his story and then to discuss in more detail its main features.

---

[1] *Gahmuret Anschevin* (Oxford, 1923), Preface. See also Ernst Cucuel, *Die Eingangsbücher des Parzival und das Gesamtwerk* (*Deutsche Forschungen*, vol. 30, Frankfurt am Main, 1937).

Gahmuret

The plot is as follows. Gahmuret, the younger son of King Gandin of Anschouwe (Anjou[1]), sets out upon the death of his father in search of adventure. He rapidly gains pre-eminent fame, especially in the East, where he takes service with the greatest prince of all, the *bâruc* of Baldac (Caliph of Baghdad). On one occasion he delivers a Moorish queen, Belakane, from her attackers, and she rewards him with her hand and two kingdoms. But thirst for adventure drives him to desert her within a year and, having outshone all others in a tournament, he is now claimed in marriage by the queen of Waleis (Valois or Wales). In spite of the rival claims of both Belakane and Queen Amphlise of Franze (Ile de France)—a lady who had gained his allegiance in his youth—he is awarded by the judge to Herzeloyde of Waleis. Before marrying her, he makes the condition that he may fight as often as he wishes and, although he is now king of Waleis and Norgals, Herzeloyde's two kingdoms, and also, as a result of his brother's death, of Anschouwe, he soon rides away to help his former lord, the *bâruc*, in whose service he is killed. He leaves behind two sons, one by each wife. Feirefiz, the child born of Belakane, re-enters the story at the close of the work, when he is taken to the Grail by his half-brother, Parzival.

This is a typical story of knight-errantry, and it is from this point of view that I shall first consider the opening book. What drives Gahmuret to leave home upon the death of his father is not necessity—Wolfram makes a point of the generous love shown by the elder brother Galoes, who would have preferred his former companion to stay with him—but pure love of adventure. And it is this same restless spirit which later prevents Gahmuret from staying at home with either of his wives; it is

[1] Some of the place-names in *Parzival* are historical, some purely fictional. I include in brackets the probable identification of the more important historical ones, though even some of these are open to doubt. On Wolfram's apparent glorification of the Angevin dynasty, see F. Panzer, *op. cit.*, and Willem Snelleman, *Das Haus Anjou und der Orient in Wolframs Parzival* (Nijkerk, 1941).

at once his glory and his limitation. He himself gives expression to it when he takes leave of Galoes:

> mîn herze iedoch nâch hœhe strebet:
> ine weiz war umbez alsus lebet,
> daz mir swillet sus mîn winster brust.
> ôwê war jaget mich mîn gelust? (9, 23–26)

Gahmuret does not understand the emotions of his heart, nor where they will lead him; but follow he must. What he hopes to gain are honour and wealth, both of which, rightly enjoyed—wealth, for instance, imposes generosity (*milte*) upon the owner—are accepted as positive qualities by the code of chivalry (7, 27–8, 7). Further, Gahmuret hopes his deeds will win the favour of women:

> ob mich gelücke wil bewarn,
> so erwirbe ich guotes wîbes gruoz. (8, 10 f.)

Nor is a greeting all he requires from women but, after remarking his brother's success in love, he adds: 'wan kunde ouch ich nu minne steln!' (8, 24). The phrase 'stealing love' is characteristic. Gahmuret has no thought of a great lifelong passion, nor yet of the Christian sacrament of matrimony. All his life he seeks fulfilment in battle, and accepts that the labour (*arbeit*) imposed on the knight is war. What he requires from women is the inspiration to fight well, and the reward for so doing. In the code of chivalry these can take the form of a wave of the hand, the exchange of a token, an invitation to bed; they can be granted always by the same lady, or on different occasions by different ladies—provided that the knight's zeal is kindled by the knowledge that some noble lady has his welfare at heart, then *minne* is fulfilling its proper function.

The exalted state of mind engendered by *minne* is described in medieval German as *hôher muot* (cf. 736, 6–8); there is no exact equivalent in modern English—'high spirits' lacks the ethical component, 'exaltation of heart' is too mystical—but the underlying reality survives. Now as then graciousness and sympathy on the part of one person can raise another's spirits and give him fresh courage to undertake his allotted task; but where the chivalric ethic differed from our own was in making *hôher muot* a moral virtue and in stressing its dependence on sexual love. The opposite of *hôher muot* is the state of being *verzaget*: depressed, apathetic, unable to undertake anything—and for the knight that meant unable to fight, cowardly. This is the sin of *accidia* (sloth or apathy) from which it was the ladies' duty to preserve their men.

Gahmuret of course, as 'der helt unverzaget', never for one moment looks like falling into the sin of apathy; nevertheless his meeting with Belakane does demonstrate how even his valour depends to some extent on feminine encouragement. On arrival in the town of Patelamunt, he shows no particular desire to help the besieged, but asks for a promise of payment:

> oder daz sim sageten umbe waz
> er solte doln der vînde haz.   (17, 13 f.)

The natives' black skins bore him, and only reluctantly does he decide to stay; nor does he take any pleasure in the kiss of salutation given him by the wife of his host, the city marshal. Such lack of interest does not augur well for the besieged, who are fortunate that their queen gradually wins the noble guest round. She feels at once the attraction of his manly beauty, but his formal offer of service betrays no answering quickening of his heart. Yet when his inquiry about the origin of the war has led her to tell how her lover Isenhart was killed in her service, the heartfelt grief and tears which the memory evokes in her do at last affect him:

> Gahmureten dûhte sân,
> swie si wære ein heidenin,
> mit triwen wîplîcher sin
> in wîbes herze nie geslouf.   (28, 10–13)

Heathen or no, she did inspire Isenhart to risk his life for her, and she does feel truly for his death: she is clearly capable of *minne*. Moreover, the shy looks she casts at Gahmuret even through her tears reveal that he too has stirred her interest. His

realisation of her essential womanliness and in particular of her
feeling for him lead Gahmuret to return her glances. By the
time the first interview terminates, the attraction is mutual
(29, 14–16).

The queen does not leave the matter there however, but later,
when Gahmuret is dining with the marshal, herself comes to
wait upon her guest. She kneels down and with her own hand
serves him food and drink, and he closely observes her behaviour and is much moved. Such honour has never been done
him before, and by the time she departs he is deeply in love.
Her attentions have so changed his boredom and lack of sympathy that that night he is unable to sleep for impatience to try
his strength:

> den helt verdrôz
> daz sô lanc was diu naht.
> in brâhte dicke in unmaht
> diu swarze Mœrinne,
> des landes küneginne.
> er want sich dicke alsam ein wit,
> daz im krachten diu lit.
> strît und minne was sîn ger:
> nu wünschet daz mans in gewer.
> sîn herze gap von stôzen schal,
> wand ez nâch rîterschefte swal.
> Daz begunde dem recken
> sîne brust bêde erstrecken,
> sô die senwen tuot daz armbrust.
> dâ was ze dræte sîn gelust.   (35, 18–36, 2)

Unable to await the full light of day, Gahmuret rides out before
his host the marshal is awake, and single-handed engages one
after the other all the leading knights of the two besieging
armies. His military prowess fortunately proves now as always
the equal of his reckless spirit, and he triumphs over them all.
His cousin Kaylet picturesquely comments that such glory
would make even a devil taste sweet to the ladies:

> ich muoz des eime tiuvel jehen,
> des fuor ich nimmer wirde vrô:
> het er den prîs behalten sô

>an vrävelen helden sô dîn lîp,
>für zucker gæzen in diu wîp.   (50, 12–16)

From this incident it can be seen that, if the favour of the ladies follows upon glory in battle (*prîs*), the feats of arms which win such glory must also be inspired by the hope of this reward. Gahmuret's delivery of Belakane testifies to her worth as well as his, for if he saved her country, she inspired him to do so. They are well matched, and she accordingly rewards his service with her hand and both her kingdoms. In so doing she sets the seal upon his pre-eminence in the mutually dependent fields of love (*minne*) and of war (*strît*).

Gahmuret's limitations are shown by his inability to progress beyond this stage, beyond the stage, that is, of knight-errant. He should now presumably settle down to rule the lands of Zazamanc and Azagouc, but it is doubtful if he ever for a moment intends to do so. His heraldic anchor, specifically the device of a knight in search of a port (99, 13–16), is not now abandoned as it is later when he inherits Anschouwe from his brother. Furthermore immediately after the wedding feast Gahmuret orders the magnificent pavilion of Belakane's dead lover Isenhart, which has been presented to him, to be taken on board his own ship:

>dô begunderm volke sagn,
>er woldez füern in Azagouc:
>mit der rede er si betrouc.   (54, 14–16)

It is just possible but not necessary to explain this 'deceit' away as unintended at the time; Gahmuret's honour would not thereby be saved, and even his son Feirefiz later plainly says it had suffered from his desertion of Belakane (750, 20–23). Gahmuret stays about a year—until he discovers that *minne* now prevents rather than aids his participation in *strît*, and then without attempting to discover a solution furtively makes off:

>dâ was der stolze küene man,
>unz er sich vaste senen began.
>daz er niht rîterschefte vant,
>des was sîn freude sorgen phant.   (54, 17–20)

It is not that he is not deeply attached to Belakane—directly after the passage just quoted the narrator insists that he is—but that, as appears later (90, 29 f.), he cannot fulfil himself in her service, for she maintains a close watch on him to prevent his engaging in combat, and this he cannot bear. The excuse he lamely offers as he sails away—that Belakane is only a heathen— is proved false by her immediate reaction: to keep him she would willingly adopt his faith (56, 25–57, 8). It seems he wanted not that, but to return to his life of adventure.

This episode also raises the whole question of the attitude adopted by Christian chivalry to heathendom. Gahmuret's initial distaste for the black skins of the inhabitants of Patelamunt is paralleled by Belakane's express fear that he will on the same account despise her:

> er ist anders denne wir gevar:
> ôwî wan tæte im daz niht wê! (22, 8 f.)

Yet the narrator emphasises that such scorn would be wrong, that her colour is no guide to her worth:

> ist iht liehters denne der tac,
> dem glîchet niht diu künegin.
> si hete wîplîchen sin,
> und was abr anders rîterlîch,
> der touwegen rôsen ungelîch.
> nâch swarzer varwe was ir schîn. (24, 6–11)

Conventionally a courtly lady should be fair as the day, the redness of her cheeks and lips reminding her admirers of a dewy rose. Belakane lacks such beauty, but her courtesy and true womanliness cannot be denied; and Gahmuret himself, as he tells Kaylet after his desertion of his wife, eventually comes to find her blackness beautiful:

> nu wænt manc ungewisser man
> daz mich ir swerze jagte dane:
> die sah ich für die sunnen ane.
> ir wîplich prîs mir füeget leit:
> si ist (ein) bukel ob der werdekeit. (91, 4–8)

Such a statement leaves no doubt that, so far as purely

chivalrous values are concerned, heathens can be regarded as
fully the equals of their Christian contemporaries.

The heathen problem is, however, also considered in *Parzival*
in its religious aspect. Although Wolfram is aware that some
heathens have fair skins (29, 4 f.), he nevertheless allows the
black skins of the inhabitants of Patelamunt to symbolise their
pagan state, and they are referred to on one occasion as 'die nâch
der helle wârn gevar' (51, 24). Being coloured like hell does not,
however, necessarily mean that one is predestined to hell,
though such an outlook might well be attributed to the squire
who, reporting the details of Gahmuret's burial, insists that
no heathen was permitted to help erect the cross over his
tomb:

> wir tâtenz âne der heiden rât:
> ir orden kan niht kriuzes phlegn,
> als Kristes tôt uns liez den segn.
> ez betent heiden sunder spot
> an in als an ir werden got,
> niht durch des kriuzes êre
> noch durch des toufes lêre,
> der zem urteillîchen ende
> uns lœsen sol gebende. (107, 16–24)

The exclusive nature of the redemption brought by Christ[1] to the
Christian world is here made plain; the heathens may worship
him as *one* of their gods, but they are ignorant of the role
of the Cross and of baptism at the last Judgment. Similarly,
in the opinion of Herzeloyde, Gahmuret's non-sacramental
marriage to a heathen can and should be set aside in favour
of a Christian union (94, 11–15); and similarly Kaylet considers the black-skinned and unbaptised knights of Azagouc and
Zazamanc as inferior (49, 13–17).

If such incidents reveal the heathen in *Parzival* as undeni-
ably handicapped by their paganism, others show that this
handicap need not prove fatal. Amongst these, the passage

---

[1] Not that the use of *Krist*, as here, is rare in *Parzival*. *got* is usual,
reference to the Trinity or its persons exceptional (cf. 817, 11–22).

which declares Belakane's *kiusche* and the tears she shed for Isenhart to have the value of baptism is the most famous:

> ir kiusche was ein reiner touf,
> und ouch der regen der si begôz,
> der wâc der von ir ougen flôz
> ûf ir zobel und an ir brust.
> riwen phlege was ir gelust,
> und rehtiu jâmers lêre. (28, 14–19)

Elsewhere the narrator prays that God, to whom nothing is impossible, may redeem the heathen prince Razalic even though he died unbaptised:

> ... der küene swarze heiden.
> des lop was virrec unde wît:
> starb er âne toufen sît,
> so erkenn sich über den degen balt
> der aller wunder hât gewalt. (43, 4–8)

Inner worth can thus triumph over the handicaps of paganism in the sphere of religion as well as of *minne*.

Yet if that is so, if there really are good heathen, it seems a pity that they cannot be reconciled with Christ; that is the problem latent in Gahmuret's encounter with the Orient. A tentative solution is offered at the end of the work where Feirefiz, having been escorted to the Grail by Parzival, accepts baptism in order to win the hand of Repanse de Schoye, the bearer of the Grail. In this way his heritage of *minne* leads him to Christ and, as ruler over much of the Orient, he introduces Christianity into it:

> Feirefîz hiez schrîben
> ze Indyâ übr al daz lant,
> wie kristen leben wart erkant:
> Daz was ê niht sô kreftec dâ. (822, 28–823, 1)

The son of Feirefiz and Repanse de Schoye is the famous Prester John. This development makes it appear at the end of *Parzival* as though the heathen problem raised in the opening books will one day be solved by the conversion of all pagans. (This possible solution seems, however, to be abandoned in

Wolfram's second work, *Willehalm*, which largely turns on the Christian attitude to the heathen as heathen.)

Book II tells of Gahmuret's second marriage. Some time after leaving Patelamunt, he arrives at Kanvoleis, by chance just when a tournament has been announced to decide who shall marry the queen, Herzeloyde of Norgals and Waleis. Again his conduct throws light on the relationship between *minne* and *strît*. On the evening before the tournament Gahmuret joins in the *vesperîe* with his usual success. Initially he takes the field solely on behalf of his cousin Kaylet, who is using the occasion to settle a private feud with his old adversary Hardiz. Even though Gahmuret is clearly conscious of the interest Queen Herzeloyde takes in him and has himself been impressed with the distant glimpse he catches of her beauty, he at first rides into the fray without particular enthusiasm. The reason for this is nowhere specified, but it may be taken as certain that no contest can bring him much joy which is not inspired by the hope of *minne*. The one glance he exchanges with Herzeloyde does not suffice to divert his thoughts from his own wife to her.

Gahmuret's interest is at last aroused by the intervention of a third lady, a fact which seems to indicate that true concern for his welfare on the part of any (sufficiently noble) lady can kindle his adventurous heart. During a pause in the contest he receives an embassy from Amphlise, Queen of Franze, who, lately widowed, remembers her earlier love for him—of which nothing has previously been said—and offers him her hand and throne. In particular she commands him in her letter:

> du solt ouch mîn ritter sîn
> ime lande ze Wâleis
> vor der houbtstat ze Kanvoleis. (77, 8–10)

As Gahmuret puts on his armour once again, all grief for the wife he has abandoned is forgotten; another lady has called upon him and, without a thought for the complications to

which her offer of marriage may lead, he hastens eagerly into
the battle. The narrator comments 'Gahmureten trûren flôch'
(77, 22), and later explains why:

> aldâ wart von Gahmurete
> geleistet Ampflîsen bete,
> daz er ir ritter wære:
> ein brief sagt im daz mære.
> âvoy nu wart er lâzen an.
> op minne und ellen in des man?
> grôz liebe und starkiu triuwe
> sîne kraft im frumt al niuwe.   (78, 17–24)

Gahmuret's exploits now do not outshine his previous performance—that would hardly be possible—but the spirit in
which they are undertaken is transformed. Now once again
minne and *strît* go hand in hand.

At the end of the day Gahmuret's pre-eminence amongst the
participants is only too evident; Herzeloyde proclaims that

> ... Gahmuretes tât
> den hœsten prîs derworben hât.   (82, 3 f.)

Moreover, so many prisoners have been taken in this *vesperîe*
that the tournament proper on the morrow has to be cancelled.
The queen accordingly claims the victor's hand at once—and
the latent crisis is precipitated. Gahmuret himself, who with-
drew from the fray before the end on hearing of his brother's
death, wants no part in the general happiness and attempts
several times to escape the claims made upon him by stating
that sorrow can find no place for love's reward. Herzeloyde,
however, who has already lost one husband killed before the
marriage could be consummated, is in no mood to be shamed
now by the refusal of the victor of the appointed contest to wed
her (88, 27–30). Nor does she feel secure against the claims of
Amphlise, to whom Gahmuret readily admits an immense debt
of gratitude:

> jâ diu ist mîn wâriu frouwe.
> ich brâht in Anschouwe
> ir rât und mîner zühte site:

18

> mir wont noch hiute ir helfe mite,
> dâ von daz mich mîn frouwe zôch,
> die wîbes missewende ie flôch.　　　(94, 21–26)

It was Amphlise who first instilled into Gahmuret the ideals of
chivalry and who endowed him with the means to put them into
practice; she must always be his 'lady' par excellence. Lastly
there is also Belakane, who has no one at Kanvoleis to press her
claims but whom Gahmuret's *triuwe* cannot altogether forget:

> ich sen mich nâch der künegîn.
> ich liez ze Pâtelamunt
> dâ von mir ist mîn herze wunt,
> in reiner art ein süeze wîp.
> ir werdiu kiusche mir den lîp
> nâch ir minne jâmers mant.
> si gap mir liute unde lant.
> mich tuot frô Belakâne
> manlîcher freuden âne:
> ez ist doch vil manlich,
> swer minnen wankes schamet sich.　　　(90, 18–28)

Gahmuret feels ashamed of his desertion of Belakane, but as he
repeats in the following lines, life was impossible for him under
her constant surveillance—and in fact her cause is now lost. So
too is that of Amphlise, for the judge to whom Herzeloyde
appeals awards Gahmuret to her.

Curiously the poet emphasises that it is the lady for whom
Gahmuret feels least who gains his hand. It is not personal
preference but the law of chivalry which marries Gahmuret to
Herzeloyde; his last message to Amphlise explains that in the
circumstances she who made him a knight could not expect
him to behave otherwise:

> dô si mir gap die rîterschaft,
> dô muos ich nâch der ordens kraft,
> als mir des schildes ambet sagt,
> derbî belîben unverzagt.
> wan daz ich schilt von ir gewan,
> ez wær noch anders ungetân.
> ich werdes trûric oder geil,
> mich behabt hie rîters urteil.　　　(97, 25–98, 2)

Gahmuret is bound completely by the code of his class. For good or ill he must now wed Herzeloyde—but, as he tells Amphlise's messengers, that in no way prevents him from continuing to serve the lady who taught him chivalry:

> vart wider, sagt ir dienest mîn;
> ich sül iedoch ir ritter sîn.
> ob mir alle krône wærn bereit,
> ich hân nâch ir mîn hœhste leit. (98, 3–6)

However much this message may owe to the courteous desire to soften the blow of his refusal of Amphlise's hand, it does make it plain that Gahmuret is still free to serve whom he wishes. *minne* is still no exclusive passion for him, but a simple concomitant of *strît*.

Herzeloyde's persistence in demanding Gahmuret's hand and her success in gaining it are to some extent justified by her ability as his wife to solace him for all he has lost. It is a function of *minne* to restore *hôher muot* to the dispirited, and both Gahmuret's sorrow for his brother and his longing for Belakane quickly vanish in Herzeloyde's arms:

> juncfrouwen unt diu künegîn
> in fuorten dâ er freude vant
> und al sîn trûren gar verswant.
> entschumphiert wart sîn riwe
> und sîn hôchgemüete al niwe:
> daz muose iedoch bî liebe sîn. (100, 8–13)

A condition which Gahmuret imposes upon his second marriage is that he shall be permitted to fight as often as he likes; otherwise he threatens to run away again (96, 23–97, 4). Herzeloyde agrees to this condition, and in this respect, which is for him most important, his second marriage is more successful than his first. His wife's chemise, which he wears on top of his armour into battle and which, torn and tattered, Herzeloyde replaces on her bare skin on his safe return, is the symbol of their perfectly harmonious union.

Gahmuret is finally treacherously slain while helping to defend his former lord the *bâruc* against his enemies. Dr

Richey, conscious of the relative shallowness of Gahmuret's feelings for the various women who love him, suggests that the man for whom he laid down his life surely evoked a 'stronger bond of fellowship, a love perfect in understanding, fostered in battle and knit together in unity of purpose with the service of shield and spear' (p. 77 f.), but there is no evidence that the *bâruc* called forth a so much deeper affection in Gahmuret than did the women he loved. The *bâruc*'s distress provides an excuse for battle, just as on an earlier occasion did the quarrel of Gahmuret's nephew Kaylet with Hardiz; chivalry demands that ties of friendship and kinship be upheld, and Gahmuret is all too eager to fight to uphold them. Always, however, it is the love of women which adds zest to his fighting; that is demonstrated before Patelamunt and Kanvoleis, and it surely remains true of Gahmuret's last campaign. Certainly he died for the *bâruc*, as is stated in *Willehalm* (73, 25 f.); but when the narrator says he died for love (*Parzival*, 751, 27 f.; *Titurel*, 74, 4), he surely means in the service of his wife. That Gahmuret wore Herzeloyde's chemise in the last campaign is stated specifically, and his widow even tries to put on once more the blood-stained relic. Moreover, both the whole context of the following address to *frou minne* and the association with his brother Galoes who died fighting for the lady Annore, surely prove that, in reference to Gahmuret's death as normally in *Parzival, minne* refers to heterosexual love:

> Gâlôesen und Gamureten,
> die habt ir bêde übertreten
> daz ir se gâbet an den rê.   (586, 19–21)

It is ultimately his thirst for adventure, his innate and ineradicable knight-errantry, which leads Gahmuret to his death—but all his adventures are spiced by the love of women.

Gahmuret's name does not disappear from the story with his death; on the contrary, reference is made back to him throughout, and in particular Parzival and Feirefiz reflect their father's characteristics in different ways. As is shown by his desertion of Belakane within a year, Gahmuret, although dependent upon *minne* for inspiration, yet fails to find complete satisfaction in his first marriage; later he hesitates between three different ladies, and even while agreeing to marry one of them swears homage to another. In this respect Feirefiz, who is always cheered by the mention of women—'diu wâren et sîn selbes lîp' (754, 6)—is the true son of his father; and he also deserts a heathen for a Christian wife. Parzival by contrast inherits a purer and more chaste form of love from his mother, and after attaining maturity reveals none of his father's tendencies to philander. He too, however, as Gahmuret's son, is aware of the honour as well as the pleasure which a lady's love confers, especially upon a newly-made knight:

> sît er tumpheit âne wart,
> done wolte in Gahmuretes art
> denkens niht erlâzen
> nâch der schœnen Lîâzen,
> der meide sælden rîche,
> diu im geselleclîche
> sunder minn bôt êre.   (179, 23–29)

Liaze admittedly is soon forgotten; and the great love Parzival bears his wife not only perpetuates the tradition embodied in his father's career of gallantry, it also transcends it.

As Gahmuret explains in his letter of farewell to Belakane, any male child of his will inherit not only *minne* but also *strît*:

> werde unser zweier kindelîn
> anme antlütze einem man gelîch,
> deiswâr der wirt ellens rîch.
> erst erborn von Anschouwe.
> diu minne wirt sîn frouwe:
> sô wirt ab er an strîte ein schûr,
> den vînden herter nâchgebûr.   (55, 28–56, 4)

Gahmuret himself long appears invincible, and his death is only brought about by a trick: his adamantine helmet, made soft as a sponge by the application of goat's blood, is penetrated all too

22

easily by an opponent's lance. After his death his fame lives on in his two sons. Feirefiz's behaviour in the last scenes of the work testifies to this and to the truth of his father's prediction (cf. 814, 1–3); Artus comments that nothing else could be expected from the son of such a father:

> von dem vater dîn,
> Gahmurete, dem neven mîn,
> ist ez dîn volleclîcher art,
> in wîbe dienst dîn verriu vart.　　　(769, 1–4)

And when Parzival first learns from Gurnemanz the rudiments of tilting, it is his *inherited* prowess which unseats his opponents:

> der junge süeze âne bart,
> den twanc diu Gahmuretes art
> und an geborniu manheit,
> daz ors von rabbîne er reit
> mit volleclîcher hurte dar,
> er nam der vier nagele war.
> des wirtes ritter niht gesaz,
> al vallende er den acker maz.　　　(174, 23–30)

Similarly towards the end of the work King Artus says to the squires of Gramoflanz, whom Parzival has forced for the first time to admit defeat:

> der mit iwerm hêrren vaht,
> dem was der sig wol geslaht:
> er ist Gahmuretes kint.　　　(717, 21–23)

Courage and supremacy in battle are thus inherited characteristics; they constitute a major part of Parzival's paternal heritage, and it is not by chance that at crucial moments during his struggle to win the Grail, especially at the outset (333, 15) and the triumphant conclusion of the quest (781, 3), he is referred to as the son of Gahmuret. The father's simple but superlative knight-errantry gives promise of the son's distinction in the more earnest task he inherits through his mother.

This hereditary chain (*art*) is not in *Parzival* confined to the two generations of Gahmuret and his children, even though these alone are portrayed in detail. Gahmuret in his turn, as is made plain when he comes to marry Herzeloyde, inherits his compulsive need for love:

> sîn art von der feien
> muose minnen oder minne gern.
> des wolt in friundîn dâ gewern.   (96, 20–22)

The fairy in question is Terdelaschoye,[1] from whose marriage to the mortal Mazadan are descended Utepandragun, Artus and Gawan on the one hand, Gandin, Galoes, Gahmuret, Parzival and Feirefiz on the other.[2] A long apostrophe to *frou minne*, occasioned by Gawan's persistence even when wounded in his service of Orgeluse, enumerates many of the descendants of Mazadan and Terdelaschoye who have suffered for love, beginning:

> muoterhalp al sîn geslehte
> daz stuont iu gar ze rehte
> sît her von Mazadâne,
> den ze Fâmurgâne
> Terdelaschoye fuorte,
> den iwer kraft dô ruorte.
> Mazadânes nâchkomn,
> von den ist dicke sît vernomn,
> daz ir enkein iuch nie verliez.   (585, 11–19)

It is a genealogy predestined to *minne*, and no single member of the race has escaped untouched. Much later it appears that there is also another great family in the story, the Grail family to which Parzival's mother belongs; and so in Parzival himself the two are united.[3]

If such men as Gahmuret live primarily for battle, it is not

---

[1] In Wolfram's version the French name for the fairy's land has become her personal name (Terdelaschoye), and her personal name has become the name of her land (Famurgan). This confusion used to be regarded as evidence of Wolfram's poor French, but is now usually considered an example of his deliberate whimsy: cf. below, p. 181.

[2] See genealogical table, p. xx.

[3] J. Schwietering restates and expands his interpretation of *art* in *Parzival* in 'Natur und *art*', *Zeitschrift für deutsches Altertum*, vol. 91 (1961).

inappropriate that they should also die in battle. As Gahmuret writes to Belakane:

> wizzen sol der sun mîn,
> sîn an der hiez Gandîn:
> der lac an rîterschefte tôt.
> des vater leit die selben nôt . . . (56, 5–8)

And Gahmuret himself goes on fighting until he gets himself killed. For the menfolk such an end seems fitting and final; but what of the women whose duty it has been to inspire such deeds of valour and who are now left to solitude and sorrow? For a time they may find consolation in their sons, but, as the account given to Gahmuret of the fate of Schoette his mother shows, even that does not long endure:

> dô ir erstarp Gandîn
> und Gâlôes der bruoder dîn,
> unt dô si dîn bî ir niht sach,
> der tôt och ir daz herze brach. (92, 27–30)

Having devoted her life to husband and sons, Schoette dies at last of a broken heart. A similar pattern is represented by Annore, the lady to whom Galoes offers his services; he meets a knightly end while wooing her, she dies for love of him:

> diu kom och sît nâch im in nôt,
> si lag an klagenden triwen tôt. (81, 3 f.)

Belakane herself at first sets her price too high, encouraging Iscnhart to fight unarmed to show the quality of his love. His death, however, does not kill her, though much is made of her grief and possibly it is this unhappy experience which leads her to try to keep Gahmuret from risking his life. That attempt, however, only forces him to desert her, and as Feirefiz later informs Parzival she too then dies for love of her husband:

> sîn wîp, von der ich wart geborn,
> durh minne ein sterben nâch im kôs,
> dô si minne an im verlôs. (750, 24–26)

Thus the ladies of whom the opening books of *Parzival* tell live only to inspire their men to battle, and, when the men die,

have no further purpose in life and die too. Herzeloyde epito-
mises their common lot. Before meeting Gahmuret she has
already, like Belakane before her, lost one lover; yet she agrees
without reserve to Gahmuret's condition that he may fight as
often as he will, and her participation in his *strît* is indicated by
his wearing of her chemise. On receiving news of his death she
faints, and after she has recovered consciousness has only one
hope: that the shock has not killed the child in her womb. This
fruit of their love is all that remains of her husband:

> mir sol got senden
> die werden fruht von Gahmurete.
> daz ist mînes herzen bete.
> got wende mich sô tumber nôt:
> daz wær Gahmurets ander tôt,
> ob ich mich selben slüege,
> die wîle ich bî mir trüege
> daz ich von sîner minne enphienc,
> der mannes triwe an mir begienc.   (110, 14–22)

Careless of the bystanders, Herzeloyde rips open her clothes
and presses the milk out from her breasts, exulting in this
herald of the new life within her. This milk—to which she now
speaks—has the significance of a sacrament:

> du bist von triwen komn.
> het ich des toufes niht genomn,
> du wærest wol mîns toufes zil.
> ich sol mich begiezen vil
> mit dir und mit den ougen,
> offenlîch und tougen:
> wand ich wil Gahmureten klagn.   (111, 7–13)

Prevented from putting on the blood-stained chemise—which is
buried in the church together with the lance-head that killed
her husband—Herzeloyde finds solace in the new Gahmuret
who is born a fortnight later and whom, comparing herself to
Mary the mother of Jesus, she feeds from her own breast:

> si dûht, si hete Gahmureten
> wider an ir arm erbeten.   (113, 13 f.)

So the opening books, narrating the life and death of

26

Gahmuret, end with the picture of the widow sorrowing for her
dead husband but delighting in the new-born son:

> sich begôz des landes frouwe
> mit ir herzen jâmers touwe:
> ir ougen regenden ûf den knabn.
> si kunde wîbes triwe habn.
> beidiu siufzen unde lachen
> kunde ir munt vil wol gemachen.
> si vreute sich ir suns geburt:
> ir schimph ertranc in riwen furt.   (113, 27–114, 4)

The traditional association of *triuwe* with *riuwe*—they are often
rhymed together in Middle High German—finds its most
moving expression in these final scenes which, moreover, provide the motivation for Herzeloyde's attempt to bring up her
child ignorant of chivalry, and which explain why, when she
fails and Parzival leaves her in order to become a knight, she too
collapses and dies of a broken heart:

> der werlde riwe aldâ geschach.
> dô si ir sun niht langer sach
> (der reit enwec: wemst deste baz?),
> dô viel diu frouwe valsches laz
> ûf die erde, aldâ si jâmer sneit
> sô daz se ein sterben niht vermeit.
>   ir vil getriulîcher tôt
> der frouwen wert die hellenôt.
> ôwol si daz se ie muoter wart!
> sus fuor die lônes bernden vart
> ein wurzel der güete
> und ein stam der diemüete.   (128, 17–28)

Herzeloyde's self-sacrificing love is rewarded in heaven; as too
according to his squire is Gahmuret's knight-errantry:

> diu manlîche triwe sîn
> gît im ze himel liehten schîn,
> und ouch sîn riwic pîhte.   (107, 25–27)

So God sets his seal upon the pattern of chivalry revealed in
the story of Parzival's parents; the co-ordinated efforts of
knight and lady to the common end of *strît* are of ultimate

value. Yet Herzeloyde's rebellion against that pattern empha-sises in conclusion how unbearable is the sorrow which it im-poses on society. Were the Gahmuret story an independent and self-contained work, then Wolfram's sum picture of human life would be one of misery—for which compensation can only be had in heaven. But in fact the epic of the Grail King, the son of Gahmuret and Herzeloyde, restores the balance; in it the renunciation of worldly happiness, imposed indiscriminately upon all the ladies of the opening books, appears as a special vocation to which particular individuals such as Sigune are called. To the rest a chivalrous life, blessed by God through the medium of the Grail, can bring joy even on earth.

III

PARZIVAL'S CHIVALRY

dir hete got den wunsch gegebn,
ob du mit witzen soldest lebn.[1]

Books III to VI of *Parzival* tell of the hero's youth, which is characterised by exceptional *tumpheit*.[2] A moderate dose of such foolishness, begotten of ignorance and inexperience, is regarded in the work as a normal component in the make-up of all young people. In the natural course of growing up their experience teaches them better, and with added years should come increased wisdom, rash *tumpheit* yielding to sober *wîsheit*. On one occasion Trevrizent admits that this natural order is sometimes reversed: when he is considering the sins into which *tumpheit* led Parzival. He reminds himself that, being old and therefore properly wise, he should not condemn these sins disproportionately and should encourage rather than dishearten his suppliant (489, 1–21). Foolishness in the old is truly lamentable, whereas youthful folly may be forgiven if it matures to a ripe wisdom; a hope which eventually the hero, described in the Prologue as slow to mature, *træclîche wîs* (4, 18), eventually fulfils gloriously.

The wisdom Parzival at first lacks is twofold: he is ignorant of the ways of chivalry and has but a superficial understanding of religion. From a descendant of Mazadan a special insight into Christian truth is not expected; as has been seen in Gahmuret's case, a whole-hearted and successful devotion to the vocation of chivalry is itself pleasing to God. Parzival's early adventures show how quickly and brilliantly he enters into this chivalrous heritage. The handicaps imposed on him

---

[1] 124, 19 f.
[2] See Heinz Rupp, 'Die Funktion des Wortes *tump* im *Parzival* Wolframs von Eschenbach', *Germanisch-Romanische Monatsschrift*, vol. 38, new series 7 (1957).

by Herzeloyde's attempt to deprive him of his birthright are soon overcome and, in Book VI, King Artus, the present head of the Mazadan dynasty, crowns Parzival's knightly distinction by making him a member of the Round Table. Yet from Parzival, who is through his mother a member of the Grail family, more is demanded: at the very moment of his Arthurian triumph Cundrie, the messenger from the Grail, proclaims him unworthy. He has failed in the task imposed on him by his maternal heritage, failed to redeem Anfortas and himself become Grail King. Failure in this sphere indicates a sinfulness that is primarily religious; acts such as the killing of Ither, which might be forgiven any purely Arthurian knight as due solely to ignorance in the customs of chivalry—Ginover, Artus's queen, does in fact formally forgive Parzival for this deed (310, 25–30)—reveal in the heir to the Grail a deeper wickedness, which prevents him from succeeding in his mission at the Grail castle of Munsalvæsche. Moreover, Cundrie's pronouncement that Parzival's failure at the Grail renders him unfit even to be a member of the Round Table, and his voluntary withdrawal from this company, show that for him at least, in whom the heritages of Mazadan and of the Grail are united, the spheres of chivalry and of religion cannot be kept apart (cf. 255, 26 f.). It is the task of Parzival to explore the religious foundation of Christian chivalry; his initial failure in his particular task is for him total failure, revealing once again his more than ordinary *tumpheit*.

In this chapter I propose to trace the stages of Parzival's progress in the art of chivalry, and in the next to indicate how in making this progress he involves himself ever more deeply in religious guilt; the culmination of the one development is marked by membership of the Round Table, the culmination of the other by Cundrie's denouncement of the new Arthurian knight. The two aspects of his growing up can of course only artificially be separated; but it is convenient to treat them separately, and some justification may be seen in the fact that at the time Parzival is only conscious of the progress he makes towards knighthood, and not till later does the sinfulness of his course become apparent.

Upon the birth of her son, Herzeloyde withdraws from her court into the wilderness of Soltane, where she leads a pastoral life, instructing her servants never to mention chivalry to the boy, who is brought up ignorant of all knightly pursuits (except hunting):

> der knappe alsus verborgen wart
> zer waste in Soltâne erzogn,
> an küneclîcher fuore betrogn . . .
>
> (117, 30–118, 2)

This lack of a proper upbringing not only provides the poet with many opportunities of portraying the naïveté of an uninhibited child—of which he makes amusing use—but also serves to demonstrate that Parzival is a complicated character. His skill and strength as a huntsman are outstanding, his love of birdsong apparently inherited—'des twang in art und sîn gelust' (118, 28)—though he bursts into tears when he succeeds in killing the birds he shoots at. And when his mother tries to solve this problem too by radical evasion—she orders all the birds to be destroyed—this does not suit Parzival either (118, 4–119, 11). In his childish way he can accept the complexities of life better than she can. This life is, however, eventually interrupted when one day, apparently by chance, the young boy encounters four knights. But it is not the chance itself so much as what Parzival makes of it that counts: his attraction is so strong that he leaves his mother to seek the king who shall make him too such a knight (120, 11–128, 15).

Much is made at this point of the shining beauty of both Parzival and the knights. He, indeed, having heard from his mother that God is Light, mistakes them for gods; and they in turn are much impressed by his beauty. Their leader Karnahkarnanz, who is engaged in the characteristic chivalrous task of rescuing a lady from the hands of a scoundrel who would rape her, recommends Parzival to Artus with the comment:

'ir mugt wol sîn von ritters art' (123, 11). And the narrator explains:

> von den helden er geschouwet wart:
> Dô lac diu gotes kunst an im.
> von der âventiure ich daz nim,
> diu mich mit wârheit des beschiet.
> nie mannes varwe baz geriet
> vor im sît Adâmes zît.
> des wart sîn lob von wîben wît.　　(123, 12–18)

Beauty is a God-given asset, a sign of chivalry which reveals to all who behold him Parzival's worth. That it is no idle token appears, moreover, from his behaviour, for once he has encountered knights and learnt that he too can become one, he leaves all to do so. So the years of Parzival's isolation from the world come to an abrupt end, his mother's attempt to keep him from chivalry being thwarted by chance—or 'providence'—and by his own desires.

For two eventful days after his departure Parzival remains under the influence of his mother. In the vain hope that he will be driven by the world's mockery to return to her, she dresses him in fool's attire; and the contrast between this *tôren kleit* (127, 5) and both his own beauty underneath and the fine armour he later wears on top symbolises the contrast between his uncourtly upbringing and his knightly nature and aspirations. Nor can he, the untaught and inexperienced child of the forest, profit much from what advice his mother has time to give him before he rushes away into the world. Her warning against treacherous fords leads him to make unnecessary detours to avoid a perfectly safe one (127, 15–18; 129, 7–13), and he rather spoils the effect of his polite greeting of everyone he meets by adding 'sus riet mîn muoter' (138, 8). Most of all is his *tumpheit* displayed in his discourteous interpretation of his mother's advice on *minne* (about which more will be said directly); so that altogether it is fortunate that on the second day he meets a 'grâ wîse man' to whom, as Herzeloyde suggests

(127, 21), he can turn for instruction in courtly etiquette (*zuht*). One function of the adventures he encounters in these first two days is undoubtedly to give him the experience to profit from such instruction: only after he has failed to gain acceptance in courtly society on his own untutored merit is he willing to submit patiently to advice.

Two of his first adventures particularly illustrate Parzival's disastrous lack of *zuht*. The few words his mother addresses to him on the subject of love contain a clear statement of courtly doctrine:

> sun, lâ dir bevolhen sîn,
> swâ du guotes wîbes vingerlîn
> mügest erwerben unt ir gruoz,
> daz nim: ez tuot dir kumbers buoz.
> du solt zir kusse gâhen
> und ir lîp vast umbevâhen:
> daz gît gelücke und hôhen muot,
> op si kiusche ist unde guot.   (127, 25–128, 2)

The favour of a virtuous lady, whether expressed in a ring, greeting, kiss or other embrace, brings joy to a knight, as we have seen from Gahmuret, and is a worthy goal for him to seek. That it must be freely given is of course essential for true chivalry, but this has not been explained to Parzival who, coming upon Jeschute asleep in the forest, uses force to win her kiss, ring and clasp (130, 26–131, 21). His lack of courtliness is further emphasised in the unconcern he shows for the lady while he eats her food, and later by the casual way he barters her clasp to a fisherman for a night's lodging. Clearly he is anxious to obey his mother's commands, but has no understanding of the spirit behind them. Yet the narrator's comment, that had Parzival learnt his father's ways he would have tilted with Jeschute to better effect (139, 15–19), is two-edged: for if Parzival is less gallant than his father, he is also less sensual in his dealings with women and, as a later meeting with another lady, Orgeluse, confirms, does not share Gahmuret's tendency to philander (see below, p. 142). For the moment, however, it

33

is the unchivalrous aspect of his behaviour which is important; it results in Jeschute suffering great hardship at the hands of her somewhat overbearing husband, Orilus, who believes her faithless (132, 28–137, 30). (Orilus is the type of the proud, inconsiderate knight who uses the chivalrous code to cause others suffering. He it was who killed Gahmuret's brother Galoes, and he it is who kills Sigune's sweetheart Schionatulander, see below, p. 50; moreover, his brother Lähelin has conquered two of Herzeloyde's lands. Such knights are clearly contrasted in the work with those of the Round Table, see below, p. 70; their role is, however, small, as indeed is that of Orilus, who is easily defeated by Parzival when the occasion arises, see below, p. 43.)

Unaware of Jeschute's fate, Parzival proceeds on his way and, after meeting with Sigune—who will be discussed in the next chapter—and passing the night with the surly fisherman, arrives the next morning at Nantes, where he finds Artus and his court. His lack of *zuht* here appears from his clothes, from his rudeness to Artus—he demands rather than begs to be made a knight, and refuses either to wait a day or to be beholden to the king for his armour—and above all by his so unchivalrous duel with Ither. The latter, the precise nature of whose relationship with Artus Wolfram leaves obscure—it would seem that not only has he accidently offended Queen Ginover by spilling wine over her, but has also laid claim to the kingdom of Bertane to which he believes himself and not Artus to be the rightful heir[1]—requests the boy to convey on his behalf a challenge to the court (146, 13–147, 10). This challenge is, however, not immediately taken up, as one might expect it to be, and in the end Parzival with difficulty obtains permission from Artus to fight Ither himself. His aim in so doing is not to champion Artus or Ginover, but to win Ither's red armour for himself. Ither is, not unnaturally, offended by the boy's presumption and, after some provocation, strikes him on the head with the

[1] See Margaret F. Richey, 'Ither von Gaheviez', *Modern Language Review*, vol. 26 (1931).

butt of his lance. For answer Parzival hurls his child's javelin at Ither. It pierces his eye and kills him.

This act, prompted ultimately by the entirely selfish coveting of his neighbour's goods, testifies to Parzival's lack of chivalry in a drastic manner; as the narrator implies, only his unreflecting youth could in any way excuse it:

> sîn harnasch im verlôs den lîp:
> dar umbe was sîn endes wer
> des tumben Parzivâles ger.
> sît dô er sich paz versan,
> ungerne het erz dô getân. (161, 4–8)

The ludicrous manner of Ither's death seems to make the matter worse (159, 9–12), as does also Parzival's unconcerned stripping of the dead man's armour (*rêroup*, 475, 5). Altogether the boy's attempt to prove his worth as a knight has succeeded only in demonstrating the opposite; that he should at this point insist on retaining his *tôren kleit* beneath his armour is pathetically revealing.[1]

A further incident which occurs at Artus's court serves to contrast the glorious future which awaits Parzival with his present *tumpheit*. When the laugh of the unlaughing lady Cunneware and the speech of the silent Antanor proclaim Parzival as the one destined to win the greatest glory of all, Keie the Seneschal, whose duty it is to uphold the proprieties of the court, spanks both for delivering so ridiculous a prophesy:

> ez ist dem künge Artûs
> ûf sînen hof unt in sîn hûs
> sô manec werder man geriten,
> durch den ir lachen hât vermiten,
> und lachet nu durch einen man
> der niht mit ritters fuore kan. (152, 7–12)

Parzival, unable to throw his javelin at Keie because of the throng surrounding the queen, feels acutely the disgrace of the incident. For the first time he realises that he is not yet acceptable in court society—and accordingly declines to return

---

[1] See Wolfgang Mohr, 'Parzivals ritterliche Schuld', *Wirkendes Wort*, vol. 2 (1951).

to Artus after killing Ither (158, 17–159, 4). Herzeloyde's efforts have resulted in the son of Gahmuret being mocked at for lack of *zuht*; he does not, however, abandon his quest for knighthood, as she had hoped, but journeys on to find the mentor he needs. His persistence testifies to the strength both of his urge and of his will.

For the last time Parzival's chivalrous *tumpheit* controls his every action on his arrival at the castle of Gurnemanz on the evening of the day following his departure from his mother: tiredness makes him hold his shield so awkwardly that his host later comments that many shields have hung better on the wall (173, 12–17); the boy repeatedly tells Gurnemanz that it is on his mother's advice that he seeks help from an older man; he long refuses to dismount from the horse he associates with the status of knighthood (163, 21–164, 4); and when he is finally relieved of his armour, the fool's attire appears underneath. The suggestion that he might be so dressed at the behest of a lady is ridiculed: no lady would accept a suitor who lacked all notion of courtly behaviour. Once again it is only Parzival's beauty which proclaims his noble birth and great promise.

In such circumstances Gurnemanz, 'der houbetman der wâren zuht' (162, 23), is exactly the right person for Parzival to have encountered. He does not teach his gawkish pupil about his peculiar sinfulness—of which indeed neither is yet aware since neither Herzeloyde's death nor the blood-relationship linking Parzival to Ither has yet come to their knowledge—but he instructs the boy in that *ritters fuore* for the lack of which Keie had mocked him. So far *zuht* is all that Parzival feels the need of, and therefore it is in *zuht* alone that Gurnemanz educates him. It is a very necessary and entirely positive quality in any knight, particularly so in one who is to be king of Munsalvæsche where, as Parzival is soon to learn, courtly etiquette is very much in evidence.

So Gurnemanz tells Parzival to cease quoting his mother so

36

much; never to act unashamedly, never to bring shame upon himself; if he is born to rule, as seems likely, always to behave graciously to his inferiors; to strike a proper mean between miserliness and extravagance—'gebt rehter mâze ir orden' (171, 13)—not to ask too many questions but to speak when spoken to; to show mercy to a vanquished opponent unless he has caused him especial sorrow; to seek happiness in true love (170, 7-173, 6). It is a courtly version of the sort of advice still to be found in books of etiquette: not profound but practical, and very necessary to a brash youth entering for the first time into a highly conventional society.

In addition Gurnemanz keeps Parzival with him for a fortnight, from the very first ministering to his wounds with a father's love, and finally coming to feel like a father to him. He instructs the boy in the Mass—on which the narrator comments 'daz noch die sælde mêrte' (169, 18)—and teaches him the art of tilting, in which Gahmuret's son immediately excels. Lastly Gurnemanz, whose own three sons have been killed in battle, tries to make good his loss by kindling in his protégé a love for his daughter Liaze. So by advice, practical help and warm affection does Gurnemanz make Parzival for the first time a member of chivalrous society. His reward is but further suffering, for so well has Parzival come to understand the essence of chivalry that he is reluctant to enjoy a love which he has not merited (177, 2-4), and rides off to earn Liaze's *minne*. Gurnemanz rightly feels that his 'fourth son' will not return; Parzival's destiny takes him beyond Liaze's reach.

The Parzival who leaves Gurnemanz is no longer *tump* in matters of chivalry; as the narrator says:

> Dannen schiet sus Parzivâl.
> ritters site und ritters mâl
> sîn lîp mit zühten fuorte . . .   (179, 13-15)

Nor can the son of Gahmuret stop thinking about the fair Liaze (179, 23-29). He has fully inherited his father's birthright, and it is time his knightly prowess was put to the test.

37

Appropriately he comes upon a lady, Queen Condwiramurs of Brobarz, who is besieged in her castle of Pelrapeire. She is the niece of Gurnemanz and it is in her service that one of his sons was killed; Parzival's service of her is therefore, as she tells him, also service of Gurnemanz. (In this way the exploit in which Parzival proves his chivalry is fittingly associated with the man who taught him.) Moreover, Parzival's attraction to Liaze leads directly to his full love for her cousin Condwiramurs. In regarding the latter Parzival is reminded of the former—though we are assured there is no real comparison:

> Lîâzen schœne was ein wint
> gein der meide diu hie saz,
> an der got wunsches niht vergaz ...   (188, 6–8)

That Parzival forgets Liaze once Condwiramurs has proffered him her love, is not held against him in the work. Sinfulness lies in the failure to fulfil one's God-given destiny, not in any necessary infliction of sorrow which this destiny may involve. For Parzival, Gurnemanz and Liaze represent a stage on the way, not the goal itself. In the sphere of *minne* that goal is embodied in Condwiramurs; Gurnemanz and Liaze must look for consolation elsewhere.

The fate which threatens Condwiramurs on Parzival's arrival is that of being forced to marry against her will. She herself would sooner die than wed the man who killed her cousin Schenteflur; but King Clamide cares little for her wishes and is attempting to starve her into surrender (194, 14–195, 6). Such negation of the courtly ethic, which insists that knights should respect the wishes of ladies and never attempt to force a favour (cf. Trevrizent, 502, 4 ff.), is typical of the sort of problem with which Arthurian knights are called upon to deal. Thus the first knights Parzival ever met were pursuing Meljahkanz who had seized a lady by force; thus too Parzival himself in his *tumpheit* sins against Jeschute; similarly does Orilus abuse his power as Jeschute's husband. The *zuht* which Gurnemanz teaches is specifically directed against such behaviour, as a noble page who criticises the same Meljahkanz—whose reputation

38

it is never to have won a lady's love except by force (343, 23–30)—later indicates:

> da ist och sîn sun Meljacanz.
> het den erzogen Gurnamanz,
> sô wær sîn prîs gehœhet gar . . .   (356, 21–23)

That the first task which falls to Parzival after leaving Gurne-manz is to free Condwiramurs from the unwanted attentions of Clamide is therefore appropriate, for it provides a fitting test of his chivalry.

In the event first Clamide's seneschal Kingrun and later the king himself are defeated by Parzival without great trouble. The narrator considers their previous behaviour to reveal a sinful pride (215, 17 f.)—note that Clamide would risk the fate of a Pilate or a Judas just to embrace Condwiramurs (219, 19–220, 6)—which is now humbled by a hero who can be described at least from the chivalrous point of view as 'der unlôse niht ze hêr' (201, 18). The defeated pair are sent as prisoners to Cunne-ware at the court of Artus. Since both are Artus's enemies and neither has ever been defeated before, their submission brings Artus great glory—and of course seems to corroborate Cunne-ware's prophecy. The next time Artus appears on the scene he is accordingly riding out to invite Parzival to join the Round Table company (280, 1–18).

Parzival's liberation of Condwiramurs thus proves him a stout warrior, whose strength is ranged on the side of Artus in his struggle to uphold the ethics of chivalry against the selfish claims of brute force. The customary reward for such service in Arthurian romances is the hand of the lady concerned and, accordingly, Parzival now marries Condwiramurs and accepts from her the throne of Brobarz. In this way the courtly pattern of love set by Gahmuret is followed by his son—but with a difference. Where Gahmuret in serving Belakane is inspired primarily by the thought of his own advantage, Parzival at Pelrapeire is moved above all by pity for Condwiramurs. Correspondingly the scene on the eve of the battle is given colour in the one case by the magnificence of Gahmuret's entry into the Moorish city and the loving attentions paid him by Belakane, in the other by the famine prevailing in the besieged town and the desperate plea of the sleepless Condwiramurs for help. Gahmuret, one might say, responds primarily to the stimulus of *amor*, Parzival to that of *caritas*. For Wolfram the two are by no means incompatible: Gahmuret expresses his willingness to help Belakane before he feels the attraction of her person (24, 21–28), and the effect of his desire for her is to make him fight better and so rescue her more quickly. 'Der dienst gebende Parzivâl' (195, 9) hopes to prove himself worthy of Liaze's love, and is not insensible to the beauty of that 'other Liaze', Condwiramurs: 'daz fuogte ir gaste grôze nôt' (188, 14). Yet the absolute selflessness of Parzival's offer of aid is stressed in a way that would have been inappropriate to Gahmuret.

The night of Parzival's arrival Condwiramurs herself visits the bed-chamber of her guest. Silently she steals from her maids-in-waiting and her chamberlains to enter the room where he lies alone. The setting is clearly suited for that stolen love which Gahmuret left home to seek, and one feels that Belakane, having stirred his desires as she did, could hardly have visited him thus with safety the night before the battle. But Condwiramurs, kept from sleep by sorrow, seeks only help from the man who, by sharing with the townsmen the food sent by the queen's hermit uncles to welcome him, has already revealed his readiness to share that sorrow:

> dô gienc diu küneginne,
> niht nâch sölher minne
> diu sölhen namen reizet
> der meide wîp heizet,
> si suochte helfe unt friundes rât. (192, 9–13)

Nor is her confidence abused for, as the narrator insists, Parzival no more thinks of love-making than she does. Since no seat is at hand, she lies alongside him on his bed, in a chaste intimacy that expresses their spiritual harmony. She gives her sorrow into his keeping, he promises to do all he can to relieve her of it; there is no need to tempt a Parzival with promise of reward, no place in the nature of either of them for casual eroticism. As she leaves him at break of day, Condwiramurs simply thanks him (196, 2–4).

After the victory, however, she gives herself wholeheartedly to the man who has freed her from affliction:

> nu wart gecondwieret
> Parzivâl zer küncgîn.
> diu tet im umbevâhens schîn,
> si druct in vaste an ir lîp,
> si sprach 'in wirde niemer wîp
> ûf erde decheines man,
> wan den ich umbevangen hân.'   (199, 22–28)

The queen helps take off Parzival's armour, but does not immediately lead him to bed, as Belakane does Gahmuret. Instead attention is directed once more to the lack of food in the town—

> nâch sîner grôzen arbeit
> was krankiu wirtschaft bereit   (200, 1 f.)

—and not until the hunger of all the citizens has been alleviated by the arrival of victuals by sea is there any question of consummating the marriage. Even then Parzival's scruples testify both to the selflessness of his motives in serving his lady, and to his humble awareness of the value of the reward she offers. The narrator first criticises women whose superficial chastity cloaks erotic desires, and then describes how a noble-minded man might behave:

> des mâze ie sich bewarte,
> der getriwe stæte man
> wol friwendinne schônen kan.
> er denket, als ez lîht ist wâr,
> 'ich hân gedienet mîniu jâr
> nâch lône disem wîbe,
> diu hât mîme lîbe
> erboten trôst: nu lige ich hie.
> des hete mich genüeget ie,
> ob ich mit mîner blôzen hant
> müese rüeren ir gewant.
> ob ich nu gîtes gerte,

41

untriwe es für mich werte.
solt ich si arbeiten,
unser beider laster breiten ?'   (202, 2–16)

Such a man is reluctant to take advantage of the service he has
rendered his lady; as reward he would be content with a touch of
her garment, to claim her body would be to betray them both.
Clearly the reader is here being invited to reflect on the unusual-
ness of the behaviour of both Parzival and Condwiramurs, on
the unselfishness and lack of casual sensuality in their love.
This love is indeed remarkably pure, and its purity later appears
as one of Parzival's qualifications for the redemption of Anfortas—who has sinned in this very sphere of *minne*.[1]

That Condwiramurs is a fitting companion for such a man is
shown by her reaction to Parzival's failure to consummate the
marriage on the first night. Many women, says the narrator,
would feel cheated by such behaviour; but the purity of
Condwiramurs, her affection for and perfect trust in Parzival
make it impossible for her to doubt him:

Den man den rôten ritter hiez,
die künegîn er maget liez.
si wânde iedoch, si wær sîn wîp:
durch sînen minneclîchen lîp
des morgens si ir houbet bant.
dô gap im bürge unde lant
disiu magetbæriu brût:
wand er was ir herzen trût.   (202, 21–28)

Although technically unmarried, Condwiramurs feels herself
Parzival's wife, binds her hair accordingly and formally makes
her lands over to him. He is indeed the darling of her heart,
and so on the third night his scruples vanish and he takes her to
him. So the love of Parzival and Condwiramurs, based on the
disinterested service of the helping knight and the total self
surrender of the rescued lady leads to a union in which (in ideal
Christian fashion) the flesh is the willing servant of the spirit.
In such a relationship the *dienst-lôn* convention of courtly *minne*

[1] On the relationship of Parzival's love for his wife to his Grail destiny see
Carl Wesle, 'Zu Wolframs Parzival', *Beiträge zur Geschichte der deutschen
Sprache und Literatur*, vol. 72 (Halle, 1950).

is at the same time perfectly embodied and transcended. Unlike the more selfish and erotic union of Gahmuret and Belakane, that of Parzival and Condwiramurs will withstand every test and eventually find acceptance at Munsalvæsche.

After about a year Parzival leaves his wife to seek his mother —and further adventure (223, 15–25). His journey leads him to the Grail castle and to Sigune, and then on to Jeschute and finally to Artus. The first two of these adventures will be treated in the next chapter, the latter two reveal the progress Parzival has made in chivalry since he first left his mother, and so will be discussed here. Not at once recognising Jeschute in the lady who rides in a torn chemise on a starved nag, Parzival denies that he ever harmed a woman since becoming a knight:

> jane wart von mîme lîbe
> iu noch decheinem wîbe
> laster nie gemêret
> (sô het ich mich gunêret)
> sît ich den schilt von êrst gewan
> und rîters fuore mich versan. (258, 17–22)

And of course it was before he was acquainted with *rîters fuore* that Parzival behaved in so unchivalrous a manner to Jeschute; but now the pupil of Gurnemanz and husband of Condwiramurs is permitted to undo that former wrong. He vanquishes Orilus in battle and swears on a holy relic that Jeschute never betrayed her husband; the two are reconciled—and Orilus also sent as prisoner to (his sister) Cunneware.

Parzival himself rides on and sleeps that night in the open. The next morning the intensity of his love for his wife is revealed by the trance into which he falls on beholding three drops of red blood which a wild goose, wounded by a falcon, has let fall on the white snow.[1] They remind him of the beauty of Condwiramurs:

> des heldes ougen mâzen,
> als ez dort was ergangen,

[1] See Herbert Kolb, 'Die Blutstropfen-Episode bei Chrétien und Wolfram', *Beiträge zur Geschichte der deutschen Sprache und Literatur*, vol. 79 (Tübingen, 1957); and Erich Köhler, 'Die drei Blutstropfen im Schnee', *Germanisch-Romanische Monatsschrift*, vol. 40, new series 9 (1959).

zwên zaher an ir wangen,
den dritten an ir kinne.
er pflac der wâren minne
gein ir gar âne wenken.
sus begunder sich verdenken,
unz daz er unversunnen hielt:
diu starke minne sîn dâ wielt.　　　　(283, 10–18)

Unwittingly Parzival has halted not far from the camp of Artus, and his lance is raised as though for battle. Two knights therefore challenge him to fight, but, lost in thought of his wife, he neither hears them nor feels the blow the second one deals him with the butt of his lance. At the first challenge, however, his well-trained horse turns to take up position for combat, while his second opponent himself turns Parzival's horse's head. Each time, with the vision gone, Parzival's wits return and he unseats his challenger—only to return once more to contemplation of the drops of blood. Such evidence of the power of love calls from the narrator criticism of *frou minne*, whose supreme control over all earthly beings is not always exercised for good. But not only is the capacity for love Parzival has inherited from both father and mother (300, 14–19) boundless, also the direction of his love is constant, its nature pure. So, as the narrator several times remarks, all that his hero suffers this day is suffered out of *triuwe*. The episode thus shows how Parzival's love, founded as it is upon spiritual values, survives without loss physical separation. He has come to understand better than at first his mother's instructions about love, has lived to demonstrate in his own person the truth of Gurnemanz's teaching of the mystical union of man and woman:

ich wil iu mêr von wîbes orden sagn.
man und wîp diu sint al ein;
als diu sunn diu hiute schein,
und ouch der name der heizet tac.
der enwederz sich gescheiden mac:
si blüent ûz eime kerne gar.
des nemet künsteclîche war.　　　　(172, 30–173, 6)

It is Gawan who, from his own experience of the ways of love, succeeds in restoring Parzival to himself by covering the drops of blood with a cloth. Then Parzival learns that the second of the two vanquished knights is Keie, whose right arm and left leg are broken by his fall. With this last triumph Parzival has finally freed himself from the disgrace which the Seneschal's spanking of Cunneware had brought upon him on his first visit to Artus's court. On this, his second visit, Cunneware appropriately takes care of him, and so it is in the company of the lady who had first proclaimed his knightly pre-eminence that Parzival now goes to meet Artus. The king calls an assembly of the Round Table, which Parzival agrees to join; and at this assembly Ginover formally forgives him for killing Ither. With this Parzival's progress to chivalry is complete; the two sins he committed against the knightly code in the first days after leaving Soltane, together with the disgrace in which they involved him, have been wiped out. (And Parzival is now able to arrange the marriage of Cunneware to Clamide, thus providing a neat solution to their emotional entanglements—a solution which anticipates the various marriages arranged by Artus and Gawan in Book xv, see below, p. 147.) The man who has brought Artus more glory than any other is fully worthy to join the Arthurian circle; and the narrator comments:

> als mir diu âventiure maz,
> an disem ringe niemen saz,
> der muoter brust ie gesouc,
> des werdekeit sô lützel trouc.   (311, 9–12)

werdekeit is Wolfram's term for chivalrous worth—a quality no Arthurian knight can now deny to his hero. Parzival has already at this stage realised to the full the potentialities he inherits from his father.

IV

PARZIVAL'S SINFULNESS

wê waz ist got? [1]

At the very moment of his Arthurian triumph, Parzival is denounced by Cundrie. That his maternal heritage lays him under any further obligation beyond that of following in his father's footsteps, the young knight has not yet realised. The function of Cundrie's denunciation is to compel this realisation upon him, to make him aware of that other sphere in which he has proved such a failure. But it is only much later, with the help of his maternal uncle Trevrizent, the brother of the Grail King, that Parzival comes to understand how justified is Cundrie's attack. From the viewpoint of an Arthurian knight he can no more comprehend his peculiar sinfulness than can the other members of the Round Table.

Yet of Parzival such an understanding is required. As the son of Herzeloyde he has to realise that not only purely chivalrous characteristics are handed on from generation to generation; so too is the capacity for good and evil. In the words of Trevrizent:

> Von Adâmes künne
> huop sich riwe und wünne,
> sît er uns sippe lougent niht,
> den ieslîch engel ob im siht,
> unt daz diu sippe ist sünden wagen,
> sô daz wir sünde müezen tragen.   (465, 1–6)

Sorrow and joy, sin and salvation are inherited too, for all men are related both to Adam and to God. In this way Wolfram gives to the concept of kinship a specifically Christian meaning. It is a meaning which, he recognises, few men are granted by God fully to understand—but his story is of such a

[1] 332, 1.

one. Parzival is permitted by God to sin and is disgraced by God for that sin because he, the future Grail King, can profit from such testing. (It is therefore suggestive that whereas in the forest of Soltane Parzival was babied by his mother as 'bon fîz, scher fîz, beâ fîz', 140, 6, and after taking Ither's armour was generally known as 'der rîter rôt', e.g. 276, 21, cf. 315, 11, now at last when he is finally singled out from all other men his particular name of 'Parzival' is publicly proclaimed by Cundrie, 325, 17 ff.) Admirable as this may be for others, Parzival is not allowed to be content with membership of the *tavelrunder*, but must realise his own higher vocation; nor is this realisation granted lightly to a son of Adam, but it must be won through suffering with the help of God.

In the light of this concept of inherited sin and salvation,[1] Parzival's *tumpheit* gains an added significance. In the boy who lacks all education, who is a member of no society and is entirely unselfconscious, can be seen the double heritage of man in its extreme form. Whereas Parzival can blame his education for his failure at the Grail Castle of Munsalvæsche, he can never attempt to justify the sins he commits before meeting Gurnemanz. They reveal to him his own inherited sinfulness; and after he has recognised them (475, 13–476, 30) he takes upon himself the burden of the later self-conscious sin also (488, 1–20). The *tumpheit* of young Parzival now remains to be re-examined from this point of view; we have to trace not what leads to Keie and Gurnemanz, but what leads to Cundrie and Trevrizent.

Of the story of man's sin and salvation, which is thus to prove so important for his development, young Parzival appears to know nothing. All his mother manages to impress upon him is that God is brighter than the sun and a certain help in trouble. And even this she only mentions in reply to a question of his. His susceptibility to bird-song had led her to wish all the birds

[1] See Julius Schwietering, 'Parzivals Schuld', *Zeitschrift für deutsches Altertum*, vol. 81 (1944); reprinted in J. Schwietering, *Mystik und höfische Dichtung im Hochmittelalter* (Tübingen, 1960).

killed; he begs mercy for them, and she sees her error and asks
rhetorically why she should undo God's handiwork:

> der knappe sprach zer muoter sân
> 'ôwê muoter, waz ist got ?'
> 'sun, ich sage dirz âne spot.
> er ist noch liehter denne der tac,
> der antlitzes sich bewac
> nâch menschen antlitze.
> sun, merke eine witze,
> und flêhe in umbe dîne nôt:
> sîn triwe der werlde ie helfe bôt.
> sô heizet einr der helle wirt:
> der ist swarz, untriwe in niht verbirt.
> von dem kêr dîne gedanke,
> und och von zwîvels wanke.'   (119, 16–28)

The conception of God revealed here is indistinguishable from
that expounded by Trevrizent in Book IX; it is, however, so
lightly sketched in that it is liable to misinterpretation—and, as
has been seen, the boy does in fact misinterpret it, showing
himself soon afterwards quite unable to distinguish between a
knight and God. Part of his future trouble can be traced to this
childish anthropomorphism. It would, however, in my view be
wrong to blame Herzeloyde for herself having an inadequate
conception of God; her fault lies not in her own religious views,
but in her attempt to seclude the child from life, involving as this
apparently does not only keeping him ignorant of chivalry, but
also telling him too little of religion.

One of the two great sins of which Trevrizent accuses
Parzival in Book IX is that of causing his mother's death (499,
20–25). When Parzival tells his mother of his encounter with the
knights, she faints; he, however, is apparently unmoved, and on
her regaining consciousness he repeatedly demands that she
give him a horse. On this he rides off the next morning:

> des morgens dô der tag erschein,
> der knappe balde wart enein,
> im was gein Artûse gâch.
> (frou) Herzeloyde in kuste und lief im nâch.

der werlde riwe aldâ geschach.
dô si ir sun niht langer sach
(der reit enwec: wemst deste baz?)
dô viel diu frouwe valsches laz
ûf die erde, aldâ si jâmer sneit
sô daz se ein sterben niht vermeit.   (128, 13–22)

The boy is so entirely taken up with his own desire to become
a knight, that his mother's collapse makes no impression on
him; he rides rough-shod over her feelings and breaks her
heart. Such childish thoughtlessness may appear natural in a
boy; but that does not prevent its being evil, the product of the
innate selfishness of a descendant of Adam. (A similarly serious
view might be taken of Parzival's forcing of his will on Jeschute;
but in this instance the outcome is not so disastrous, and the
chivalrous Parzival of a year later is allowed to make good this
particular fault.)

It is not of course Parzival's desires in themselves which are
sinful, but the self-centred execution of these desires at the
expense of others, the complete lack of feeling for others where
his own wishes are concerned. That under different circumstances the boy can show sympathy is revealed by his encounter
with Sigune—who is added by Wolfram almost entirely independently of his source, and is of such importance in his story
that a short digression is needed here to introduce her.

Sigune too is a member of the Grail family, the daughter of
Herzeloyde's sister Schoysiane, and so Parzival's cousin. Her
mother died in giving her birth. Her father Kyot von Katelan-
gen together with his brother Manpfilot thereupon gave up
their profession of arms; they are the two hermit uncles of
Condwiramurs who provide food on Parzival's first arrival.
For the first five years of her life Sigune was brought up
together with Condwiramurs, but then the latter's father was
killed, and Sigune went to live with Herzeloyde. She is thus
by birth and upbringing closely linked to Parzival, to whom
indeed she first reveals his name (which she interprets as
meaning 'right through'—because his father pierced his

49

mother's heart right through with sorrow, 140, 16–20). She appears to have been nearing maturity when Gahmuret married Herzeloyde and introduced Sigune to his squire Schionatulander. The story of the ill-fated love of these two is told in Wolfram's fragmentary poem *Titurel*. In a manner reminiscent of Belakane, Sigune demands excessive services of her lover, who is killed by Orilus when seeking for her a particular dog's lead. (He is also in some sense serving Parzival when he fights Orilus, as Orilus's brother Lähelin had conquered two of Herzeloyde's lands, cf. *Parzival*, 141, 2–24.)

Parzival, who leaves Jeschute just before her husband returns from the combat with Schionatulander, is the first person to come upon Sigune in her sorrow. Crying and tearing her hair, she sits on the ground with her dead lover in her lap. The sorrowful scene corresponds closely to that used in the later Middle Ages for the Pietà, and the suggestion has been made that it is a sort of precursor of this.[1] Sigune is the epitome of sorrow. The sorrow of the various women in the first two books points towards her; and as Parzival passes through the various stations of his journey to the happiness of Munsalvæsche—in which directly or indirectly nearly all the figures of the main story have a share—Sigune goes to her death. When Parzival next meets her, she sits in a tree (trees were the refuge of various legendary medieval hermits) with the embalmed Schionatulander in her arms; all her beauty has now faded. On the third occasion she occupies a hut in which is placed Schionatulander's coffin; and on the fourth, after Parzival has been proclaimed Grail King, Sigune lies dead across that coffin, which is then opened so that she can be laid beside her lover.

It is the unparalleled *triuwe* of Sigune—

> al irdisch triwe was ein wint,
> wan die man an ir lîbe sach   (249, 24 f.)

—which causes her such equally unparalleled *riuwe*; of all the

---

[1] See Julius Schwietering, 'Mittelalterliche Dichtung und bildende Kunst', *Zeitschrift für deutsches Altertum*, vol. 60 (1923).

characters of the main part of the work that rhyme of the first two books really fits her alone. That *triuwe* should lead to *riuwe* is the common experience of all the women associated with Gahmuret; even Herzeloyde, who rebels against it, has it finally forced upon her. Of the women around Parzival (if his mother who dies at the beginning of the main story is excluded) only Sigune is called upon to endure the loss of her beloved; by her complete acceptance of her destiny—that is by her perfect *kiusche*—she appears to free the others from that general condemnation.

For anyone to witness Sigune's distress and not feel sorry for her, would be *untriuwe*, comments the narrator:

> swenz niht wolt erbarmen,
> der si sô sitzen sæhe,
> untriwen ich im jæhe.   (249, 18–20)

Parzival is fortunately not such a one. On his first encounter with his cousin his emotion is apparent from his immediate offer of help:

> ich hân hie jæmerlîchen funt
> in iwerm schôze funden.
> wer gap iun ritter wunden?...
>
> ob ich in müge errîten,
> ich wil gerne mit im strîten.
>   (138, 28–30; 139, 7 f.)

Clearly where there is no clash of wills, Parzival's instinctive sympathy and desire to help are as readily expressed as his selfish needs elsewhere—and such *caritas* receives recognition from Sigune:

> du bist geborn von triuwen,
> daz er dich sus kan riuwen.   (140, 1 f.)

Nor is this *triuwe* of Parzival's in any way inhibited by the *zuht* he learns from Gurnemanz, for when he meets Sigune a second time (directly after his failure at Munsalvæsche!), although he does not recognise her, he reacts in the same way. He is evidently quite capable of feeling for others, but only so long as his own interests are not involved.

51

Parzival's second great sin is to kill Ither, who, as it later transpires, is his own kinsman—although a rather distant one. Admittedly this relationship is not known to the boy at the time, but the evil nature of his own motives takes from him all justification. Parzival covets Ither's fine armour, and will have no other. Rather than be beholden to the king for a gift, indeed, he is prepared to risk a knight's life; and he shows no regret for his death, but is utterly absorbed by the problem of getting off the dead man's armour and putting it on himself. Such wilful disregard of others is of course a childish characteristic, as the narrator emphasises at the time (161, 4–8), but Trevrizent later condemns the sinfulness of such childishness in no uncertain terms: were God to exercise justice, he says, Parzival's own life would be forfeit (475, 24 f.). Clearly *tumpheit* does not absolve from sin; it may indeed be an expression of natural wickedness. Unless Parzival obtains God's forgiveness and is upheld by his grace, the sins into which it leads him must condemn him out of hand; the murder of Ither is proof of it.

Parzival's love for Condwiramurs, which has been discussed at length in connection with his chivalrous development, also requires a mention here; for its exceptional purity shows that, at least in the sphere of *minne*, Parzival is specially graced. Condwiramurs gives herself to him even before he is conscious of desiring her—so that here there is no clash of wills and no occasion for Parzival to disregard her wishes in seeking his own ends.

The revelation of Parzival's third sin nearly brings Trevrizent to despair at first (488, 21–30), whereas later he seems to consider it more as an inevitable consequence of the other two (501, 1–5). A careful examination may perhaps reveal the relevance of each point of view.

Parzival's maternal uncle Anfortas, who is king of the Grail, has sinned against the Grail; as a result he suffers from a wound which God will only allow to heal if a stranger, having penetrated to Munsalvæsche, asks spontaneously what ails the king.

Then the wound will heal and the stranger become Grail King in place of Anfortas (472, 21–473, 4; 483, 19–484, 8). This destiny is of course reserved for Parzival, who is, apart from Anfortas himself and his hermit brother Trevrizent, the only remaining male descendant of the Grail line. Accordingly when, on leaving Condwiramurs, Parzival allows his horse a free rein, it takes him safely through the lines of knights guarding Munsalvæsche to the lake where the sick king is fishing; and Anfortas then directs him to the castle. Clearly this is Parzival's supreme test, his great chance of fulfilling his destiny; the sin which prevents him from asking the necessary question is the final proof of his wickedness.

To determine the nature of this sin, it is necessary first to decide the nature of the question to be asked and then the reasons which prevent Parzival from asking it. What Parzival finds at Munsalvæsche is a noble company of knights and ladies who participate before his eyes in a strange ceremony. The two oddest things about this ceremony are that at a certain stage the whole company breaks out into loud lamentation, and that it culminates in a feast, the food and drink for which are provided by a miraculous stone—the Grail. Since the cause of the lamentation is the suffering of the Grail King, it is probable that a question about either phenomenon would lead to a further question about the other; and that may be why Wolfram does not draw a rigid distinction between a question motivated by curiosity about the Grail and one motivated by sympathy for Anfortas.[1] But the latter's attempt to draw the question from Parzival by giving him his own sword and referring as he does so to the wound God inflicted upon him (239, 18–240, 6), suggests that it is the suffering rather than the stone which the stranger is required to investigate. (Parzival incidentally appears to wear two swords from now on, Ither's which may be associated with the Round Table, and that of Anfortas. Both serve him well, though the Grail sword has to shatter and be magically repaired

[1] See further Bernard Willson, 'Das Fragemotiv in Wolframs Parzival', *Germanisch-Romanische Monatshefte*, vol. 43, new series 12 (1962).

before it is finally secure, 253, 24–254, 15. On Ither's sword, see below, p. 162.) The emphasis on the suffering of Anfortas receives confirmation later from Trevrizent's version of the question: 'hêrre, wie stêt iwer nôt?' (484, 27), as also from the version Parzival successfully uses at the end of the work: 'œheim, waz wirret dier?' (795, 29).

What should move Parzival to ask such a question is not primarily curiosity—though that may play some small part—but, as Signe plainly tells him when he has failed, compassion:

> iuch solt iur wirt erbarmet hân,
> an dem got wunder hât getân,
> und het gevrâget sîner nôt.   (255, 17–19)

Similarly Cundrie curses Parzival for not having been moved by Anfortas's suffering to show the sympathy which would have cured him:

> hêr Parzivâl, wan sagt ir mir
> unt bescheidt mich einer mære,
> dô der trûrge vischære
> saz âne freude und âne trôst,
> war umb irn niht siufzens hât erlôst.
>   Er truog iu für den jâmers last.
> ir vil ungetriwer gast!
> sîn nôt iuch solt erbarmet hân.   (315, 26–316, 3)

And both Trevrizent (484, 25) and Parzival, when he finally realises his sin (488, 17), consider the crime to consist in a lack of feeling in the face of true sorrow (*den rehten kumber*). As a matter of fact the pain suffered by Anfortas on the occasion of Parzival's first visit is greater than ever before or since (492, 11–493, 14), and the general lament of the company, which Parzival witnesses, should have made him conscious of the special nature of the wound, which, as he is specifically told, God has inflicted on the king. Yet the man who, both before and after his visit to Munsalvæsche, demonstrates his capacity for sympathy by proffering help to Signe, now fails to ask the question which would set the seal upon his *triuwe*.

Parzival's Sinfulness

A lack of feeling for others, that is a lack of *triuwe* or *caritas*, is often explained by an excessive concern for oneself; and that explanation exactly fits Parzival's conduct at Munsalvæsche. To understand this it is necessary to go back a little. On a previous occasion, at Artus's court, Parzival had been disgraced because he had no *zuht*; Gurnemanz had then taught him *zuht*, but there is evidence, so far passed over, that even then he remained for some time unsure of himself. When he first meets Condwiramurs, he embarrasses her by not speaking until spoken to—and the narrator indulges in irony at the new knight's expense:

> sîn manlîch zuht was im sô ganz,
> sît in der werde Gurnamanz
> von sîner tumpheit geschiet
> unde im vrâgen widerriet,
> ez enwære bescheidenlîche,
> bî der küneginne rîche
> saz sîn munt gar âne wort,
> nâhe aldâ, niht verre dort.
> maneger kan noch rede sparn,
> der mêr gein frouwen ist gevarn.   (188, 15–24)

Such gaucheness is not at all what Gurnemanz intended, but Parzival's inexperience excuses it, and Condwiramurs is sufficiently humble not to take it amiss. Accordingly Parzival's concern with the propriety of his own behaviour rather than with the embarrassment of Condwiramurs does not this time lead to disaster.

At Munsalvæsche, however, it is Parzival's feeling for others which is on test—but he is so preoccupied by his own worries that he does not realise it. What makes the greatest impression on him is clearly not the miraculous power of the Grail nor the sorrow of Anfortas and his court, but the degree of ceremony with which everyone behaves. The courtly etiquette of the knights and ladies of Munsalvæsche is more pronounced than that of any other characters in the work. Before embarking on his long description of the Grail ritual, the narrator promises to tell 'wie dâ mit zuht gedienet wart' (232, 8), and the word *zuht*, which is repeated six more times in the following 200 lines, does indeed characterise the ceremony which follows. The bearing in and out of the Grail and the serving of the meal are performed with a propriety which leaves no doubt that, had Parzival not passed through the hands of Gurnemanz, he would have been totally out of place in such a company—though he might of course have blurted out the question. As it is the young knight suppresses his wonder and his curiosity—there is little suggestion that he has any compassion to suppress—for fear of committing once again a breach of etiquette:

> wol gemarcte Parzivâl
> die rîcheit unt daz wunder grôz:
> durch zuht in vrâgens doch verdrôz.
>   er dâhte 'mir riet Gurnamanz
> mit grôzen triwen âne schranz,
> ich solte vil gevrâgen niht.
> waz op mîn wesen hie geschiht
> die mâze als dort pî im?
> âne vrâge ich vernim
> wiez dirre massenîe stêt.' (239, 8–17)

It has been suggested that it is not exclusively Parzival's fault that he thinks more about the propriety of his own behaviour than about the distress of his host, and that Wolfram is really criticising in Parzival the courtly obsession with outer form (*zuht, fuoge*) at the expense of inner feeling. There are, however, a number of reasons for querying too sharp an antithesis between Arthurian convention and Grail sincerity. Gurnemanz who, as 'der houbetman der wâren zuht' (162, 23), has been the particular object of criticism, reveals considerable depth of feeling both for his dead sons and for Parzival; he is indeed also described as 'der fürste ûz triwe erkorn' (177, 13); and his suffering plunges his court into sorrow just as surely as does that of Anfortas (175, 7–18). Schoette and Annore, respectively the wife of Gandin and the beloved of Galoes, die of grief just as do Herzeloyde and Sigune, even though they are

not members of the Grail family. Even the apparent heartless-
ness of Orgeluse, who eventually marries Gawan, Artus's
nephew and the Arthurian knight par excellence, is explained
as due to *triuwe*; and both she and Itonje, Gawan's sister, fail on
occasions to control their feelings, and behave in an uncourtly
manner. To state bluntly that the Arthurian ethic upholds
form at the expense of feeling is therefore erroneous—though
no more so than to suppose that at Munsalvæsche feeling leaves
no room for form.

Conventional behaviour is a quality demanded equally in the
Arthurian and the Grail societies, but in both, as anywhere else,
it is not always in place. Parzival's mistake is to worry about
the superficialities of convention when they are inappropriate.
Such behaviour is not typical of Arthurian knights; it is, however, in keeping with the character of the boy who, when intent
on becoming a knight, spared no thought for either his mother
or Ither. Now he is intent on avoiding disgrace, anxious to
prove his *zuht* equal to the occasion—and so he fails to appreciate the suffering of his host. The sin which brings disgrace
upon Parzival is not arbitrary, nor is it imposed by courtly
convention: it is characteristic and innate. It testifies moreover,
as will be shown, to the inherited self-centredness of a descendant of Adam. Parzival's failure to redeem Anfortas proves that
the boy who could unthinkingly kill his mother and his cousin
is not fit to become Grail King.

(In *Der Ritter zwischen Welt und Gott*[1] W. J. Schröder has
stressed a different aspect of Parzival's visit to Munsalvæsche.
He points out that what goes on there is a religious cult of
central importance to the chivalrous world the Grail sustains,
and that Parzival's task is to restore that cult. It is true,
Schröder admits, that Parzival's failure reveals a lack of compassion, but more important is that it shows a lack of instinctive appreciation of the point and value of the cult itself. I
doubt myself if this emphasis is correct, though I do see that
the breakdown of the Grail cult through Anfortas's sin over-

[1] Weimar, 1952.

shadows the whole work, and that Parzival's development is essentially a development to the point at which he is fit to restore the cult, and himself take over its administration. But surely the work shows that this point is reached when Parzival has resolved his troubled relationship to man and God, rather than when he has understood the function of ritual? The two do, however, as Book IX shows, interlock.)

When Parzival wakes at Munsalvæsche the following morning, he finds the castle deserted; as he departs, the portcullis drops behind him, and a concealed page abuses him for not putting the vital question. Parzival finds no answer, but cries out with anguish. Later that day Sigune asks him if he has cured Anfortas, and his delay in replying seems to indicate an awareness of failure. When he does tell her, she curses him for lack of *triuwe*, proclaims his 'êre und rîterlîcher prîs' destroyed, and denies him any hope of atonement. He breaks out in sweat, not only on account of the heat of the day, but also because of his regret that he did not ask what ailed Anfortas. Parzival feels bitterly the shame of his disgrace, but his facile offer to make amends—'ich wandel, hân ich iht getân' (255, 23) —reveals no adequate consciousness of his sin. Nor does the condemnation of Cundrie convince him of it.

Cundrie is an exceptionally ugly woman who, with her equally ugly brother Malcreatiure, was sent as a curiosity to Anfortas by the heathen Queen Secundille (519, 18–23). Both are characterised by a total lack of sexual attractions which the narrator says derives from the *ungenuht* of certain of Adam's daughters (518, 1–29), and which perhaps qualifies them for their unusual roles. Malcreatiure is presented by Anfortas to his lady Orgeluse, and later plays a minor part in the work as her servant. Cundrie's role on the other hand is the major one of Grail messenger; she and she alone travels freely between Munsalvæsche and the outer world. The attack she launches on Parzival at the court of King Artus therefore originates at the Grail. According to her the Round Table is dishonoured

by the presence of Parzival, who with all his beauty is less
seemly (*gehiure*) than the hideous creature addressing him:

> gunêrt sî iwer liehter schîn
> und iwer manlîchen lide.
> het ich suone oder vride,
> diu wærn iu beidiu tiure.
> ich dunke iuch ungehiure,
> und bin gehiurer doch dann ir.   (315, 20–25)

This accusation does not expose the superficiality of the courtly
emphasis on beauty—a quality which, like *zuht*, particularly
characterises the assembly at Munsalvæsche—but reveals the
depths to which Parzival, in betraying the high promise of his
looks, has fallen.

Similarly Cundrie denounces Parzival for failing to perpe-
tuate the *triuwe* of his parents:

> nu denke ich ave an Gahmureten,
> des herze ie valsches was erjeten.
> von Anuchouwe iwer vater hiez,
> der iu ander erbe liez
> denn als ir habt geworben.
> an prîse ir sît verdorben.
> het iwer muotr ie missetân,
> so solt ichz dâ für gerne hân,
> ir möht sîn sun niht gesîn.
> nein, si lêrte ir triwe pîn . . .
>
> Nu ist iwer prîs ze valsche komn.
> ôwê daz ie wart vernomn
> von mir, daz Herzeloyden barn
> an prîse hât sus missevarn!
>   (317, 11–20; 318, 1–4)

Clearly Cundrie believes that parents bequeath to their children
their own characteristics, and what horrifies her is that Parzival
should have betrayed his *art*. He who in every way was
destined for the heights has fallen so low. He is, she says, condemned of God, and should be rejected by men too; *valsch*
such as his is unprecedented:

59

gein der helle ir sît benant
ze himele vor der hôhsten hant:
als sît ir ûf der erden,
versinnent sich die werden.
ir heiles pan, ir sælden fluoch,
des ganzen prîses reht unruoch!
ir sît manlîcher êren schiech,
und an der werdekeit sô siech,
kein arzet mag iuch des ernern.
ich wil ûf iwerem houbte swern,
gît mir iemen des den eit,
daz græzer valsch nie wart bereit
necheinem alsô schœnem man.
ir vederangl, ir nâtern zan!
iu gab iedoch der wirt ein swert,
des iwer wirde wart nie wert:
da erwarb iu swîgen sünden zil.
ir sît der hellehirten spil. (316, 7–24)

It is because he is so *schœne*, because his opportunity is so
great, that Parzival's sin is overwhelming; Christ's words 'to
whomsoever much is given, of him shall much be required'
apply perfectly to him. He is condemned utterly for what
seems a trivial error, but in his hands lay the cure of Anfortas
and the care of the Grail.

Parzival's reaction to Cundrie's attack is complex. On the
one hand his sense of shame, already apparent from his behaviour both to the page who abused him and to Sigune, leads
him now to withdraw from Arthurian society and willingly to
take upon himself the tribulations of a solitary existence.[1] Truly
sorry now for Anfortas, he realises all too late what a chance he
has missed:

mîn sol grôz jâmer alsô pflegn,
daz herze geb den ougen regn,

---

[1] Marianne Wynn interestingly contrasts the solitary wilderness in which
Parzival is brought up and which he now seeks out with the charted civilisation
in which Gawan moves, 'Parzival and Gawan—Hero and Counterpart',
Beiträge zur Geschichte der deutschen Sprache und Literatur, vol. 84 (Tübingen,
1962).

sît ich ûf Munsalvæsche liez
daz mich von wâren freuden stiez,
ohteiz wie manege clâre magt!
swaz iemen wunders hât gesagt,
dennoch pflît es mêr der grâl.
der wirt hât siufzebæren twâl.
ay helfelôser Anfortas,
waz half dich daz ich pî dir was?   (330, 21–30)

The very fact that his disgrace upsets him proves that Parzival is
not utterly degenerate; the hardness of heart which he has three
times exhibited is not total, for he can still feel shame. This is
surely the sense of the narrator's remark that, although neither
Parzival's courage nor his courtesy nor yet his *scham* saved him
from denunciation, yet the latter is a mitigating factor:

waz half in küenes herzen rât
unt wâriu zuht bî manheit?
und dennoch mêr im was bereit
scham ob allen sînen siten.
den rehten valsch het er vermiten:
wan scham gît prîs ze lône
und ist doch der sêle krône.
scham ist ob siten ein güebet uop.   (319, 4–11)

'der rehte valsch' is the unrepentant treachery of Lucifer;
that at least Parzival avoids.

On the other hand, ignorant as he is of original sin, of which
so far as we know no mention has yet been made to him by
anyone, Parzival declines to take upon himself full responsibility for his failure at Munsalvæsche. He maintains that by
keeping silent he was only obeying Gurnemanz's instructions,
and attempts to shift the blame to the latter (330, 1–6). When
Gawan, whose honour has also been called in question, commends him to God, Parzival, convinced that he has always
served God faithfully, replies by denouncing as impotent one
who thus betrays his servants:

Der Wâleis sprach 'wê waz ist got?
wær der gewaldec, sölhen spot
het er uns pêden niht gegebn,

61

kunde got mit kreften lebn.
ich was im diens undertân,
sît ich genâden mich versan.
nu wil i'm dienst widersagn:
hât er haz, den wil ich tragn.   (332, 1–8)

It is clear from this speech that Parzival conceives his relationship with God in feudal terms—though this is no proof that Arthurian society as a whole does so—and his religion at this stage may consequently be termed anthropomorphic. God has let him down and so he claims the right to leave his service and, indeed, to make war on him. Of the unpayable debt man owes to God on account of Adam's first sin—which Parzival has inherited—and of God's limitless goodness in redeeming his debtor on the Cross, the young knight knows nothing. Nor is he, in his self-centredness, willing to learn; he assumes that he is right and God wrong, and that if he only persists in his course he must triumph. Such self-righteousness is in strong contrast to Parzival's sense of shame; he knows that he has failed in his appointed task and is ashamed but, ignorant of the reasons for failure, he refuses stubbornly to admit that the fault is his. It takes four and a half years of misery—during which he gets no nearer the Grail—to break his obstinacy and make him ready to learn. Disgrace and failure are needed to bring Parzival, the child of Adam, back to God. Only when the sinner has come of his own accord to recognise his sin, does he find his way to Trevrizent, who can absolve him.[1]

There remains a third factor in Parzival's reaction to Cundrie's denunciation: his determination not to rest till he has made good his failure:

ine wil deheiner freude jehn,
ine müeze alrêrst den grâl gesehn,
diu wîle sî kurz oder lanc.
mich jaget des endes mîn gedanc:

---

[1] Friedrich Maurer takes Parzival's rejection of God, his so-called 'Gotteshass', as his gravest sin: see 'Parzivals Sünden', *Deutsche Vierteljahrsschrift für Literaturwissenschaft und Geistesgeschichte*, vol. 24 (1950).

dâ von gescheide ich nimmer
mînes lebens immer. (329, 25–30)

One who was convinced of both the shame and the injustice of
his disgrace might well fall into despair and apathy, and thus
seal his condemnation; the state of being *verzaget* is a religious
as well as a chivalrous crime. Parzival's persistence in his
attempt to recover what he has lost, in spite of many years of
vain endeavour and then considerable discouragement from
Trevrizent, proves at least that he has inherited and can put to
good use his father's gift of courage; without it he could never
have become Grail King.

In some ways Parzival's disgrace by Cundrie parallels his
earlier disgrace by Keie; then he fled the Round Table, but did
not despair, and eventually made good his claim to chivalry.
Now he once more takes leave of society, determined to find
acceptance at Munsalvæsche:

schildes ambet umben grâl
wirt nu vil güebet sunder twâl
von im den Herzeloyde bar.
er was ouch ganerbe dar. (333, 27–30)

And as Parzival on the former occasion proved his right to his
paternal heritage, so now his determination proves his worthi-
ness to be Herzeloyde's son and the heir to the Grail. It may
even connect up with that quality of *unverzaget mannes muot*
which is mentioned in the opening lines of the Prologue.

V

GAWAN'S EARLY ADVENTURES

ein manlîch höfsch man.[1]

With the exception of Book IX, the seven Books VII to XIII narrate the adventures not of Parzival but of Gawan. In Book IX Parzival spends a fortnight with the hermit Trevrizent, in Book XIV he is formally readmitted to the Round Table. Otherwise, for four and a half years before he visits Trevrizent and for two months after, he does nothing but fight. Towards the end of this period, he himself, echoing an earlier comment of the narrator (390, 9), says: 'ichn suochte niht wan strîten' (461, 8), and he adds that his life all this time has been entirely joyless:

> mirst freude ein troum:
> ich trage der riwe swæren soum.   (461, 1 f.)

It is the duty of a knight to fight; this is his particular task, for which he normally expects the reward of happiness (*freude*). The company of the Round Table, from which Parzival is absent for so long, is particularly associated with this happiness, as can be seen from the scene at the end of the work where Feirefiz is introduced to Artus (766, 1–18). By contrast the distinguishing feature of Parzival during the years of his absence from the *tavelrunder* is his total renunciation of all happiness until such time as he may make good his failure at Munsalvæsche (329, 25–30). In accordance with this vow Parzival does not see his wife again until after he has redeemed Anfortas. In the meantime, while Gawan holds the centre of the stage and mixes *freude* and *arbeit* as a knight should, Parzival only makes occasional appearances in the wings and, until the very end, never joins in the cheerful gatherings of knights and ladies either at the Round Table or elsewhere.

[1] 430, 20.

Thus in Book VII Parzival fights incognito on the opposite side to Gawan, but refuses to stay after the battle:

> si bâten in belîben vil:
> fürbaz gestôzen was sîn zil.
> dô kêrte der gehiure
> dâ grôz gemach was tiure:
> ern suochte niht wan strîten.
> ich wæn bî sînen zîten
> ie dechein man sô vil gestreit.   (390, 5–11)

In Book VIII King Vergulaht tells how a red knight had defeated him in combat and made him, like other knights defeated by Parzival in Book VII (388, 26–389, 14), promise to seek the Grail and, if not successful within a year, go as his prisoner to Condwiramurs (424, 22–425, 14). Similarly, after leaving Trevrizent, Parzival is mentioned as having defeated Orgeluse's knights and refused the reward she offered—on the grounds that he prefers his own wife and lacks the Grail alone (618, 19–619, 24). Finally in Book XIV Parzival arrives on the scene of Gawan's impending combat with Gramoflanz, simply as he says in the hope of a fight:

> von sînem boume ich einen kranz
> brach hiute morgen fruo,
> daz er mir strîten fuorte zuo.
> ich kom durch strîten in sîn lant,
> niwan durch strît gein sîner hant.   (701, 2–6)

On this occasion Parzival's eagerness for battle leads to his fighting not only Gramoflanz but also, by mistake, Gawan and Feirefiz.

Before this latter contest—which immediately precedes Cundrie's arrival with her good news of Parzival's final election to the Grail—he steals away from the Round Table to which he has just been readmitted but whose happiness he cannot share:

> sol ich mit den ougen freude sehn
> und muoz mîn herze jâmers jehn,
> diu werc stênt ungelîche...

ich pin trûrens unerlôst.
gelücke müeze freude wern
die endehafter freude gern:
got gebe freude al disen scharn:
ich wil ûz disen freuden varn.

(732, 23-25; 733, 16-20)

Thus a second time Parzival takes leave of society. God apparently will not grant him what he seeks—'got wil mîner freude niht', he says (733, 8)—and it is impossible for him to abandon his quest for the Grail and content himself with the joys of the Round Table. His knightly *arbeit*—he later lists for Feirefiz some of those whom he has defeated (771, 23-773, 6)—is distinguished from that of all other knights by its total joylessness. One function of Gawan in the work is to represent that joyful society from which Parzival is for so long excluded.

No more than Parzival, who is a member of both the Grail and the Arthurian families and whose progress is punctuated by encounters with his cousin Sigune and his uncle Trevrizent, does Gawan stand alone in the work.[1] As a child he was brought up by Artus himself, who is his mother's brother; and this relationship is here, as usually in medieval literature, one of the closest intimacy (cf. 661, 21-662, 2).[2] When Gawan's honour is impugned, Artus exclaims indignantly:

hêrre, erst mîner swester suon:
wær Gâwân tôt, ich wolde tuon
den kampf, ê sîn gebeine
læge triwenlôs unreine.
wil glücke, iu sol Gâwânes hant
mit kampfe tuon daz wol bekant
daz sîn lîp mit triwen vert
und sichs valsches hât erwert.   (322, 15-22)

[1] On Gawan in general see Georg Keferstein, 'Die Gawanhandlung in Wolframs *Parzival*', *Germanisch-Romanische Monatsschrift*, vol. 25 (1937); Wolfgang Mohr, 'Parzival und Gawan', *Euphorion*, vol. 52 (1958); and Marianne Wynn, 'Parzival and Gawan—Hero and Counterpart,' *Beiträge zur Geschichte der deutschen Sprache und Literatur*, vol. 84 (Tübingen, 1962).

[2] On the relationship of mother's brother to sister's son outside medieval literature see A. R. Radcliffe-Brown, *Structure and Function in Primitive Society* (London, 1952), ch. 1, a book which contains much that scholars might find useful in interpreting family relationships in medieval literature.

Nor is this confidence of Artus in his nephew misplaced, for the accusation against Gawan is later withdrawn. At least after the death of Ither, Gawan is known as the most distinguished of all the Round Table knights—'der tavelrunder hôhster prîs' (301, 7)—and of them all he is the only one whose reputation is such that Gramoflanz, who normally engages two opponents at once, is prepared to fight him single-handed, explaining:

> nu . . . hât Gâwân erworben
> solhen prîs vor ûz besunder
> daz ob der tavelrunder
> im prîses niemen glîchen mac . . .   (608, 25–29)

When so distinguished a representative leaves the Round Table, the narrator describes it as 'orphaned'—

> der werdekeit ein weise
> wart nu diu tavelrunder   (335, 8 f.)

—but even during his absence a link remains, for Gawan enters combat as 'der werden tavelrunder bote' (380, 11). He is in fact always associated with Arthurian chivalry, and cannot properly be understood except with reference to this; I propose therefore briefly to characterise Artus himself and his company before proceeding to the individual exploits of Gawan.

Just as Gahmuret, *der Anschevîn*, is first and foremost king of Anschouwe, which he inherits from his father, and Parzival, *der Wâleis*, should be king of Waleis, which has, however, been conquered from his mother, so Artus, *der Bertûn* or *Berteneis*, is primarily king of Bertane (Brittany). His capital is Nantes, and that is where Parzival first seeks him out. As king of Bertane, Artus is only the equal of other kings and is therefore liable to be attacked when he rides unannounced through their lands, as he is by the followers of Orgeluse (664, 18–665, 29); he does not, however, expect unprovoked attacks against himself or his knights:

> ein ieslîch künec mîn genôz
> mîn gerne möhte schônen.   (719, 24 f.)

Nevertheless Clamide, King of Iserterre, has to confess when he is sent to Artus as Parzival's prisoner:

> du weist wol daz in mîn lant
> dir manec laster ist getân . . .   (220, 14 f.)

But Artus generously pardons him. Certain Arthurian knights, having been captured on a previous occasion, appear in one of Gawan's adventures fighting on the other side to him, so that he has carefully to avoid them (382, 9–383, 16). Gawan himself remains in the service of Artus although he is the son of the deceased King Lot of Norwæge; he has a brother, Beacurs, but neither seems interested in their inheritance.

If in such ways the court of Artus is like other courts, it is distinguished from them and idealised by the customs of the Round Table. On special occasions—and only if one of his knights has met with adventure (309, 3–9; 648, 18–22)—Artus has a circular table laid out and invites those knights and ladies who are so privileged to dine at it. These form the noble company of the *tavelrunder*, into which in the course of the work Artus specially invites Parzival and Feirefiz, and which he further allows Gramoflanz, Lischoys and Florant to join after they have married into his family (776, 25–777, 1). Ladies are only permitted to be present if they have accepted the service of an Arthurian knight and have promised him reward:

> swelch frowe was sunder âmîs,
> diu getorste niht decheinen wîs
> über tavelrunder komn.
> het si dienst ûf ir lôn genomn
> und gap si lônes sicherheit,
> an tavelrunder rinc si reit.
> die andern muosenz lâzen:
> in ir herberge se sâzen.   (776, 17–24)

The customs of the Round Table thus epitomise the courtly life in which knights perform noble deeds for their ladies, who reward them with their love (cf. 217, 7–18); *freude* is the keynote at all its meetings.

In addition Arthurian society has a strong ethical bias. The

68

narrator speaks of it as a company, 'der neheiner valscheit nie geriet' (307, 16), and later remarks:

> sich moht ein bœse man wol schamn,
> ob er dâ bî den werden saz:
> die spîs sîn munt mit sünden az.   (775, 18–20)

The noble spirit (*werdekeit*) of Artus himself is widely famed, as Feirefiz points out on his arrival from heathen lands:

> du gebârest vil gelîche
> einem man des werdekeit
> ist mit mæren harte breit:
> bistu Artûs genant,
> sô ist dîn name verre erkant.   (767, 6–10)

When Parzival is accused by Cundrie of falsehood, she says he has disgraced the whole company (314, 23–315, 10); and with reference to Gawan's supposed crime, his accuser Kingrimursel generalises about the *tavelrunder*:

> der reht wære gebrochen sân,
> sæze drob ein triwenlôser man.   (322, 5 f.)

It is the unique characteristic, the law (*reht*) of the Round Table that all its members are beyond reproach; its honour depends on theirs. Were the accusations against Parzival and Gawan fully justified, it would be destroyed; at the time Cundrie goes so far as to say:

> tavelrunder ist entnihtet:
> der valsch hât dran gepflihtet.   (314, 29 f.)

The first task of all members is therefore to preserve its honour —both by behaving nobly and by defending their reputation for so doing (cf. 290, 16 f.). It is a public concern.

The adventures of Gawan most perfectly represent this especial *werdekeit* of Arthurian knights, but some light is also thrown on it by the character of Artus himself. Like Parzival on the occasion of his liberation of Condwiramurs (when he doles out the newly-arrived food to the starving citizens with his own hand and has no thought of profiting from his feat of arms, above, pp. 39-41), Artus also is described by the narrator as 'der unlôse niht ze hêr' (201, 18). Nor is this description fortuitous: modesty and caution are as much characteristics of the leading Round Table knights as is consideration for others; and the enemies of Artus are notable for their arrogance, rashness and inhumanity. The king himself always listens to the advice of others, and might indeed be thought to be almost unduly swayed by it—as when Keie persuades him to let young Parzival fight Ither, or when he allows first Segramors and then Keie to fight Parzival when the latter is lost in thoughts of his wife. The possible implications of such weakness are exploited in certain other Arthurian romances of the time, but not in Wolfram's *Parzival*. Here the contrast with the two kings Meljanz and Vergulaht, who as will be seen shortly are misled by hot-headed rashness wrongly to take up arms against the advice of their chief counsellors, makes Artus's lack of impetuosity appear as a desirable quality in a ruler. He is above all a diplomatic king who carefully considers all his actions beforehand and listens to what others have to say. Furthermore he himself clearly prefers peace to war, forbidding his knights to indulge in unnecessary fighting when the risk is serious (280, 18–281, 8), never on any occasion provoking trouble, and only once, when Orgeluse's followers set on him as he seeks out Gawan, engaging in combat himself (665, 11 f.).

Yet Artus would defend Gawan's honour in battle were he dead (322, 13–18), and acts firmly to punish rape, which, as an offence against *minne*, is the worst (civil) crime known to chivalrous society. Two knights, Meljahkanz and Urjans, are mentioned as having committed rape in the course of the work; Meljahkanz—the man whom the first knights Parzival ever sees are chasing—has the reputation of never winning love except by force (343, 23–30), Urjans commits an offence against a particular lady, of whom Gawan says:

> Diu juncfrouwe reit uns mite:
> riwebærec was ir site,
> durch daz ir hête genomen
> der nie was in ir dienst komen
> ir kiuscheclîchen magetuom. (526, 1–5)

The particularly unchivalrous nature of the crime is indicated here by the description of Urjans as 'he who had never entered the service' of the girl he deflowered. The chivalrous code prescribes *minne* as the reward of *dienst*; and Artus, in revenging the girl, is upholding the code. Indeed she claims justice from him not only in the name of womanhood and virginity, but also because she should have enjoyed special immunity as a messenger, and 'Durch der tavelrunder art' (527, 1). Artus initially condemns Urjans to death, but then, at the request of Gawan to whom Urjans had surrendered (instead of fighting to the finish), commutes the punishment to one of eating with the dogs for four weeks. Thus does the Round Table impose observance of the laws of chivalry.

Artus perhaps behaves most characteristically when, having accepted Gawan's request that he come with all his court to watch the duel between Gawan and Gramoflanz, he is then instrumental in negotiating an honourable peace between the two. In this connection the narrator refers several times to the king as 'der wîse höfsche man' (717, 1; 728, 9; cf. 699, 22), and these terms surely describe him most accurately. He and his whole company stand for prudence and courtesy.

Gawan, whom the narrator throughout distinguishes as *mîn hêr Gâwân*, is also frequently described as *höfsch* or *kurteis*, but (since he is a younger man ?) not usually as *wîse*. It is rather as 'ein manlîch höfsch man' that he appears most characteristically to his fellows (430, 20; 677, 24). The contrast is significant, for Gawan is certainly more active with lance and sword than is Artus—even as a boy he was prematurely eager to enter the lists (66, 15–22)—though in his maturity he is far removed from resembling the rash, hot-headed or proud knights who oppose the *tavelrunder*. Indeed, Gawan is distinguished by those very qualities of prudence and love of peace which characterise Artus. Thus after Segramors has been unseated and Keie disabled in attacks on Parzival, whose senses are rapt away by *minne*, Gawan quietly rebukes Keie for suggesting he is a coward and rides out leaving his arms behind him:

> er wolde güetlîche ersehen,
> von wem der strît dâ wære geschehen.   (300, 9 f.)

When he receives no reply to either his friendly greeting or his warning, his experience in love—'Gâwân was solher nœte al wîs' (301, 8)—enables him to recognise the symptoms in the other, with the result that instead of perpetuating strife, he and Parzival exchange promises of mutual service and Artus's search for the latter ends happily. Moreover, Gawan's reluctance to avenge Keie proves justified, for it was Keie who first insulted Parzival, unjustly as everyone now admits, and so the latter had the right to restore his honour.

This encounter of Gawan with Parzival leads directly to the assembly at the Plimizœl, where both are accused of shameful behaviour and take leave of the others. The parallelism of their fates is here emphasised for the first time (326, 11–14; 332 17 f.); but their divergent reactions to the fate thrust upon them reveals also an element of contrast. Parzival, who knows he has failed to redeem Anfortas, yet abandons his allegiance to a God who can visit such shame upon him when his wish at least has been to serve his Lord faithfully. Clearly a man who can thus doubt God does not have a satisfactory relationship with him. Gawan on the other hand is wrongfully accused of treacherously slaying King Kingrisin in the course of a greeting—'ime gruozer mînen hêrren sluoc' (321, 10)— wrongfully, since in fact, as it later transpires, quite another man killed Kingrisin (413, 13–20). Yet Gawan does not feel his trust in God in the least disturbed by God's permitting so false a charge to be brought against him—the charge is incidentally 'inherited', in that a similar one was brought against his father; such is their common destiny—but prays God will protect both himself and Parzival, whom he addresses thus:

> ich weiz wol, friwent, daz dîn vart
> gein strîtes reise ist ungespart.
> dâ geb dir got gelücke zuo,

> und helfe ouch mir daz ich getuo
> dir noch den dienst als ich kan gern.
> des müeze mich sîn kraft gewern.   (331, 25–30)

Whatever may be the nature and depth of Gawan's religion—
and that problem will be discussed in chapter VIII—it is clear
that his relationship with God is secure and confident from the
beginning; unlike Parzival, Gawan does not require to sin and
suffer before he can accept as good whatever God decrees.

Nor is this confidence based upon a certainty of winning the
duel to which Kingrimursel challenges him, nor upon the joy
another knight might feel at the prospect of fighting. Gawan is
warned by the others to beware of combat with such a man, and
he takes all possible precautions, wisely choosing his shields for
their toughness rather than for their ornament:

> Gâwân maz besunder
> wâ mit er möhte wol gesign.
> alt herte schilde wol gedign
> (ern ruochte wie si wârn gevar)
> die brâhten koufliute dar
> ûf ir soumen, doch niht veile:
> der wurden im drî ze teile.   (335, 10–16)

Admittedly it transpires later that Gawan does not travel alone
to his tryst but has a worthy retinue of eight noble-born squires;
nevertheless, he does not employ these to make a proud show of
the sort beloved of Gahmuret, but behaves throughout with a
modesty that is sometimes mistaken for lowliness of birth. His
reluctance to fight unless it is absolutely unavoidable is clearly
expressed at this stage when he refuses his brother's offer to
fight in his stead (which in any case Kingrimursel would not
have accepted, 324, 1–30):

> Gâwân sprach 'ich pin sô wîs
> daz ich dich, bruoder, niht gewer
> dîner bruoderlîchen ger.
> ine weiz war umbe ich strîten sol,
> ouch entuot mir strîten niht sô wol:
> ungerne wolt ich dir versagn,
> wan daz ich müesez laster tragn.'   (323, 24–30)

And throughout the adventures that follow, in which Gawan's prowess in arms is proved again and again, this passage should never be forgotten: *strît* is not in itself a source of joy to the leading knight of the *tavelrunder* but is only undertaken as unavoidable duty, as *arbeit*.

Gawan is on his way to his tryst at Barbigœl when at the beginning of Book VII, as he approaches Bearosche, his way is blocked by a large army. That it is not over chivalrous appears first from the crowd of merchants, whores and unruly foot-soldiers who follow the knights (341, 11–30). A noble-hearted squire, whom Gawan stops, confirms this impression, and tells him that the leaders are King Poydiconjunz and his proud nephew Meljanz who, accompanied by that violator of women, Poydiconjunz's son Meljahkanz, are unjustifiably making war upon Meljanz's former guardian and tutor Lyppaut. The war results from the impetuosity both of Meljanz and of Obie, one of Lyppaut's two daughters to whom Meljanz had offered his 'Minnedienst'. She arrogantly spurned him as one whose worth was still unproven, he as arrogantly took offence and declared he would avenge himself on her father who must have inspired her words. The father, whose loyalty to his charge reveals him as the type of the faithful retainer, vainly protested innocence and endeavoured to pacify Meljanz, who, however, departed without a by-your-leave and is now returning in force. All this Gawan learns from the squire, who makes his opinion clear that pride had brought about a most unchivalrous situation, in which lover is fighting lover, master fighting man (343, 19–348, 30).[1]

Gawan is thrust by this information into a predicament which the narrator, addressing his public, specifically designates as *zwîvel*:

> waz welt ir daz Gâwân nu tuo,
> ern besehe waz disiu mære sîn?

[1] See Wolfgang Mohr, 'Obie und Meljanz', in *Gestaltprobleme der Dichtung (Günther Müller Festschrift*, Bonn, 1957); and Xenja von Ertzdorff, 'Fräulein Obilot', *Wirkendes Wort*, vol. 12 (1962).

doch lêrt in zwîvel strengen pîn.
Er dâhte 'sol ich strîten sehn,
und sol des niht von mir geschehn,
sost al mîn prîs verloschen gar.
kum ab ich durch strîten dar
und wirde ich dâ geletzet,
mit wârheit ist entsetzet
al mîn werltlîcher prîs.
ine tuon es niht decheinen wîs;
ich sol ê leisten mînen kampf.'
sîn nôt sich in ein ander klampf.
gegen sîner kampfes verte
was ze belîben alze herte:
ern mohte ouch dâ niht für gevarn.
er sprach 'nu müeze got bewarn
die kraft an mîner manheit.'
Gâwân gein Bêârosche reit.   (349, 28–350, 16)

At this stage the dilemma touches Gawan's personal honour alone; he is pledged to meet Kingrimursel very shortly and if for any reason he fails to appear, his reputation will suffer. On the other hand his honour would also be affected if he deliberately avoided the battle which is about to break out before him. Unable to resolve what appears to him insoluble, Gawan commits the issue to God and rides to Bearosche, the scene of the present conflict.

The succeeding events point to the hidden working of the hand of God. Gawan rides first through the ranks of the besieging army, inquiring whether they wish to enlist his aid; but no single member of this unchivalrous company even invites him to alight: 'belîbens bete in niemen bat' (351, 15). The town gates are walled up, so Gawan dismounts beneath some trees in full view of the castle; his squires unload a mattress and cushion for him to rest on, and make themselves comfortable too. Meanwhile Lyppaut's wife and two daughters have observed him from above and discuss his identity, all their conversation being audible to him. Clearly against appearances, for no one agrees with her, the elder daughter Obie pronounces Gawan to be a merchant; pours scorn on her sister who supports him, even though he takes no part in the *vesperie*; attempts to mock Gawan himself by sending a page to buy goods from him; despatches Count Scherules, Constable of the castle, to seize the property of this presumed swindler; and finally requests her father to apprehend him as a coiner. Such conduct is no more calculated to win Gawan's allegiance than is the total disregard paid to him by Meljanz and his army; Obie like her lover is proud and churlish, and her sister rightly compares her behaviour to Gawan with her treatment of Meljanz.

Nevertheless the narrator cautions the reader against condemning Obie's whole character for this show of pride, and provides a psychological explanation (365, 1–366, 2). Obie is in the grip of love, whose workings are unpredictable; it is precisely because she loves Meljanz so much that she was hurt by his anger against her; she takes it out on others because she is so hurt; since it is her capacity for feeling which thus leads her astray, one should hesitate to blame her. This sort of comment is not isolated in the work; later a similar argument is put forward to explain the similar behaviour of Orgeluse (see below, pp. 132 and 136 f.). Orgeluse eventually marries Gawan, Obie's troubles are solved with his help: it seems that Arthurian knights can not only punish acts of rape, but also by their courage and patience help with the psychology of sex.

That Gawan is willing to assist Obie at all is due to the intervention of her younger sister Obilot who, though as yet too young for love, is filled with the true spirit of chivalry, so that to Obie's scorn of Gawan she replies:

> du zîhst in daz doch nie geschach:
> swester, des mahtu dich schamn:
> er gewan nie koufmannes namen.
> er ist sô minneclîch getân,
> ich wil in zeime ritter hân.
> sîn dienst mac hie lônes gern:
> des wil ich in durch liebe wern.   (352, 20–26)

Gawan's appearance proclaims him for Obilot, as also for all the others whom Obie tries to inflame against him, as a model of chivalry, so that she upholds his nobility to her sister and declares she will herself engage and reward his services. Accordingly after Lyppaut has welcomed Gawan but failed to overcome the latter's doubts as to whether he should risk missing his tryst with Kingrimursel—even though Lyppaut points out that Meljanz is attacking him without cause (367, 4-6)—Obilot goes herself, with her father's consent, to visit the stranger:

> ich wil den fremden ritter biten
> dienstes nâch lônes siten. (368, 17 f.)

The following scenes, which reveal the same indulgent humour with children as those describing Parzival's earliest adventures, demonstrate the power for good contained in the courtly convention of 'Minnedienst'; for Gawan, who knows full well that there is no question of his obtaining an adult reward for his service—he says plainly to the girl:

> ê daz ir minne megt gegebn,
> ir müezet fünf jâr ê lebn (370, 15)

—is nevertheless won over by her naïve plea that he take service with her in expectation of reward, and agrees in the name of *minne* to do so:

> nu dâhter des, wie Parzivâl
> wîben baz getrûwt dan gote:
> sîn bevelhen dirre magde bote
> was Gâwân in daz herze sîn.
> dô lobter dem freuwelîn,
> er wolde durch si wâpen tragen. (370, 18-23)

The recommendation to serve women alone, with which Parzival had at their parting countered Gawan's prayer to God, is an expression of a disordered allegiance which only brings Parzival unhappiness; yet for Gawan, who has just re-expressed his trust in God on approaching Bearosche, the recollection of this remark has the effect of resolving his *zwîvel* in a way which subsequent events prove correct. (Note that the contrast between the outlook of the two friends is brought home by the reminder that Parzival did not simply recommend the service of women, but specifically trusted this more than the service of God.)

There is some justification for the parallel often remarked between Gawan's *zwîvel* on this occasion and that of Parzival at Munsalvæsche, for to some extent Gawan's choice, like Parzival's, is between an excessive concern for his own honour and a sincere feeling for the suffering of others. The affair in which Gawan risks getting involved at Bearosche is no longer just any military engagement, avoidance of which might appear as cowardice, it is now specifically a matter of helping the innocent parties in response to their particular request, in a war which threatens to overwhelm them. If Gawan preferred his own interests at this stage to those of Lyppaut and Obilot, he would be guilty of a selfishness not unlike that exhibited by Parzival before Anfortas; that he does not do so reveals his essential *triuwe* within his own sphere, a *triuwe* which Obilot's offer of *minne* has helped to call forth.

Gawan and Obilot go through all the forms of a *minne* relationship from which the erotic element is totally absent— she has her first grown-up dress made, one sleeve remaining unsewn until Gawan, who enters battle with this token (*kleinœte*) pinned to his shield, returns it to her bearing evident signs of *strît*—and the joy which not only the young girl but also the experienced knight derive from this episode is considerable. When Obilot's playmate brings Gawan the sleeve, 'dô wart sîn lîp gar sorgen vrî' (375, 21) is the (perhaps somewhat ironic) comment of the narrator. Moreover, the ideal unity of the two is given frequent expression; they are one when she requests his service: 'her, ich bit iwer unde mîn' (369, 11); one when he risks his life in battle—

> ich pin wirt und wirtîn
> und wil in strîte bî iu sîn   (371, 13 f.)

—one when he defeats his opponent: 'iuch envienc hie niemen wan ir hant' (394, 18). Clearly the honour of both is enhanced by this triumph, and their joy is a united joy (395, 20–30). The contrast between such a relationship and that of Obie and Meljanz is evident; the ideal of *minne* works perfectly—so long as it remains a game. Where it is more than that, the reality varies according to the individual circumstances.

A game, however, can have a useful function, and Gawan's service of Obilot does help others. Indeed he fights in such a way that God's might is apparent in his deeds (380, 11–13), and he overthrows the despicable Meljahkanz and takes the proud King Meljanz himself prisoner, handing him over to Obilot. His hope in so doing is that he will re-establish peace between the warring lovers (392, 17 ff.), and to this end he begs his lady to dispose of her prisoner in such a manner 'daz prîs ir fuore walte' (394, 10). Obilot maliciously reproves the king for surrendering to a 'merchant', but proceeds to insist on a reconciliation:

> Meljanze si dâ nâch gebôt
> daz er sicherheit verjæhe,
> diu in ir hant geschæhe,
> ir swester Obîen.
> 'zeiner âmîen
> sult ir si hân durch ritters prîs:
> zeim hêrren und zeim âmîs
> sol si iuch immer gerne hân.
> ine wils iuch dwederhalp erlân.'   (396, 10–18)

And the narrator adds: 'got ûz ir jungen munde sprach' (396, 19). God, to whom Gawan entrusted the issue on his arrival at Bearosche, has worked out his purpose through *minne*; in serving each other, Gawan and Obilot serve God. There is no ultimate disharmony in the Arthurian world.

Greatly to Obilot's sorrow, after peace has been restored, Gawan neither remains with her nor takes her with him, but journeys on to Schamfanzun where he is to fight Kingrimursel. Book VIII opens with his arrival within sight of the castle, in front of which he encounters the young King Vergulaht, whose father he is accused of having murdered. Without revealing his identity, he gains permission to enter the castle and seek hospitality from Vergulaht's sister Antikonie, until the king should return from hunting. The consequent meeting of

Gawan and Antikonie is directly contrasted with the preceding adventure with Obilot by its open eroticism. Vergulaht himself suggests that Gawan will wish to remain alone with his sister as long as possible, and the narrator draws an intriguing parallel between Antikonie and the Margravine of Heitstein:

> ... sô daz ir site und ir sin
> was gelîch der marcgrâvin
> Diu dicke vonme Heitstein
> über al die marke schein.
> wol im derz heinlîche an ir
> sol prüeven! des geloubet mir,
> der vindet kurzewîle dâ
> bezzer denne anderswâ.　　　　(403, 29–404, 6)

Extra-literary references of this kind are numerous in *Parzival* and unfortunately require for their full enjoyment a more detailed knowledge of the times than historical records provide; we know that Elisabeth of Heitstein was a sister of Duke Ludwig of Bavaria and was widowed in 1204, and we know much about Antikonie's habits and outlook, but we do not know the point of the parallel. Even the assumption that Wolfram did not expect his contemporaries to be as shocked by frank sensuality as some modern scholars have been is not necessarily valid without further knowledge of the reputation of Elisabeth and of Wolfram's relationship to her family. Fortunately, however, the episode can be enjoyed for itself, and is as amusing in its way as the more innocent one which precedes it.

Antikonie greets Gawan with a courteous speech in which she indicates her willingness to exchange a kiss of salutation with him if he thinks this proper. Propriety in such a matter depends, according to the code of chivalry, on the rank of the people concerned, but Gawan, instead of stating his rank, replies with gallantries:

> frouwe, iwer muont
> ist sô küssenlîch getân,
> ich sol iweren kus mit gruoze hân.
> 　　　　　　　　　　　　(405, 16–18)

And the kiss which he then offers her full, warm, red lips is not that of a stranger (*ungastlîch* 405, 21). Encouraged by this beginning, Gawan asks for 'favours'; and Antikonie's consent to anything he suggests except lying together (*âne bî ligen*, 406, 6) is probably calculated to provoke him further. When he has assured her that his status is equal to her own, the assembled company retire tactfully, and indeed only just in time:

> Gâwân des gedâhte,
> dô si alle von im kômen ûz,
> daz dicke den grôzen strûz
> væhet ein vil kranker ar.
> er greif ir undern mantel dar:
> Ich wæne, er ruort irz hüffelîn.
> des wart gemêret sîn pîn.
> von der liebe alsölhe nôt gewan
> beidiu magt und ouch der man,
> daz dâ nâch was ein dinc geschehen,
> hetenz übel ougen niht ersehen,
> des willn si bêde wârn bereit . . .
>
> (406, 28–407, 9)

But Gawan and Antikonie are prevented from consummating their mutual desire by the interruption of an old knight who recognises Gawan and gives the alarm:

> ôwê unde heiâ hei
> mîns hêrren den ir sluoget,
> daz iuch des niht genuoget,
> irn nôtzogt och sîn tohter hie.   (407, 16–19)

That this new accusation of rape is no more true than the old one of murder cannot be doubted after Antikonie's behaviour and the comment on the 'thing' about to take place when they were interrupted: 'des willn si bêde wârn bereit' (407, 9); and nowhere is it suggested in the work that the attempted seduction of which Gawan might well be accused could justify the attack which follows. Indeed this onslaught on Gawan, who has not even a sword to defend himself with against knights, citizens and later even King Vergulaht, is condemned outright. As Kingrimursel, the only person beside

81

Antikonie to stand by Gawan, later points out, Gawan had come to Schamfanzun to defend his honour on the condition that nobody else at all should fight him; his immunity had been guaranteed by the king himself (415, 9–17). In addition he had entered the castle as the king's guest and had been committed by Vergulaht to the care of Antikonie, who supports him when he is attacked; both his status as guest and a lady's protection should have been additional safeguards (412, 18–20; 415, 1–5). Under these circumstances the *triuwe* of Antikonie and Kingrimursel, who risk all to support a knight who is a stranger to the one and an enemy to the other, stands out in sharp contrast to the *untriuwe* of Vergulaht in particular, who is prepared even to attack his sister and his kinsman, until others, 'dens ir triwe jach' (412, 11), persuade him to grant a truce while the affair is debated rationally. The king realises his disgrace (414, 8–12), Kingrimursel postpones his combat with Gawan for another year, and after much discussion Gawan is released on condition that he seeks the Grail in place of Vergulaht, whom Parzival has accidentally encountered and compelled to join in his own quest.

The incident thus concludes with the belated acceptance by the king and his people of the ethic of chivalry, which forbids the use of treachery or *force majeure* to exact vengeance, and insists even in the event of murder that the accused be given a fair chance to prove his innocence in single combat. This principle is incorporated in the person of Kingrimursel who, although he earlier excepted Gawan from his general commendation of the Round Table company to the care of God (324, 29 f.), thus perhaps indicating that the outcome of the duel was to be regarded as the judgment of God, yet springs to his enemy's side and even addresses Gawan as *du* when his immunity from others is threatened, and finally is content when Gawan is released and the combat arranged for a later date.

It is perhaps surprising that, from the moment when Antikonie sides with Gawan, no more mention is made of the impropriety which so scandalised the old knight who broke in upon the pair. Nevertheless the erotic element does not vanish from the scene, for much is made of the pleasure Gawan derives from contemplating his lady's pretty face and 'ant'-waisted figure during pauses in the fighting (in which incidentally they defend themselves with giant chessmen!):

> waz Gâwân dô tæte?
>   swenne im diu muoze geschach,
> daz er die maget reht ersach;
> ir munt, ir ougen, unde ir nasen.
> baz geschict an spizze hasen,
> ich wæne den gesâht ir nie,
> dan si was dort unde hie,
> zwischen der hüffe unde ir brust.
> minne gerende gelust
> kunde ir lîp vil wol gereizen.
> irn gesâht nie âmeizen,
> Diu bezzers gelenkes pflac,
> dan si was dâ der gürtel lac.
> daz gap ir gesellen
> Gâwâne manlîch ellen.   (409, 22–410, 6)

Gawan's 'minne gerende gelust' can, however, no longer be raised as an issue without involving Antikonie too, and no one appears willing to question the honour of the lady described to Vergulaht by the spokesman of the people as 'vor valscheit diu vrîe' (413, 2).

With this we return to the question of Antikonie's morals. She herself later claims to Vergulaht that the shield with which she defended Gawan consisted of her virtue alone:

> dô was ich âne wer ein magt,
> wan daz ich truoc doch einen schilt,
> ûf den ist werdekeit gezilt:
> des wâpen sol ich nennen,
> ob ir ruochet diu bekennen.
> guot gebærde und kiuscher site,
> den zwein wont vil stæte mite.
> den bôt ich für den ritter mîn,
> den ir mir sandet dâ her în:
> anders schermes het ich niht.   (414, 18–27)

That Antikonie should describe her own virtue in terms of *kiusche* and *stæte* could be dismissed as 'in character', were it not for the ardent praise the narrator extends to her after the fighting is over:

> mit lobe wir solden grüezen
> die kiuschen unt die süezen
> Antikonîen,
> vor valscheit die vrîen.
> wan si lebte in solhen siten,
> daz ninder was underriten
> ir prîs mit valschen worten.
> al die ir prîs gehôrten,
> ieslîch munt ir wunschte dô
> daz ir prîs bestüende alsô
> bewart vor valscher trüeben jehe.
> lûter virrec als ein valkensehe
> was balsemmæzec stæte an ir.   (427, 5–17)

There may be an element of irony in this praise of a lady whose sexual morals appear rather loose, but I do not think that the whole issue of Antikonie's morality can be dismissed as a product of Wolfram's notorious humour. Her name is emphasised here by being extended over a whole line, as elsewhere is that of Condwiramurs, and sense, phrase and rhythm echo various passages describing Sigune—facts which have disturbed those scholars who do not approve of Antikonie's sexual laxity. Clearly in extolling her *kiusche*, the narrator is not extolling her chastity, for if that is preserved, it is certainly not her fault. Clearly also, her merits cannot lie in a simple observance of the chivalrous code, for she has been willing to grant favours without previous service. The episode indeed seems to indicate that even where a chaste disposition and an abidance by the rule are lacking, virtue is still possible; and in this case it may be regarded as the complement of the one which precedes it: if Obilot's behaviour demonstrated the value of a naïve acceptance of the code of chivalry, that of Antikonie demonstrates the value of a personal disregard of it.

The basis of the narrator's claims for Antikonie seems to be this:

> wol si daz bescheinde,
> daz friwentlîch liebe ist stæte. (409, 20 f.)

Compared with the constancy of Sigune's love, which survives the grave, that of Antikonie may appear short-lived—there is no mention, and no likelihood, of her pining for Gawan after his departure—yet by standing by her lover in his hour of need ('si tûrte mit im in der nôt', 410, 7) she has demonstrated that, as far as is required of her, she too is constant. Antikonie is a much shallower person than Sigune, but on her own level her integrity is as complete as the other's, and that is what the narrator seems to applaud: even such an affection is sincere, it too knows no *valsch*. Not everyone is born into the Grail family; nor amongst the relatives of Artus—it is twice pointed out that Vergulaht and Antikonie are members of the Gahmuret branch of the Arthurian family (406, 4 f.; 410, 21–27)—are all called on to behave in the same manner. But each should be true to his or her own vocation, whatever it may be. Vergulaht fails:

> Welt ir hœrn, ich tuon iu kunt
> wâ von ê sprach mîn munt
> daz lûtr gemüete trüebe wart.
> gunêrt sî diu strîtes vart,
> die ze Schampfanzûn tet Vergulaht:
> wan daz was im niht geslaht
> von vater noch von muoter. (414, 1–7)

Antikonie succeeds supremely, and is greeted with praise.

The *triuwe* which distinguishes her from her brother consists primarily of the loyalty shown by her to Gawan; to that extent it is a social virtue. It also, however, involves trueness to oneself, and in so doing approximates to *kiusche*, which is one of the most difficult of Wolfram's terms to render into English. In that Antikonie's *triuwe* is vitiated by neither treachery (*valsch*) nor pride (*hôchvart*, *lôsheit*), it testifies to the incorruption, the purity and chastity of her inner self; she accepts perfectly her

85

own nature and place in society, her own destiny, and can act *naturally* well; although so different, she and Sigune are both *kiusche* because they are themselves, and these selves are in their various ways purely good. Furthermore neither fear nor anger tempts Antikonie to be untrue to herself or to Gawan; her *stæte* or constancy is also perfect, indeed it partakes of the holiness of the sacrifice, it is *balsemmæzec*.

These virtues do not exist independently for Wolfram; evidence of one is evidence of all. His characters are each called upon to behave in a particular way, a way suitable to their individual personality (sexual chastity may appear from Sigune to be the highest vocation, but not all are destined to it); and if they succeed in their particular vocation, they are essentially good, they are pleasing to man and God, they are sweet (*süeze*).[1] Hence the praise of Antikonie. But Gawan has to leave her too, for he is now pledged to seek the Grail; and so, sending his squires back to Artus, he sets out on this most arduous task of all, alone.

[1] On the meaning of *süeze* in Wolfram's work, see Werner Schröder, 'Süeziu Gyburc', *Euphorion*, vol. 54 (1960).

VI

PARZIVAL AND TREVRIZENT

wand in der wirt von sünden schiet
unt im doch rîterlîchen riet.[1]

With the ninth book of *Parzival*, which is almost entirely
Wolfram's independent work, being about seven times as long
in his version as in Chrestien's, Wolfram returns to the main
theme of his story.[2] 'frou aventiure', the lady who tells the
narrator his tale, informs him she has news of his hero, to which
he replies with the all-important question: has Parzival yet
redeemed Anfortas?

> hât er Munsalvæsche sît gesehen,
> unt den süezen Anfortas,
> des herze dô vil siufzec was?
> durch iwer güete gebt uns trôst,
> op der von jâmer sî erlôst.
> lât hœren uns diu mære,
> ob Parzivâl dâ wære,
> Beidiu iur hêrre und ouch der mîn.
>
> (433, 24–434, 1)

The reader realises from this question that there is now a
fair prospect of Parzival's quest ending successfully; and indeed,
after the narrator has indicated briefly that his hero has been
fighting all over the world since he left the Round Table—
later Parzival specifies that he has known no joy all that time
(460, 28–461, 2)—the definite statement comes: 'sîn wolte got
dô ruochen' (435, 12). God is now desirous of showing mercy
to Parzival. This remark is quite isolated, but nevertheless

---

[1] 501, 17 f.
[2] On Book IX in general see Gustav Ehrismann, 'Über Wolframs Ethik',
Zeitschrift für deutsches Altertum, vol. 49 (1908), pp. 422 ff.; and Walter
Henzen, 'Das neunte Buch des Parzival' in *Erbe der Vergangenheit*, *Festgabe
für Karl Helm* (Tübingen, 1951).

throws light on all the events of Book IX, the theme of which might be described as the gradual triumph of God's grace over human sinfulness.

As a prelude there first comes Parzival's third meeting with Sigune. At the last meeting, immediately after Parzival's visit to Munsalvæsche, his cousin had cursed him as one beyond hope of redemption. Now when, by uncovering his head, her visitor reveals his identity, she retains the distant *ir* form of address she had then adopted and asks, perhaps ironically, if he has made good his failure (440, 29–441, 2). His pathetic reply, in which he makes it clear to her that he now fully realises the extent of his loss and suffers accordingly—though there is still no sign that he regards himself as to blame—moves her to forgive him and to acknowledge once again the bond of kinship:

> diu maget sprach 'al mîn gerich
> sol ûf dich, neve, sîn verkorn.
> du hâst doch freuden vil verlorn . . .'   (441, 18–20)

Indeed Sigune, who previously stated that the Grail could only be found by one who did not seek it, now points out to Parzival the trail left by Cundrie who, she says, recently brought her her week's food from Munsalvæsche—and may well have returned thither. Her hope is that God will show his acceptance of Parzival's suffering by leading him where he wants to be:

> si sprach 'nu helfe dir des hant,
> dem aller kumber ist bekant;
> ob dir sô wol gelinge,
> daz dich ein slâ dar bringe,
> aldâ du Munsalvæsche sihst,
> dâ du mir dîner freuden gihst.'   (442, 9–14)

Such a complete reversal of attitude demonstrates the value Sigune sets on Parzival's proven willingness to suffer endless hardship and total lack of worldly happiness in order to win a second chance at Munsalvæsche: Parzival's own *kumber* may enable God, 'dem aller kumber ist bekant,' to help him.

The event proves Sigune's hope premature, for the trail fades

out and Parzival fails to find Munsalvæsche: 'sus wart aber der
grâl verlorn' (442, 30). That he is not far off, however, is shown
by his encounter with one of the knights guarding the Grail
territory. Their duty is to prevent any unauthorised person
reaching the Grail; on Parzival's first visit he had miraculously
passed through their ranks unheeded (492, 1–10), but now he has
to fight for his life. On the earlier occasion he had been destined by God to be put to the test at Munsalvæsche, whereas
now he is attempting to win the Grail in defiance of God. This
episode, the climax of Parzival's four and a half years of opposi-
tion to God, proves the vanity of such a course. For the Grail
knight, even though defeated, evades pursuit on the far side of
a ravine, and Parzival, for all his prowess in arms, is no further
forward than before:

> dô reit er, ern wist war,
> sô daz diu Munsalvæscher schar
> in mit strîte gar vermeit.
> des grâlcs vremde was im leit.   (445, 27–30)

God may indeed desire to show mercy to Parzival, but suffering
alone does not suffice to gain for a sinner what he seeks; it must
first inspire in him contrition. The narrator specifically states
that a further, not inconsiderable, period of time elapses before
this next step is taken (446, 1–5).

Then one day when Parzival is, as usual, riding fully armed
through the forest in search of adventure, he meets an old, grey-
bearded knight, Kahenis, who, with his wife, two daughters and
whole household, is returning from a penitential pilgrimage to
a hermit. All wear the coarse, drab dress of the pilgrim, and
walk barefoot on their *bîhtes verte*, their *gotes vart* (as it is
variously described). The narrator first emphasises the contrast between Parzival's knightly splendour and their humble
attire, and then makes first Kahenis and later Trevrizent
explain their garb. It is Good Friday, on which day, says
Kahenis, every knight should leave his arms at home and walk
barefoot, 'unt des tages zît begienge' (447, 18). The rest of the

year, Trevrizent later informs Parzival, a knight may seek to win
his lady's love in combat, but on Good Friday he should think
only of the love of God:

> hât iuch âventiure
> ûz gesant durch minnen solt,
> sît ir rehter minne holt,
> sô minnt als nu diu minne gêt,
> als disses tages minne stêt:
> dient her nâch umbe wîbe gruoz.   (456, 16–21)

Neither Kahenis, who is a brother-in-law of the King of Kareis,
and apparently devoted to King Artus (449, 8–13), nor the
hermit Trevrizent, ever decries the chivalrous way of life which
Parzival is pursuing. But the latter's failure to show an especial
respect for God on Good Friday, in the way Kahenis does every
year, indicates to them that his chivalry has lost touch with God
—and that is what they lament:

> dô was des grâwen rîters klage,
> daz im die heileclîchen tage
> niht hulfen gein alselhem site,
> daz er sunder wâpen rite
> ode daz er barfuoz gienge
> unt des tages zît begienge.   (447, 13–18)

The reference to Holy Week calls from Parzival a bitter out-
cry: he had faithfully served one called God, until deserted by
him, but now neither knows nor cares what day it is:

> ich diende eim der heizet got,
> ê daz sô lasterlîchen spot
> sîn gunst übr mich erhancte:
> mîn sin im nie gewancte,
> von dem mir helfe was gesagt:
> nu ist sîn helfe an mir verzagt.   (447, 25–30)

It is a similar cry to that uttered by Parzival before the court of
Artus; both are based on the obstinate conviction of his own
righteousness and therefore of God's faithlessness. In reply,
Kahenis does not even bother to ask what is the treachery of

which Parzival accuses God, but endeavours to direct the sinner's attention away from the particular episode towards the
universal truth—in the conviction that the story of man's
salvation can leave no doubt about God's everlasting *triuwe*.
Good Friday is kept sacred to his name because of the suffering
which he endured for man on that day:

> geloubt ir sîner mennescheit,
> waz er als hiut durch uns erleit,
> als man diss tages zît begêt,
> unrehte iu denne dez harnasch stêt.
> ez ist hiute der karfrîtac . . .   (448, 3–7)

Never has greater *triuwe* been seen than that which God evinced
when he was crucified for man:

> wâ wart ie hôher triwe schîn,
> dan die got durch uns begienc,
> den man durch uns anz kriuze hienc?
>   (448, 10–12)

The *durch uns* is repeated, and elaborated (though not with a
full account of Adam's fall): God died because man was condemned to death for his own sin:

> er hât sîn werdeclîchez lebn
> mit tôt für unser schult gegebn,
> durch daz der mensche was verlorn,
> durch schulde hin zer helle erkorn.   (448, 15–18)

The God who died for the sin of man cannot be guilty of
treachery; if Parzival has quarrelled with him, it is because of
his own wickedness, which God will forgive if he is penitent.
Kahenis concludes:

> ob ir niht ein heiden sît,
> sô denket, hêrre, an dise zît.
> rîtet fürbaz ûf unser spor.
> iu ensitzet niht ze verre vor
> ein heilec man: der gît iu rât,
> wandel für iwer missetât.
> welt ir im riwe künden,
> er scheidet iuch von sünden.   (448, 19–26)

91

The whole speech from which these extracts are taken is calculated to raise doubts in Parzival's mind about his own self-righteousness; to make him wonder if he may not after all be in the wrong; and to show him what action to take in that case. Kahenis achieves this by reminding Parzival what happened on the first Good Friday. The story is not recited simply as a lesson in dogma—though one does not know how much Gurnemanz explained when he instructed Parzival in the Mass (169, 15–20)—but because Parzival is now for the first time inwardly ready to profit from it, to take the lesson of man's sin and salvation to heart. All the religious instruction given to Parzival in Book IX aims in this way at breaking his sinful pride and reconciling him with God.

Kahenis, 'von des râte er [Parzival] sît gelücke enphienc'(446, 24), with his insistence on the goodness of God and the sinfulness of man, makes Parzival wonder for the first time if perhaps he has been mistaken about the divine nature. Accordingly, after he has taken leave of the pilgrim band in the consciousness of their love and trust in the God who appears to have deserted himself, Parzival finds new thoughts and feelings arising within him:

> hin rîtet Herzeloyde fruht.
> dem riet sîn manlîchiu zuht
> kiusch unt erbarmunge:
> sît Herzeloyd diu junge
> in het ûf gerbet triuwe,
> sich huop sîns herzen riuwe.
> alrêrste er dô gedâhte,
> wer al die werlt volbrâhte,
> an sînen schepfære,
> wie gewaltec der wære.   (451, 3–12)

These lines indicate the beginning of Parzival's conversion. His obstinate heart begins to soften, to feel contrition (*herzen riuwe*); for the first time (*alrêrste*) he realises, not the enormity of the shame God has visited upon him, but the greatness of the Creator himself.

This is Parzival's first religious experience of any depth, and it is significant that the narrator considers his behaviour to testify to the *triuwe* of his mother Herzeloyde. She had been the first to tell him of the love of God manifest in the incarnation (cf. above, p. 47 f.); and however little he understood, the certain conviction of the *helfe* which God always extends to the world remained with the boy; indeed, his abandonment of God's service was caused by his disillusion on precisely this point. Now, however, he is prepared to wonder once again if his mother may not have been right:

> er sprach 'waz ob got helfe phligt,
> diu mînem trûren an gesigt? . . .'   (451, 13 f.)

Parzival is once again prepared to give the God of help, whom his mother had proclaimed, a chance; in doing so he is returning to the attitude from which he should have started, returning to his maternal *triuwe*.

As Parzival had previously allowed his horse free rein before finding Munsalvæsche, but in direct contrast to his later attempt to follow Cundrie's trail thither in defiance of God, he now lays down the rein and addresses his mount—itself a Grail steed, for he captured it from the knight he defeated in the neighbourhood of Munsalvæsche—with the words: 'nu genc nâch der gotes kür' (452, 9). His action shows that he is willing for the moment to be guided by God, and he promises that if God leads him wherever is best for him—he no longer specifies where it should be—then he will praise his power:

> Er sprach 'ist gotes kraft sô fier
> daz si beidiu ors unde tier
> unt die liut mac wîsen,
> sîn kraft wil i'm prîsen.
> mac gotes kunst die helfe hân,
> diu wîse mir diz kastelân
> dez wægest umb die reise mîn:
> sô tuot sîn güete helfe schîn:
> nu genc nâch der gotes kür.'   (452, 1–9)

93

To put God to the test in this way is doubtless to exhibit a remnant of sinful pride, but God who, as the narrator said at the beginning of Book IX, wishes to show mercy to Parzival, in his graciousness accepts the challenge.

The horse leads its rider along the path made by Kahenis to Trevrizent, who is the (only) brother of Anfortas and so Parzival's maternal uncle. He, like his niece Sigune, has withdrawn from a life of chivalry, of which he later gives Parzival an extensive account, stressing in particular a meeting of his with Gahmuret and his close association with Ither (495, 13–499, 12), in order to become a hermit. His sacrifice, unlike hers, is not so much personal—though it does appear that he may have had some share in his brother's sin (458, 5–12)—as vicarious; when Anfortas received for his sin a wound the doctors could not cure, Trevrizent decided to do penance for him:

> mîne venje viel ich nider:
> dâ lobet ich der gotes kraft,
> daz ich deheine rîterschaft
> getæte nimmer mêre,
> daz got durch sîn êre
> mînem bruoder hulfe von der nôt. (480, 10–15)

Both on account of their kinship and because of Trevrizent's concern for Anfortas, it is thus appropriate that it should be to this particular holy man that Parzival comes for advice at this stage; the two do not, however, for some time discover their relationship.

Parzival has been told by Kahenis that the nearby hermit will advise him in his need and free him from sin; and when he arrives at the hermit's cell, his opening remark reveals how much the meeting with Kahenis has in fact already profited him:

> dô sprach er 'hêr, nu gebt mir rât:
> ich bin ein man der sünde hât.' (456, 29 f.)

Although still unaware of his particular sins and, as his subsequent remarks show, not yet prepared to accept responsibility for his failure at Munsalvæsche, nevertheless Parzival is at last in a penitent frame of mind. Yet the hermit does not immediately ask about his sin but, after indicating his willingness to help, courteously inquires who directed him there; then stables the horse as best he can; and finally leads his guest to a fire where he can change his armour for more comfortable clothes. The part played by such normal courtly hospitality in putting Parzival at his ease and so helping to smooth the way to his full confession should not be underrated. Parzival learns that his host comes like himself of knightly stock, and without doubt appreciates Trevrizent's chivalrous *zuht*.

Before the religious discussion reopens, they move in front of the hermit's altar. Their talk at first follows much the same course as the one with Kahenis: both times the sinner complains that God has deserted him, and the counsellor replies that the crucified Christ is incapable of such treachery—but Trevrizent considerably extends Kahenis's argument. What calls forth Parzival's complaint is his discovery that his misery has now endured for four and a half years; in his disregard of time he had remained unaware of this, and feels renewed bitterness:

> ouch trage ich hazzes vil gein gote:
> wand er ist mîner sorgen tote.
> die hât er alze hôhe erhabn:
> mîn freude ist lebendec begrabn. (461, 9–12)

No matter what anyone says of God's *helfe*, how can Parzival believe in it when his outstanding chivalry has been rewarded only with pain?

> des gihe ich dem ze schanden,
> der aller helfe hât gewalt,
> ist sîn helfe helfe balt,
> daz er mir denne hilfet niht,
> sô vil man im der hilfe giht. (461, 22–26)

To this cry of personal disillusion Trevrizent replies that God is indeed to be trusted, and will without doubt help Parzival.

Before the latter launches into further accusation, he should first hear of God's innocence:

> durch iwer zuht gedolt
> vernemt von mir sîn unscholt,
> ê daz ir mir von im iht klagt.
> sîn helfe ist immer unverzagt.   (462, 7–10)

Trevrizent then delivers a long discourse which may be divided into three parts. At the beginning he gives his authority: although a layman, he has read in the Bible of God's endless concern for man's soul; his help is always directed towards its salvation, and for that reason man should trust and serve him:

> doch ich ein leie wære,
> der wâren buoche mære
> kund ich lesen unde schrîben,
> wie der mensche sol belîben
> mit dienste gein des helfe grôz,
> den der stæten helfe nie verdrôz
> für der sêle senken.   (462, 11–17)

This general statement about the relationship between God and man is then developed, God being described in absolute terms, man—as Parzival—in personal and dependent ones:

> sît getriwe ân allez wenken,
> sît got selbe ein triuwe ist:
> dem was unmære ie falscher list.
> wir suln in des geniezen lân:
> er hât vil durch uns getân,
> sît sîn edel hôher art
> durch uns ze menschen bilde wart.
> got heizt und ist diu wârheit:
> dem was ie falschiu fuore leit.
> daz sult ir gar bedenken.
> ern kan an niemen wenken.
> nu lêret iwer gedanke,
> hüet iuch gein im an wanke.   (462, 18–30)

God is fidelity (*ein triuwe*), and knows not how to betray; he is truth (*diu wârheit*), and hates falsehood—as is proved by his incarnation.

The argument is similar to that used by Kahenis, but is put more forcefully. Trevrizent is not simply repeating the general truths of Christianity—for instance the statement that God is *ein triuwe* is parallel to but clearly not identical with the biblical 'God is love'—but he is specifically countering Parzival's accusation that God has betrayed him. He can even, as it were intuitively, take up points Parzival has only made to others: for instance his 'got heizt und ist diu wârheit' replies to Parzival's 'ich diende eim der heizet got,' said to Kahenis (447, 25; cf. above, p. 90). All in all, to Parzival's implicit accusation that God is not even fulfilling the obligation of a feudal overlord to support his faithful vassal, Trevrizent is replying that God is not merely faithful, he is fidelity itself.

Having established God's *triuwe*, Trevrizent then proceeds to narrate the story of man's *sünde*. He uses the rebellion of Lucifer to illustrate two of his points: that it is impossible to win a fight with God, and that God is not responsible for wickedness:

> Irn megt im ab erzürnen niht:
> swer iuch gein im in hazze siht,
> der hât iuch an den witzen kranc.
> nu prüevt wie Lucifern gelanc
> unt sînen nôtgestallen.
> si wârn doch âne gallen:
> jâ hêr, wâ nâmen si den nît,
> dâ von ir endelôser strît
> zer helle enpfâhet sûren lôn?...
>
> diu liehte himelische schar
> wart durch nît nâch helle var.   (463, 1–9 and 13 f.)

After Lucifer's fall, man was made, but Eve disobeyed her creator, and Cain murdered his brother. Enmity between men (*der menschen nît*, 464, 21), the mark of original sin, dates from this latter act, and has endured ever since.

There follows the crucial passage, already quoted in chapter IV, in which Trevrizent says that all men inherit not only the

7

curse of Adam but also the blessing of Christ (464, 28–465, 6). If from his kinship to Adam man must necessarily bear the burden of sin, then may God, who by his incarnation is also related to man, ever show mercy to his sinning kinsman:

> dar über erbarme sich des kraft,
> dem erbarme gît geselleschaft,
> sît sîn getriuwiu mennischeit
> mit triwen gein untriwe streit. (465, 7–10)

These words contain the essence of Trevrizent's teaching; it is God who is *getriuwe*, man who is *valsch*; the story of man's sin and salvation should prove to Parzival God's innocence of the charge of faithlessness. And as the hermit had begun by enjoining upon his guest an absolute trust in God, so now once more he commands Parzival to abandon his anger against God and seek to do penance for his sin:

> ir sult ûf in verkiesen,
> welt ir sælde niht verliesen.
> lât wandel iu für sünde bî. (465, 11–13)

So ends the first part of Trevrizent's discourse.

The hermit is, however, not content merely to absolve God from the charge of treachery; he wishes also to bring home to God's declared enemy the magnitude of his sin. He continues thus:

> sît rede und werke niht sô frî:
> wan der sîn leit sô richet
> daz er unkiusche sprichet,
> von des lône tuon i'u kunt,
> in urteilt sîn selbes munt. (465, 14–18)

To react to the suffering which sin necessarily brings with it— it was Eve's disobedience to God which first disturbed human happiness—by cursing God is to be condemned out of one's own mouth. Suffering can, as eventually in Parzival's case, lead a sinner to acknowledge his sin and return to God; that is its function in the divine order of things, and a sinner who reacts in this way to his punishment is acting with *kiusche*: in accordance with God's will. But there are also those whose pride prevents them from acknowledging their fault; they are *die unkiuschen* for whom there can be no salvation. As the prophets of antiquity foretold—Classical as well as biblical in Trevrizent's opinion—satisfaction has been given for the worst of sins; but it cannot avail those who reject it:

> si sagten dâ vor manec jâr,
> uns solde komen al für wâr
> für die hôhsten schulde pfant.
> zer helle uns nam diu hôhste hant
> mit der gotlîchen minne:
> die unkiuschen liez er dinne. (465, 25–30)

kiusche is used in this passage to denote the ultimate quality by which man is judged. It is indeed a quality Wolfram requires of every man and woman, and one he never attributes to God. In its religious significance it involves obedience to the will of God, fulfilment of God's will by each individual, 'chastity' in the sense of contentment with one's divinely appointed destiny. Parzival, at the time of his 'Gotteshass', failed in this important respect; unlike the damned spirits in hell, however, he repents while he still can. It is this penitence, already stirring in Parzival's breast when he arrives at the hermit's cell, which Trevrizent seeks to foster.

The concluding part of Trevrizent's discourse concentrates on this need for penitence. He has narrated the 'good news' (*disiu süezen mære*) of the Gospel, has told of God's *triuwe* and man's *sünde*; now he puts the alternatives squarely before Parzival: oppose God and be damned, or repent and be saved. After reminding the sinner once more of God's perfection, he takes up Herzeloyde's point that God is light, and refers to his goodwill towards man not only in terms of *triuwe* but also of *minne*:

> Von dem wâren minnære
> sagent disiu süezen mære.
> der ist ein durchliuhtec lieht,
> und wenket sîner minne nieht. (466, 1–4)

But, continues Trevrizent, it is not only God's love which is offered to every man and woman in the world, but also his enmity, his hatred:

> swem er minne erzeigen sol,
> dem wirt mit sîner minne wol.
> die selben sint geteilet:
> al der werlde ist geveilet
> bêdiu sîn minne und ouch sîn haz. (466, 5–9)

It is left to the freewill of each individual to choose which he will have:

> nu prüevet wederz helfe baz.
> der schuldige âne riuwe
> fliuht die gotlîchen triuwe:
> swer ab wandelt sünden schulde,
> der dient nâch werder hulde. (466, 10–14)

All are sinners—that Trevrizent has already demonstrated. What matters is whether the sinner remains obdurate, thus fleeing the love of God, or whether by doing penance, he serves in the hope of obtaining mercy.

This is the service to which Kahenis referred when he spoke of God, 'der stæten lôn nâch dienste gît' (449, 18); and it is widely different from Parzival's early conception of service. Parzival thought of his service of God in feudal terms, as something which laid God under the obligation of rewarding him; it gave him a claim upon God, and when this claim was not fulfilled, he was entitled to quit the service of so faithless a lord. What Trevrizent explains to Parzival is that the religious concept of service and reward is based upon the facts of man's sin and God's mercy. Man has betrayed God and can therefore never have any claim upon him; but God loves man and has promised forgiveness to all who truly repent and try to earn absolution. 'Service' of God is an endeavour to win back his favour; of his mercy God has promised to 'reward' such service with success. The penitent sinner can count with certainty upon his 'reward'; the Cross is the guarantee. God's *helfe* is always directed for the benefit of man's soul (462, 16 f.); if an individual finds himself afflicted by God in his lifetime, it is

necessarily because he deserves it, and he should accept it and
try to make amends. God will then forgive him.

Trevrizent next describes how the divine light can penetrate
even the blackness of the mind and search out secrets; what
hope can there be for the man who not only thinks but also does
evil? His soul will nowhere find refuge from God; certainly a
reliance upon mere chivalry will not avail him:

> sît got gedanke speht sô wol,
> ôwê der brœden werke dol!
> Swâ werc verwurkent sînen gruoz,
> daz gotheit sich schamen muoz,
> wem lât den menschlîchiu zuht?
> war hât diu arme sêle fluht? (466, 29–467, 4)

Only by isolating them from their context can these lines be
interpreted as an attack on chivalry (*zuht*); even in the hermit's
cell Trevrizent behaves to his guest with every possible courtesy, as also does Sigune (cf. 437, 29–438, 28). Trevrizent's
point is not that courtesy is bad, but that, as a human convention, it can avail nothing unless subordinated to the divine will.
Parzival has been complaining that God has not rewarded his
chivalry, he has relied on his knightly prowess to win him the
Grail in defiance of God; what Trevrizent maintains is that no
human effort of this kind, no purely chivalrous virtue can profit a
man whose actions have offended God. In conclusion he once
again enjoins his guest to abandon his 'Gotteshass' and seek to
win God's love:

> welt ir nu gote füegen leit,
> der ze bêden sîten ist bereit,
> zer minne und gein dem zorne,
> sô sît ir der verlorne.
> nu kêret iwer gemüete,
> daz er iu danke güete. (467, 5–10)

Thus Trevrizent concludes the speech, in which he proclaims
to Parzival God's innocence, with a warning: if after this he
continues to anger God, he is surely lost.

Parzival thanks Trevrizent for his information about God—

> der nihtes ungelônet lât,
> der missewende noch der tugent   (467, 14 f.)

—but does not at once appear converted by so general a lesson. When asked for details of his sorrow and sin, he replies with generalities which lead Trevrizent to talk about the Grail (which will be discussed in the next chapter); and on hearing that the knights guarding Munsalvæsche free their souls from sin by deeds of chivalry, he bursts out:

> Mac rîterschaft des lîbes prîs
> unt doch der sêle pardîs
> bejagen mit schilt und ouch mit sper,
> sô was ie rîterschaft mîn ger.
> ich streit ie swâ ich strîten vant,
> sô daz mîn werlîchiu hant
> sich næhert dem prîse.
> ist got an strîte wîse,
> der sol mich dar benennen,
> daz si mich dâ bekennen:
> mîn hant dâ strîtes niht verbirt.   (472, 1–11)

Parzival declares it always has been his hope to win both worldly glory and eternal salvation by following the profession of chivalry; and certainly his prowess has won recognition on earth. Why then, since the knights guarding Munsalvæsche attain this double end, why does God not recognise his valour and send him there? He feels sure he would prove worthy of the call.

Such an argument reveals how little Parzival has as yet absorbed of the hermit's teaching about original sin; he still believes his chivalry to constitute a claim upon God. Trevrizent immediately deplores the pride inherent in this attitude:

> dô sprach aber sîn kiuscher wirt
> 'ir müest aldâ vor hôchvart
> mit senften willen sîn bewart.
> iuch verleit lîht iwer jugent
> daz ir der kiusche bræchet tugent.
> hôchvart ie seic unde viel.'   (472, 12–17)

The comparatively mild tone of this reproof perhaps, however, suggests that there is yet hope for Parzival, whose pride is after all the pride of youth, his sin still the sin of *tumpheit*. Nevertheless pride, the cause of Lucifer's fall, is the basic sin of all— by opposing *hôchvart* to *kiusche* Trevrizent supports the interpretation of the latter as acceptance of the divine will—and the story Trevrizent now tells his guest reveals how direly God punishes pride, even when just apparently a youthful extravagance. Anfortas's youth and glorious heritage led him into pride, for which God has afflicted him with a terrible wound. This is part of the Grail story and so must be left till later; its relevance to Parzival's spiritual position is, however, clear.[1]

As a question about Parzival's sin led to the narration about the Grail, so this eventually leads back to Parzival's sin. Trevrizent inquires if his guest is Lähelin, for that would account for the Grail mark on his horse, Lähelin having once killed a Grail knight and stolen his horse. The two look into each other's eyes as Parzival replies that he is not Lähelin but the son of Gahmuret, and if ever he robbed the dead it was in the ignorance of youth:

> genam ich ie den rêroup,
> sô was ich an den witzen toup.
> ez ist iedoch von mir geschehn:
> der selben sünde muoz ich jehn.
> Ithêrn von Cucûmerlant
> den sluoc mîn sündebæriu hant:
> ich leit in tôten ûffez gras,
> unt nam swaz dâ ze nemen was.   (475, 5–12)

Here Parzival refers to the slaying of Ither and the theft of his armour as sins; but the tone of his speech, though regretful, suggests self-exculpation rather than self-accusation. Parzival has long known that his behaviour was unchivalrous, but is still ready to excuse it as due to youthful ignorance.

[1] Herbert Kolb interprets Parzival's whole story as a struggle between pride and humility, 'Schola humilitatis', *Beiträge zur Geschichte der deutschen Sprache und Literatur*, vol. 78 (Tübingen, 1956).

An Introduction to Wolfram's 'Parzival'

Trevrizent replies in a very serious tone; he is much moved by the discovery that his guest is his nephew, and has special cause to lament the killing of Ither—for, as Parzival now learns for the first time, Ither too was his relative; and blood-relationship, however distant, cannot be lightly dismissed:

> dô sprach er 'lieber swester suon,
> waz râtes möht ich dir nu tuon?
> du hâst dîn eigen verch erslagn.
> wiltu für got die schulde tragn,
> sît daz ir bêde wârt ein bluot,
> ob got dâ reht gerihte tuot,
> sô giltet im dîn eigen leben . . .'   (475, 19–25)

By his own act Parzival is condemned, for if justice were done, he would owe God his life in exchange for that of his kinsman. Trevrizent goes on to stress how blameless had been Ither's life—and presumably how inexcusable Parzival's crime—but it is interesting that it is for killing, not so much an innocent man, as his own flesh and blood (*dîn eigen verch*), that the sinner is primarily condemned.

Blood-relationship (*sippe*) appears in all Wolfram's work as one of the great unifying forces in the world.[1] By relating his characters to one another—to an extent without parallel in his source—the poet builds up in *Parzival* the two great families descended from Mazadan and from Titurel, representing two different kinds of chivalry, but united in the person of the hero; and in *Willehalm* he constructs the two families of Heimrich von Narbon and of Terramer, representing the opposing armies of christendom and heathendom, but also united by Willehalm's marriage to Arabel-Gyburc, who begs—in God's name—that her Christian allies will spare her heathen relatives (*Willehalm*, 306–310). In this way *sippe* not only binds each human society together internally, but also links one society to another. The ties of kinship know no limits, for all men are

[1] See Julius Schwietering, 'Wolframs Parzival' in *Von deutscher Art in Sprache und Dichtung*, vol. 2 (Stuttgart and Berlin, 1941).

children of 'unser vater Adâm' (*Parzival*, 518, 1; cf. 82, 1 f.);
and Arabel-Gyburc suggests that heathen as well as Christian
are children of the heavenly Father (*Willehalm*, 307, 26–30).
Father and son, brother and brother are joined, like man and
wife, in a mystical union; they are as Arnalt says to his brother
Willehalm, one body—

> man mac wol zeime teile
> unser zweier lîbe zeln   (*Willehalm*, 119, 24 f.)

—and they should have all interests in common. To offend against
sippe is thus to threaten the ultimate unifying structure of
Wolfram's poetic world. Even if Parzival is only related to
Ither through his great-great-great-grandfather Mazadan, who
was Ither's great-grandfather, yet the crime of which he is
accused is that of slaying his own flesh and blood. And, says
Trevrizent later, if Parzival does not recognise the bond of kinship, God does:

> von Ithêr du bist erborn:
> dîn hant die sippe hât verkorn:
> got hât ir niht vergezzen doch,
> er kan si wol geprüeven noch.   (499, 13–16)

The ties of *sippe* are thus upheld in the last resort by God, to
whom Parzival's life is forfeit for having slain his kinsman;
may God forgive him for it:

> got daz erbarmen müeze
> daz de ie gefrumtest selhe nôt!   (476, 10 f.)

Not only, however, has Parzival killed Ither, but he is also, as
Trevrizent now informs him, responsible for the death of his
mother. Till now he did not even know she was dead, and this
information shocks him at last out of his complacency:

> 'neinâ hêrre guoter,
> waz sagt ir nu?' sprach Parzivâl.
> 'wær ich dan hêrre übern grâl,
> der möhte mich ergetzen niht
> des mærs mir iwer munt vergiht . . .'   (476, 14–18)

For the first time Parzival is aware of a sorrow for which no earthly happiness can compensate him, not even his election as Grail King. Neither his relationship to Ither, nor the death of his mother seems credible to him, and he begs Trevrizent to show the *triuwe* of a maternal uncle and tell him if these things are really true. In reply the hermit reveals to his nephew further details of the Grail family of which they are both members. In particular he tells of the knight—of whose identity he is yet ignorant—who failed to ask the question that would have cured Anfortas. At the end of this speech, the narrator comments: 'si bêde wârn mit herzen klage' (485, 1); the brother who is doing penance for him, and the nephew who failed to redeem him, are both sorrowing for Anfortas. It seems as though Parzival's barrier of sinful pride is at last crumbling before the revelation of his own crimes—and, content with this progress, Trevrizent puts an end to their first conversation by suggesting it is time for a midday meal.

As a hermit, Trevrizent eats nothing but the roots he finds in the forest; trusting each day to God to lead him to them, frequently fasting all day in honour of his Lord. Nor can he offer any other fare to Parzival, though he twice assures his nephew that there is no one who would more willingly entertain him sumptuously, were he able. But so devoted is Parzival now to his uncle that the hermit's penitential fare seems to him better not only than the normal supply provided by Gurnemanz but even than the one that issued from the Grail:

> Parzivâl mit sinne,
> durch die getriwe minne
> dier gein sînem wirte truoc,
> in dûhte er hete baz genuoc
> dan dô sîn pflac Gurnemanz,
> und dô sô maneger frouwen varwe glanz
> ze Munsalvæsche für in gienc,
> da er wirtschaft vome grâle enpfienc.   (486, 13–20)

The narrator, who has the endearing characteristic of jesting about serious and even sacred situations (see below, p. 182),

remarks that the two men hardly needed to wash their hands
after a meal which would certainly not have satisfied him; were
he a falcon, he would have flown away at once in search of meat.
The jest allows the reader to relax for a moment, but only for a
moment, for after rebuking himself for impiety, the narrator
reminds the reader why the two men are fasting—and states that
God rewarded them for it:

> ir hât doch wol gehœret
> waz in rîcheit hât gestœret,
> war umb si wâren freuden arm,
> dicke kalt unt selten warm.
> si dolten herzen riuwe
> niht wan durch rehte triuwe,
> ân alle missewende.
> von der hôhsten hende
> enpfiengens umb ir kumber solt:
> got was und wart in bêden holt.   (487, 13–22)

Trevrizent and Parzival are atoning for sin, the sin of Anfortas
and of Parzival. That has taken away their happiness; but
willingly now, first the uncle and then the nephew have accepted the burden of sorrow. By doing so they have demonstrated
their *triuwe*, their 'trueness', to Anfortas, to themselves, to God.
Pleased with such behaviour, God can and will reward them.
By making Parzival share in this way in Trevrizent's life of
atonement—he remains with his spiritual mentor for two weeks,
as he had also done with his chivalrous mentor, Gurnemanz—
Wolfram demonstrates most clearly that the object of all
Trevrizent's instruction is to move to penitence the proud heart
of the knight who had denied the message of Good Friday.

After the luncheon break—a pause which gives Parzival time
to face his sin—there comes the great confession. The revelation
of his crimes against Ither and Herzeloyde makes it impossible
for Parzival any longer to deny responsibility for his failure at
Munsalvæsche. Accordingly, speaking not only as sinner to
man of God but also specifically as a nephew who has failed his
uncle, Parzival begs Trevrizent to have mercy upon him.

Whereas atonement had seemed to him an easy matter when Sigune first cursed him for his crime, now he realises that he can never truly make amends, but can only pray for forgiveness:

> ich hân sô sêre missetân,
> welt ir michs engelten lân,
> sô scheide ich von dem trôste
> unt bin der unerlôste
> immer mêr von riuwe. (488, 9–13)

Dramatically he uncovers to Trevrizent his further guilt:

> der ûf Munsalvæsche reit,
> unt der den rehten kumber sach,
> unt der deheine vrâge sprach,
> daz bin ich unsælec barn:
> sus hân ich, hêrre, missevarn. (488, 16–20)

To make clear the distance which Parzival has come, it is necessary to compare this confession with the outburst in which he attacked God on the occasion of Cundrie's denunciation of him to the Round Table. There the one certain fact appeared to him to be the faithfulness he had till then shown to God, whom he accordingly both then and later accused of treachery; in reality he was, however, consumed with pride, blinded to the truth by his own self-righteousness. No trace of this attitude survives the discussion with Trevrizent this Good Friday morning, four and a half years later. Now, looking at himself, Parzival sees only an 'unsælec barn' whose misdeeds leave him no claim to happiness; the sense of shame (*scham*) which on the earlier occasion drove him from the Round Table for fear of scandal, now, when he has realised all his guilt, threatens to overwhelm him. Yet in his new humility he does not despair— to do so would be to rise up in pride once again against God's ordinance—but, as the opening words of his confession show, puts his trust in his hermit uncle:

> hêrre und lieber œheim mîn,
> getorst ichz iu vor scham gesagn,
> mîn ungelücke ich solde klagn.

daz verkiest durch iwer selbes zuht:
mîn triwe hât doch gein iu fluht. (488, 4–8)

So Parzival is now not only aware of and sorry for his sin, but also eager to be forgiven; his conversion is complete.

That Trevrizent recognises the change in Parzival is shown by his anxiety to comfort him. Admittedly the discovery that it was his nephew who failed Anfortas, wrings from him at first a heartfelt lament, but then he recollects his responsibilities as Parzival's spiritual counsellor and advises the penitent not to abandon himself to grief:

du solt in rehten mâzen
klagen und klagen lâzen. (489, 3 f.)

There follows the passage mentioned at the beginning of chapter III on the tendency of youth to sin and the need for older men to exercise discretion. The goal which Trevrizent now sets himself is to restore Parzival's self-confidence and confidence in God, so that he may yet make good what he has lost:

möht ich ... dîn herze alsô erküenen
daz du den prîs bejagtes
unt an got niht verzagtes,
so gestüende noch dîn linge
an sô werdeclîchem dinge,
daz wol ergetzet hieze. (489, 13–19)

These lines are of considerable importance, implying as they seem to that the hermit charges his nephew not to leave the world as he himself has done, but to return to it. Later when the narrator says that Parzival rejoiced in the weeks of penance shared with Trevrizent, because the latter released him from the bondage of sin while yet permitting him to remain a knight—

wand in der wirt von sünden schiet
unt im doch rîterlîchen riet (501, 17 f.)

—it must be to this statement (if to any included in the work) that he is referring. In spite of his sin, Parzival is not called upon to sacrifice to God all that is sweet to him on earth—as does

Trevrizent—but to serve God by seeking compensation for the joys he has lost.

Precisely what form this compensation should take is, naturally enough, not specified by Trevrizent. To interpret *den pris* (489, 15) as referring definitely to the Grail is unjustified; there are parallel instances where the phrase refers quite generally to chivalrous renown (e.g. 612, 3), and in this sense Parzival's *pris* is restored at the later meeting of the Round Table (cf. 699, 1–16). Similarly when Trevrizent hopes that Parzival will succeed in a cause so noble that it will be adequate compensation for him, he may be making a veiled allusion to the possibility of his nephew winning the Grail, or he may simply mean that true service of God must bring with it an appropriate reward. The important point is not that he is encouraging Parzival against his better knowledge to seek the Grail—such false encouragement would be misplaced, and anyway Parzival does not in fact look like falling into the sin of despair—but that Trevrizent expresses his confidence that Parzival can win final happiness in the chivalrous life. And in voicing this opinion he speaks in the name of God:

> got selbe dich niht lieze:
> ich bin von gote dîn râtes wer. (489, 20 f.)

Trevrizent now gives Parzival still more information about the Grail, and finally concludes this first day's talk with a brief review of his nephew's spiritual position. He reminds him of the two great sins he has committed against Ither and his mother, and subsequently adds to them the sin against Anfortas. If now, says Trevrizent, returning to the theme first broached by his nephew, Parzival wishes to serve God faithfully, then he must do penance for the murder of Ither:

> wilt du gein got mit triwen lebn,
> sô solte im wandel drumbe gebn. (499, 17 f.)

The sinner should think of the salvation of his soul:

> nu volge mîner ræte,
> nim buoz für missewende,

unt sorge et umb dîn ende,
daz dir dîn arbeit hie erhol
daz dort diu sêle ruowe dol.   (499, 26–30)

This passage reveals the ultimate religious significance of *arbeit*: it is the toil and suffering inflicted upon man after the Fall, not only as a punishment, but also as a means to salvation. Parzival is to seek *arbeit* on earth so that he may win peace (*ruowe*) in heaven. Apart from the fourteen days he now spends with Trevrizent, his *arbeit* will include more months of fighting: the penance of the knight consists primarily of *strît*.

The fourteen days themselves are passed over in almost total silence; only for the last day is a further conversation recorded. Then Trevrizent commends to Parzival the service of both ladies and clerics, who cannot defend themselves. And finally the holy man takes from his nephew that burden of sin to which Parzival had confessed on their first meeting (456, 30):

er sprach 'gip mir dîn sünde her:
vor gote ich bin dîn wandels wer.
und leist als ich dir hân gesagt:
belîp des willen unverzagt . . .'   (502, 25–28)

To whatever these last two lines refer—and there is no evidence that Trevrizent is reminding Parzival of any one particular part of his advice rather than another—in general the hermit's final speech leaves no doubt about the overall function of his nephew's visit. For four and a half years Parzival had been separated from God by his sin, and during that time he had known no happiness. Now he has truly confessed his sin and received absolution for it. He can go back into the world with a new confidence and a new hope, for he has been reconciled with God.

VII

THE GRAIL

swaz iemen wunders hât gesagt,
dennoch pflît es mêr der grâl.[1]

With a passion for explanatory detail that is characteristic of the German poets of his time, Wolfram not only provides in Book IX a history of the Grail from the earliest times, but also includes an explanation of how this history came to be recorded. This information is not to be found in the French version of Chrestien de Troyes, from which indeed Wolfram deviates considerably in his whole conception of the Grail—justifying his deviation by claiming a different and more correct source, the Provençal poet Kyot:

> Ob von Troys meister Cristjân
> disem mære hât unreht getân,
> daz mac wol zürnen Kyôt,
> der uns diu rehten mære enbôt.   (827, 1–4)

Whether such a person as Kyot ever existed is by no means certain; there is no other evidence for him than Wolfram's bare statement. And since Bodo Mergell has shown that the ways in which Wolfram differs from Chrestien in *Parzival* are very similar to those in which he diverges from his undisputed source *Aliscans* in *Willehalm*,[2] there remains no reason to doubt Wolfram's possible independence. Quite likely he invented 'Kyôt der meister wol bekant' (453, 11) in order to mask his own originality. There was a convention at the time that all tales told should be historically true, and so all poets continually asserted this (often at the precise moment when they were altering the traditional story); and so perhaps Wolfram invented

---

[1] 330, 26 f.

[2] *Wolfram von Eschenbach und seine französischen Quellen*: Part I, *Wolframs Willehalm*; Part II, *Wolframs Parzival* (Münster in Westfalen, 1936 and 1943).

Kyot and the circumstantial details of his discovery of the truth about the Grail to protect himself against his rival's damaging accusation that he was an inventor of wild tales. It is unlikely, however, that we shall ever be quite sure about Kyot's existence.[1]

In Wolfram's version, Kyot's interest in the Grail began when, in Dolet (Toledo), he came upon an account written down in heathen language (Arabic) by a heathen astrologer named Flegetanis. From the stars Flegetanis had discovered that there was a thing called the Grail which a certain company (of angels) had left on earth when they returned to heaven, and which was in the care of a particularly worthy company of men (453, 11–454, 30). From another reference it would seem that Flegetanis further recorded the whole story of Parzival, or at least part of it (416, 25–27). Kyot's interest was aroused by his discovery, and he began to search in Latin works for a record of a people worthy enough to guard the Grail, and eventually he found in Anschouwe the entire tale not only of the Grail and its earlier kings but also of the Arthurian descendants of Mazadan (455, 1–22). It is this story, narrated by Kyot in *franzoys* (French), which the narrator claims to have translated into German (416, 25–30). I propose in this chapter to concentrate first of all on what Wolfram, through his narrator and characters, tells us about the company who have charge of the Grail, and then on what he tells us about the Grail itself.

Trevrizent, from whom we obtain most of our knowledge, elaborates Flegetanis's brief reference to the first company who were to be found near the Grail. When Lucifer rebelled against the Trinity, there was a group of angels who did not take either side; these 'neutral' angels were, according to Trevrizent, sent down to earth to the Grail. Although it has frequently been assumed that they brought the Grail with them, there is no

[1] For diverging views on this age-old problem see H. and R. Kahane, 'Wolframs Gral und Wolframs Kyot', *Zeitschrift für deutsches Altertum*, vol. 89 (1958–9); Franz Rolf Schröder, 'Parzivals Schuld', and Walter Johannes Schröder, 'Kyot', both in *Germanish-Romanische Monatsschrift*, vol. 40, new series 9 (1959).

8

evidence for this; and all that can definitely be said of the Grail's first state is that it was already to be found on earth before the rebellion of Lucifer. How long these neutral angels remained near the Grail is not known, but in Book IX Flegetanis and Trevrizent both say that they have left it, possibly to return to heaven. Later, in Book XVI, Trevrizent denies that they could possibly have so returned, and insists they are damned eternally; but throughout it remains clear that after a while they left the Grail.

The function of these angels in the work has never been satisfactorily explained. The suggestion that their apparent wavering between heaven and hell in Book IX symbolises Parzival's own position, while gaining in credibility from a later poet's description of them as *zwîvelære*,[1] yet carries little conviction: for Parzival nowhere behaves as a neutral but rather as a rebel against God, and his attitude reminds Trevrizent not of the neutral angels but of Lucifer himself (463, 1–5).

Since the departure of the neutral angels, the Grail has remained in the custody of a single family, that of Titurel and his descendants. Titurel himself was called to the Grail by an angel from God (471, 26–28; cf. *Titurel*, stanza 6); when in his old age he was lamed by gout, his son Frimutel succeeded him (474, 10–13); upon Frimutel's death in battle his eldest son, the present King Anfortas, was elected as his successor (478, 1–6). Frimutel's other children were Trevrizent, Herzeloyde, Schoysiane who died giving birth to Sigune, and Repanse de Schoye who is as yet unmarried.

The election of Anfortas was presumably effected by the company of knights and ladies whom God had decreed should assist the king in his task; they are referred to by Trevrizent in connection with Parzival's first visit to Munsalvæsche:

> es suln meide pflegn
> (des hât sich got gein im bewegn)
> des grâls, dem si dâ dienden für.

---

[1] See *Heinrichs von Meissen des Frauenlobes Leiche, Sprüche, Streitgedichte und Lieder*, edited L. Ettmüller (1843), no. 86, p. 74.

der grâl ist mit hôher kür.
sô suln sîn rîter hüeten
mit kiuscheclîchen güeten.   (493, 19–24)

The maids, led by Repanse de Schoye, by whom alone the
Grail can be carried, are its attendants; the knights defend it
against the attack of other knights who have not been called to
the Grail (473, 5–11). (Whether either have any other duties is
uncertain; certainly no other duties are specified.) Those who
are there at present all arrived as children, and were called
individually by God, their names and family appearing miraculously on the Grail itself (470, 21–471, 9). As Trevrizent states
in Book IX (468, 12–16) and Parzival confirms upon his eventual
nomination as Grail King, it is impossible to attain the Grail
without such a calling:

Parzivâl sîn rede alsus huop an.
en franzoys er zin allen sprach
als Trevrizent dort vorne jach,
daz den grâl ze keinen zîten
niemen möht erstrîten,
wan der von gote ist dar benant.   (786, 2–7)

After this public pronouncement such attempts to win the
Grail as those of Gawan and Vergulaht in support of Parzival,
and of the heathen knight whom Anfortas killed (479, 18–480,
2), are abandoned; and so the Grail remains still, as God intended, hidden from the world at large (786, 8–12).

The Grail is kept in the castle of Munsalvæsche, which is
surrounded by a wild forest, which comprises Anfortas's whole
domain of Terre de Salvæsche. That Wolfram correctly interpreted *salvæsche* (from the Old French form of *sauvage*, Latin
silvaticus) as meaning 'wild' is indicated by his comparison of
the Grail castle with that of Wildenberc, where he was apparently resident when he wrote Book V (cf. 230, 13).[1] The

[1] Wildenberc is usually taken to be the ruined castle near Amorbach in
the Odenwald, though voices have been raised in protest: see Peter P.
Albert, *Die 'Gralsburg' Wildenberg im Odenwald und die historische Kritik*
(Buchen, 1949).

Grail is wild in that the forest which surrounds it, defended as it is by the Grail knights, renders Munsalvæsche itself inaccessible and the approach exceedingly dangerous to ordinary knights. Thus when Artus's search for Parzival brings him near Terre de Salvæsche, ignorant as he is of the exact location of the Grail castle, he prudently prepares for battle:

> wir nâhen Anfortases her,
> daz von Munsalvæsche vert
> untz fôrest mit strîte wert:
> sît wir niht wizzen wâ diu stêt,
> ze arbeit ez uns lîhte ergêt.   (286, 10–14)

But while no degree of intimacy with the mysteries (*tougen*) of the Grail is ever permitted to the outside world, it is revealing that the cells of both Sigune (cf. 804, 8) and Trevrizent (at Fontane la Salvæsche, cf. 456, 1–4) seem to lie within the confines of Terre de Salvæsche. This is evidently not only a wild but also a blessed land, and it is therefore perhaps permissible to take *salvæsche* to suggest not only *silvaticus* but also *salvationis*: the wild land and the wild mountain are also the land and mountain of salvation.

From *Titurel* we learn that, when the first Grail King was summoned by God, he received a rule of life—'dâ vant ich geschriben al mîn orden' (stanza 6)—which, although nowhere set out in full, can be deduced in part from the words of Trevrizent. The information the latter gives Parzival in Book IX leaves no doubt that first and foremost an especial degree of *kiusche* and *diemuot* are required of all servants of the Grail. These qualities, and particularly *kiusche*, are regularly mentioned by Trevrizent—and elsewhere by others, Flegetanis for example (454, 28)—as attributes of the various members of the Grail family. Above all it would be impossible for Repanse de Schoye to carry the Grail were she not so *kiusche*:

> Repanse de schoy si hiez,
> die sich der grâl tragen liez.
> der grâl was von sölher art:
> wol muoser kiusche sîn bewart,

> die sîn ze rehte solde pflegn:
> die muose valsches sich bewegn.   (235, 25-30)

Here *kiusche* is opposed to *valsch*: the bearer of the 'pure' Grail—'der stein ist immer reine' (471, 22)—must be free of all falsehood, all treachery. She must, in fact, be entirely devoted to God and to the service of the Grail. Never must she fall into *ungenuht*, never become dissatisfied with her lot and seek other things than those God has intended for her; for *ungenuht*, as Cundrie tells Parzival, is foreign to the Grail, is the one quality the Grail will not bestow on him as its king:

> wan ungenuht al eine,
> dern gît dir niht gemeine
> der grâl und des grâles kraft
> verbietent valschlîch geselleschaft.   (782, 23-26)

When rebuking Parzival for the sin of claiming a place at Munsalvæsche as his right, Trevrizent, as has been seen, indicates that such *hôchvart* would be out of place there, and proceeds to lament that Parzival's youth so easily leads him away from *kiusche*; and this incident leads the hermit on to talk of the lack of *kiusche* and *diemuot*, the sinful *lôsheit* and *hôchvart* formerly exhibited by Anfortas. Such behaviour, to which we now turn, is most inappropriate in a Grail King.

Anfortas, by seeking in his youth to win the love of Orgeluse de Logroys—the very lady who is won so meritoriously by Gawan in Books x-xii—disobeys the one specific condition imposed upon all members of the Grail company (by contrast with Arthurian knights and ladies): to abandon all thought of human love, except as required by divine messages appearing on the Grail. The implications of this condition may be emphasised: it is precisely the highest inspiration of Arthurian chivalry, as incorporated in Gahmuret or in the pre-eminent Round Table knight Gawan, which Grail knights are called upon to renounce. They must serve God, not through the ladies, but through the Grail:

> swer sich diens geim grâle hât bewegn,
> gein wîben minne er muoz verpflegn.   (495, 7 f.)

Perpetual celibacy is not, however, imposed on all, for the Grail King may take a wife named by the Grail, and other knights may be required to leave the Grail and marry the queen of some lordless land (495, 9–12)—as Grail maidens may be summoned to marry Christian kings—but outside these limits *minne* is forbidden:

> swelch grâles hêrre ab minne gert
> anders dan diu schrift in wert,
> der muoz es komen ze arbeit
> und in siufzebæriu herzeleit.　　(478, 13–16)

And since *minne* is liable to attack all men in the pride of their youth—'mit selher jugent hât minne ir strît' (478, 10)—a stronger self-discipline, a greater self-sacrifice seems to be required of the knights of the Grail than of those of the Round Table.

The opportunity for self-expression which sexual love presents to a Gahmuret or a Gawan is not considered by Trevrizent as entirely—or, if the following quote is intended ironically (as seems likely), as at all—conducive to humility. Therefore such *minne* is forbidden to Anfortas, whose earlier battle-cry of *Amor* indicated his pride:

> Amor was sîn krîe.
> Der ruoft ist zer dêmuot
> iedoch niht volleclîchen guot.　　(478, 30–479, 2)

Anfortas's father, Frimutel, is remembered as one whose perfect love for his wife—who presumably was chosen by God and named on the Grail—should serve as a model for Parzival to follow (474, 14–20). When Frimutel's son failed to realise his high vocation, he was punished by God (239, 26 f.) with a wound, symbolically localised in the genital organs, which he received while fighting for worldly *minne* and which God would not allow to heal (479, 3–12; 481, 18).[1]

It seems, however, to be recognised that those Grail knights

---

[1] See H. B. Willson, 'The Grail King in Wolfram's *Parzival*', *Modern Language Review*, vol. 55 (1960).

The Grail

and ladies who do observe their particular rule of life manifest their *kiusche* in a higher spiritual form than do their worldly equivalents. For one thing they are referred to as a *rîterlîche bruoderschaft* (470, 19), and, presumably in conscious imitation of the not altogether dissimilar order of the Knights Templar, as *templeise*. Then, in defending the Grail against marauding knights, they specifically atone for any sins they have committed:

> die selben templeise,
> swâ si kumbr od prîs bejagent,
> für ir sünde si daz tragent.   (468, 28–30)

Lastly, the whole Grail company is especially graced by God:

> vor sündebæren schanden
> sint si immer mêr behuot,
> und wirt ir lôn ze himel guot.
> swenne in erstirbet hie daz lebn,
> sô wirt in dort der wunsch gegebn. (471, 10–14)

Thus if the *kiusche* required of the servants of the Grail is of a higher order than that demanded of members of Arthurian society, the king, knights and ladies of the Grail are correspondingly more blessed.

The Grail itself is kept in a temple at Munsalvæsche (816, 15) —this is perhaps the immediate justification for the designation *templeise*—and is only brought out on festive occasions (807, 16–18).[1] The one full description we have of such an occasion is on Parzival's first visit, when the Grail is produced in expectation of Anfortas's cure (807, 19–24). The ceremony which Parzival then witnesses is, however, not typical, since it contains certain extraneous elements inserted solely on account of the suffering of Anfortas. The spear whose aspect calls forth such general lamentation is the one which wounded Anfortas; its

---

[1] See Hermann J. Weigand, 'A Jester at the Grail Castle in Wolfram's *Parzival*?', *Publications of the Modern Language Association of America*, vol. 67 (1952).

poisoned head is thrust into his wound when, at a certain con-
junction of the planets, this grows terribly cold; the one pain
then relieves the other. The pair of silver knives which are also
paraded were specially made by the famous smith Trebuchet to
cut away the hard ice which forms around the spear during this
operation (489, 22–490, 30). (In these explanations, which are
not found in Chrestien, historians of literature see that rationalisation of traditional mystical elements which is so typical of
Wolfram and his age. The knives admittedly are Wolfram's
own invention, perhaps owing their existence to his mistaken
interpretation of Chrestien's *tailleor*, meaning platter. But the
presence of the lance in Chrestien may possibly be attributed to
an earlier identification of it with the spear with which Longinus
pierced Christ's side.[1] Compare also the rationalisation of the
traditional symbolism of the fisherman (Christ): Anfortas's
wound stinks so foully that he has to be carried into the fresh
air of the lake Brumbane:

> dâ von kom ûz ein mære,
> er wær ein fischære. (491, 13 f.)

In this introduction to *Parzival*, we are of course only concerned
with what Wolfram made of the story, not also with the significance of earlier versions.)

The spear and the knives are presumably abandoned once
Anfortas is cured; except for them the ceremony attendant
upon Parzival's installation as Grail King (808, 23–27) seems
just the same as that described in Book v. The knights being
seated, twenty-four maidens enter in procession through the
steel door of the Grail temple, bow to the king, set up tables and
bring in lights. Then Repanse de Schoye bears in the Grail,
places it before the king and joins the twenty-four, who stand
in order on one side. Pages, assisted by clerks, attend on the
knights during the meal, after which the maidens, once more in
procession, take away what they previously brought in. Queen

[1] But see Werner Richter, 'Wolfram von Eschenbach und die blutende
Lanze', *Euphorion*, vol. 53 (1959).

Condwiramurs (on the second occasion) is the only lady to join in the banquet; otherwise knights and ladies do not feast together as they do at the Round Table. Yet even more at Munsalvæsche than elsewhere does ceremonial etiquette seem to matter; the narrator continually stresses the *zuht* of the whole company (see above, p. 55 f.), and describes 'wie unfuoge den palas vlôch' (809, 19).

The focal point of the ceremony is of course the Grail itself, described by Trevrizent as a stone of very pure nature, which is known both as *der grâl* and as *lapsit exillis* (469, 3–7 and 28). The number of manuscript variants for this latter name suggests that the medieval scribes did not understand it themselves, and its interpretation has defeated modern scholars.[1] Neither of the more popular interpretations is satisfactory; for we have no evidence for *lapis elixir* until some time after *Parzival* was written; and since the neutral angels did not bring the stone with them from heaven, the reading *lapsit ex coelis* (and similar ones) lacks support. Friedrich Ranke has revived Ehrismann's suggestion that the reference may be to the stone Alexander found at the gate of Paradise: *lapis exilis*, the little stone or stone of humility.[2] But this is no more than a conjecture; such a name for the Grail appears nowhere else (if Albrecht's *Titurel*, which is itself based on Wolfram, is disregarded), and its significance is uncertain. Neither, for that matter, do we know for certain the derivation of the word *grâl*; but this at least was taken over by Wolfram from Chrestien.[3]

Wolfram's conception of the Grail differs directly from that of his predecessors, who make it a vessel, either a (communion) cup or, as with Chrestien, a container (of uncertain shape) for the Host, whereas he insists it is a stone. The change is clearly important, and is I think rightly interpreted as indicating a loosening

---

[1] Willy Krogmann is much too definite in his article 'wunsch von pardis', *Zeitschrift für deutsches Altertum*, vol. 85 (1954–5).

[2] 'Zur Symbolik des Grals bei Wolfram von Eschenbach', *Trivium*, vol. 4 (1946).

[3] See H. and R. Kahane, 'Wolframs Gral und Wolframs Kyot', *Zeitschrift für deutsches Altertum*, vol. 89 (1958–9).

of the traditional, and especially the liturgical, associations of the central symbol of the story: however much the Grail and its functions may resemble a religious sacrament, it cannot in Wolfram's version be identified with any historical, mythological or ritual vessel. And if, as a stone, it is reminiscent of other stones, there is no justification for stressing any particular other stone, since all we are told about this one is that it is pure (469, 4)—which may imply a precious stone, may indicate holiness—and large enough for inscriptions to appear at one end (470, 23 f.). No clearer picture is possible; attempts to gain one are doomed. Wolfram's Grail stands on its own, must be interpreted from within the work, and remains essentially imprecise.

Its attendants are laymen, not priests; when a Church sacrament such as baptism is sought at Munsalvæsche—which occurs during the visit of Parzival's half-brother Feirefiz in Book XVI—a priest appears to administer it. The baptism neverthless takes place in the Grail temple, and the baptismal font is filled with warm water by the power of the Grail. No mention is made of Mass being celebrated at Munsalvæsche, but Parzival and Condwiramurs do attend Mass within Terre de Salvæsche on the morning of their final reunion (802, 22 f.). It is impossible to tell whether the presence and power of the Grail makes Mass unnecessary within the castle itself; it may, however, be noted that Sigune has little need of it, since her life is one whole prayer:

> Sigûne doschesse
> hôrte selten messe:
> ir leben was doch ein venje gar.   (435, 23–25)

She of course dwells within Terre de Salvæsche and is brought food from the Grail. To conclude from these facts, as some scholars have done, that the Grail ceremony may be identified with the sacrament of Mass is false; the change from chalice to stone, the substantial nature of the nourishment it provides and the fact that it is attended by laymen, all support the main consideration: that at its ceremonies no reference is made to the Last Supper or the death of Christ. Nevertheless, there exists an analogy between the Mass and the Grail, an analogy which includes points of difference as well as points of resemblance, and this it remains to investigate.

The Grail is sacramental in nature in the sense that it mediates between God and man; not only do the Grail company turn towards it when they kneel in prayer, as Christians face the altar, but God's answer to such prayer may be inscribed on the Grail, as for example when it is stated that through the question of an unknown knight Anfortas's suffering may be cured by the hand of the Highest:

> unt hât der kumber ende
> von der hôhsten hende. (484, 5 f.)

Many such texts make it certain that these inscriptions always reveal the will of God.

Moreover, the Grail possesses specific powers, and these derive according to Trevrizent from a holy wafer which a dove from heaven (clearly resembling the Holy Ghost) places upon the Grail each Good Friday—in obvious remembrance of Christ's Passion:

> der stein ist ouch genant der grâl.
>   dar ûf kumt hiute ein botschaft,
> dar an doch lît sîn hôhste kraft.
> Ez ist hiute der karfrîtac,
> daz man für wâr dâ warten mac,
> ein tûb von himel swinget:
> ûf den stein diu bringet
> ein kleine wîze oblât.
> ûf dem steine si die lât:
> diu tûbe ist durchliuhtec blanc,
> ze himel tuot si widerwanc. (469, 28–470, 8)

It is this heavenly wafer which specifically enables the Grail to fulfil its central function: the provision of every sort of food and drink to be found on earth for members of the Grail company (470, 9–20). The pages who serve the knights on festive occasions fill all the dishes from the Grail, which also fills each individual's cup with whatever sort of wine he desires. The Grail company and Sigune—whose food is brought her once weekly from Munsalvæsche by Cundrie (438, 29–439, 8)—are thus to some extent freed from the curse God laid on man after the Fall: if certain duties are required of them, they yet do not have to eat bread 'in the sweat of their face' (Genesis III, 19). Consequently it is perhaps not pure hyperbole when the narrator refers to the Grail which provides this nourishment (235, 21), and later to the nourishment itself (470, 14), as the 'wunsch von pardîs': the conditions of Eden are in part restored in the Grail kingdom.

The nourishment provided is primarily the food of the body, not of the spirit. Not only does the sinful Parzival partake of it on his first visit, but so also does Feirefiz before he is baptised (when he cannot even see the Grail). Clearly this Grail food is not to be identified with the Body of Christ. It signifies an especial blessing of certain men in their life on earth, not a gateway to eternal salvation. The Grail King can therefore share it with his guests when these visit Munsalvæsche in accordance with instructions received from the Grail, but this does not mean that these guests have necessarily found favour with God in the same manner as have the permanent members of the Grail company.

The Grail also has the power of keeping alive for the space of one week anyone who gazes on it; and all who regularly gaze on it retain for ever the beauty of their early youth (469, 14–27). In consequence the very aged Titurel, who occupies a chamber adjoining the Grail temple, although both grey-haired and suffering from gout, yet lives and keeps a fresh complexion (501, 19–30). And Anfortas is kept alive against his will by the Grail company, who never lose hope that he will one day be cured (788, 13–20). Furthermore, when this cure is effected, his regained beauty far surpasses even that of Parzival—a fact on which the narrator comments: 'got noch künste kan genuoc' (796, 16). It is in this context that Trevrizent's statement

occurs that the phoenix derives its peculiar properties from the
Grail:

> von des steines kraft der fênîs
> verbrinnet, daz er zaschen wirt:
> diu asche im aber leben birt.
> sus rêrt der fênîs mûze sîn
> unt gît dar nâch vil liehten schîn,
> daz er schœne wirt als ê.   (469, 8–13)

The association with the Grail of this mythological bird, which
rises new-born out of the flames that consume it, was presumably suggested by the rejuvenating effect the Grail has on men;
but nothing more is heard of the phoenix in the work. That,
however, those who remain constantly near the Grail retain
their youthful beauty into old age and never die, is perhaps a
further reminiscence of the Garden of Eden.

Yet another power of the Grail illustrates the parallel position which it occupies within its own realm to that occupied by
minne in the outside world: as love gives strength to its servants
in battle, so does the Grail to those who serve it. In the few
months which elapse between his departure from Trevrizent
and his proclamation as Grail King, Parzival is already regarded
by the narrator as the true servant of both Condwiramurs—
who is to be called to Munsalvæsche with him—and of the Grail.
Accordingly when he unwittingly engages in battle with his
half-brother Feirefiz, whereas the latter is protected by *minne*
alone (740, 7–12; note that the precious stones which adorn
him give him courage, 743, 5–8, but are nowhere claimed as
'protection'), Parzival's defeat is averted not only by the love
of his wife, but also by the power of the Grail. The narrator
accordingly modifies his fears for his hero:

> ich sorge des den ich hân brâht,
> wan daz ich trôstes hân gedâht,
> in süle des grâles kraft ernern.
> in sol ouch diu minne wern.
> den was er beiden diensthaft
> âne wanc mit dienstlîcher kraft.   (737, 25–30)

For a (future) Grail King, whose *minne* is in accordance with the Grail's requirements, service of his lady and service of the Grail go hand in hand; the other *templeise* are presumably dependent on the Grail alone. But whether the immediate object of service and source of strength is a lady or the Grail, no doubt is left in *Parzival* that ultimately such service, in so far as it accords with God's will, is devoted to God, from whom all strength ultimately derives. Thus the narrator prays that God may preserve both Parzival and Feirefiz:

> got ner dâ Gahmuretes kint.
> der wunsch wirt in beiden,
> dem getouften unt dem heiden:
> die nante ich ê für einen. (742, 14–17)

And when Parzival is saved from the sin of killing his half-brother, this is ascribed to the direct intervention of God (744, 10–16). As the power of God can be conveyed through *minne*, so it can through the Grail; most knights can only receive it one way or the other, but through the peculiarly 'chaste' love of the Grail King both sources of divine strength are open to him.

The Grail King is indeed blessed above all other knights. The fullest description of this blessing is that given by Sigune to Parzival when he comes from his first visit to Munsalvæsche, and she thinks he may have asked the vital question:

> sô wehset unde kernet
> immer sælden kraft bî dir:
> lieber neve, geloube mir,
> sô muoz gar dienen dîner hant
> swaz dîn lîp dâ wunders vant:
> ouch mahtu tragen schône
> immer sælden krône
> hôhe ob den werden:
> den wunsch ûf der erden
> hâstu volleclîche:
> niemen ist sô rîche,
> der gein dir koste mege hân,
> hâstu vrâge ir reht getân. (254, 18–30)

It appears here that all the wonders of the Grail are at the disposal of its king, who is in consequence the richest man on earth. He is even, according to Cundrie, at liberty to extend his power over all the world (782, 18–21). His happiness will ever increase and bear fruit; to him, above all others, belongs the crown of bliss. Everything which is desirable in this world (*der wunsch ûf der erden*) is altogether his.

In conclusion one may say that Munsalvæsche symbolises an especially blessed way of life to which God calls certain of his elect. They are not priests, but constitute a particular order of knights and ladies. Their order demands of them a greater self-sacrifice, a more nearly perfect surrender to God, a higher degree of *kiusche* than is required of others. Should they succeed in serving God in the way required, they are rewarded with a life of perfect happiness which is reminiscent of the Garden of Eden. Indeed the Grail, around which their service centres and from which their blessings derive, is described as a heaven upon earth:

> . . . der grâl was der sælden fruht,
> der werlde süeze ein sölh genuht,
> er wac vil nâch gelîche
> als man saget von himelrîche.　　(238, 21–24)

In the order of the Grail is embodied the most perfect of all possible relationships between a knight and his God.

VIII

GAWAN'S LATER ADVENTURES

er reit al ein gein wunders nôt.[1]

The concluding line of Book VIII, used as a motto for this chapter, indicates the strange and perilous nature of the adventures Gawan seeks out in Books X–XII. These adventures are not connected with Kingrimursel—in the opening section of Book X the narrator dismisses the duel which has for so long threatened Gawan with the brief explanation that his innocence was proved in time and the dispute peacefully settled—but with Orgeluse and Schastel Marveile. A certain effect of anti-climax is conveyed by the petering out of the earlier motif—does Gawan only have to hold out long enough for all his problems to solve themselves?—but this effect is considerably modified by the intervening ninth book: the relaxation of tension which the encounter with Trevrizent brings to Parzival extends to Gawan also. The interdependence of the two plots is felt strongly here: Parzival is freed from the sin which had caused his disgrace; Gawan's honour, which had been attacked at the same time as Parzival's, is at last generally recognised to have been intact all the time. Both have reached a turning point, yet neither rejoins the Round Table for a time. Gawan, like Parzival, is seeking the Grail (503, 21–30), and this common goal will lead them on distinct yet parallel courses, Gawan to Schastel Marveile and marriage to Orgeluse, Parzival to the Grail and reunion with Condwiramurs. Both will meet again at the Round Table, and there their roads will part; for Parzival alone does the further way to the Grail lie open. It is mistaken, however, to suppose, as has usually been done, that Gawan simply returns in the end to his starting point: the Round

[1] 432, 30.

Table. The very fact of his marriage indicates a certain progression. Moreover, as Marianne Wynn has shown in a study of the geography of *Parzival*, the lands of Orgeluse, which Gawan acquires by marriage, are not contiguous to either Arthurian or Grail territory[1]; and Gawan's relative geographic isolation should I think be taken to indicate a relative personal independence also.[2] But it is not Gawan's story with which the poet is primarily concerned; and so we do not follow Gawan beyond the meeting of the Round Table, at which he and Parzival are reinstated.

In this chapter I shall first consider the relationship between Gawan and Orgeluse, and then Gawan's adventures at Schastel Marveile, and the Round Table reunion: in doing so I shall be separating what is interrelated in the work, but the material is more easily organised thus. Finally I shall reconsider the relationship of Arthurian and Grail societies, indicate a parallel between Wolfram's ordering of his poetic world and a particular trend of medieval thought, and summarise Wolfram's usage of one relevant word.

The individual episodes which form Gawan's second series of adventures interlock to make a compact whole; the first of them, and superficially the most trivial, is significant because of what it leads to; had Gawan not entered upon it, the others also would have eluded his grasp. On espying a battered shield tied on a lady's palfrey, he investigates it with erotic intent (504, 15–30)—only to find not joy but sadness:

> der linden grôz was der stam.
> och saz ein frouwe an freuden lam
> derhinder ûf grüenem klê:
> der tet grôz jâmer als wê,
> daz si der freude gar vergaz.
> er reit hin umbe gein ir baz.

---

[1] 'Geography of Fact and Fiction in Wolfram's *Parzival*', *Modern Language Review*, vol. 56 (1961).

[2] Whether Marianne Wynn would herself draw this conclusion seems doubtful, see her article 'Scenery and Chivalrous Journeys in Wolfram's *Parzival*', *Speculum*, vol. 36 (1961), p. 417.

9

ir lac ein rîter in der schôz,
dâ von ir jâmer was sô grôz.   (505, 9–16)

This sorrowful picture is unmistakably reminiscent of Sigune, as Parzival first sees her, but here as elsewhere Gawan's experience is less disturbing than Parzival's: the knight lying in this lady's lap is not dead but wounded. In reply to Gawan's greeting and inquiry, the lady (who is nowhere identified) begs the help which his greater experience of wounds must command; and indeed Gawan's medical skill—'er was zer wunden niht ein tôr (506, 14)—saves the knight's life. Gawan then learns that a certain Lischoys Gwelljus is responsible for the wound, which he promptly offers to avenge. Nor can this spontaneous *triuwe*, to which his original eroticism has yielded, be checked by the knight's warning that to seek vengeance is dangerous (the first of many such warnings in the episodes which follow), but Gawan's purpose is firm, and he rides off to find Lischoys.

Lischoys, as transpires later, is a suitor for the hand of Orgeluse, Duchess of Logroys, in whose land Gawan now finds himself; that the wish to avenge the wounded man should lead Gawan to Orgeluse is therefore natural enough. On their meeting near her castle, the narrator compares Orgeluse's beauty with that of Condwiramurs and emphasises in particular her sexual attractions (508, 14–30). As among Christian knights Gawan, 'der tavelrunder hôhster prîs' (301, 7), is second only to Parzival (whom Cunneware's laugh had proclaimed the finest knight of all), so among their ladies, after the incomparable Condwiramurs, the loveliest is Orgeluse. It is therefore poetically fitting (and in accord with the literary conventions of the time) that Orgeluse and Gawan should pair up as the other two had done. Gawan, who in the past has experienced little difficulty in leaving behind lesser beauties to whom he has on particular occasions offered his services, recognises at once the exceptional quality of Orgeluse's attractions—

mîn lîp muoz ersterben sô
daz mir nimmer wîp gevellet baz   (509, 8 f.)

—and sets out to win her. To Orgeluse, however, Gawan is as yet just another knight attracted by her beauty—she never sees his face uncovered until after her eventual acceptance of his suit (622, 5 f.)—and only when he has proved himself willing and able to perform whatever she asks without any immediate prospect of reward, does she acknowledge his outstanding merit.

Gawan's conventional offer of service is first scorned by Orgeluse, and then, when he replies firmly that he cannot help himself, accepted with a warning: the outcome is less likely to bring him honour than disgrace. The attitude of each to the other is clearly expressed in the exchange which follows:

> dô sprach mîn hêr Gâwân
> 'wer mac minne ungedienet hân?
> muoz ich iu daz künden,
> der treit si hin mit sünden.
> swem ist ze werder minne gâch,
> dâ hœret dienst vor unde nâch.'
> si sprach 'welt ir mir dienst gebn,
> sô müezt ir werlîche lebn,
> unt megt doch laster wol bejagn.
> mîn dienst bedarf decheines zagn.' (511, 11-20)

Throughout, Gawan's hope in serving Orgeluse is that he will win her love; all the adventures which follow have some bearing on his suit. Orgeluse, however, does not play the part of a conventional courtly lady; not only does she hold out little prospect of her lover's success, she also loses no opportunity of pouring scorn upon him. When after collecting her palfrey from a nearby orchard, Gawan offers to lift her onto it, she disdains his assistance, and even refuses to ride together with him:

> si bat in daz er rite für.
> 'ez wære et schade, ob ich verlür
> Sus ahtbæren gesellen,'
> sprach si: 'got müeze iuch vellen!'
> (515, 29-516, 2)

Such extravagant rudeness for a long time characterises

Orgeluse's whole behaviour to Gawan, but the narrator warns his readers not to hold it against her until he has revealed to them the state of her heart; then they will excuse her all (516, 3–14). She is clearly reminiscent of Obie; the two represent a type with which Gawan is apparently well fitted to deal. His long-suffering patience, unwavering purpose and strength of arm provide the stability which they lack, and resolve in the end their psychological problems; because he can tolerate women who behave badly when they are upset, he can help them to recover their balance. Why they are upset is apparently less important than how they react, and how Gawan copes with their reaction; and only after he has coped with it, can they explain their behaviour to themselves or to him. Accordingly we shall follow the narrator in observing how Gawan wins Orgeluse round, before we investigate the cause of her trouble—which indeed by then will be of little account.

Although Gawan's primary objective is to gain his lady's love for himself, nevertheless many of the adventures he encounters in her service reveal an altruism which Orgeluse's shrewishness helps to throw into relief. Thus when any apparent conflict exists between his own interests and those of others, Gawan unhesitatingly puts the need of others first. He culls a herb from the fields through which he and Orgeluse pass in the hope of once more meeting the wounded knight, and is not deterred by the scorn with which she greets his new profession of doctor from applying the herb to the wound when the opportunity arises:

> mit triwen Gâwânes hant
> die wurz ûf die wunden bant. (521, 21 f)

Such *triuwe* is, however, ill-requited, for the knight steals Gawan's horse and rides off, leaving the man who saved his life to proceed on foot—to Orgeluse's express delight. On departing the ingrate reveals himself as Urjans, whose earlier crime of rape had been punished by Artus with Gawan's help. Clearly he remains as false as ever, and even Orgeluse is now moved to arrange for the outrage against the lady—not, she insists, that against Gawan—to be further punished. And since Gawan later recovers his horse from Orgeluse's servants, justice is presumably done. Gawan's *triuwe* is thrown into relief in this episode by comparison with the *valsch* of Urjans, which is apparently irremediable; it is not, however, at all certain at this stage whether the gallant and long-suffering knight is going to come out very well from this series of adventures. His undiscriminating goodwill has brought him no thanks, but only damage and mockery; one wonders if, after all, his persistent optimism is not going to be exposed as inadequate. Orgeluse's proceedings against Urjans on the other hand reveal that, however she may behave towards Gawan, her ethical code in general is that of Arthurian society.

Orgeluse leads Gawan to a tilting-ground by the ford in front of Schastel Marveile; and there, as Lischoys Gwelljus approaches for combat, she leaves him, remarking as she goes that the vast company of ladies lining the battlements will see how he does. The desperate duel which follows calls forth the narrator's censure: the search for glory (*prîs*) does not justify the risk of bloodshed (538, 1–8). However, the consideration that they are both fighting for love (*minne*) prevents a fatal issue, for Gawan eventually spares Lischoys (whose honour forbids him to surrender) in the name of Orgeluse (543, 9–26).

Orgeluse has now disappeared, and Gawan is offered hospitality by the ferryman Plippalinot, who has been won over by Gawan's generosity (*milte*). Custom dictates that the ferryman be given the horse of every knight defeated on that field, but Lischoys is riding the horse Urjans had stolen from Gawan, and Gawan wants it back. In lieu Gawan gives Plippalinot Lischoys himself—presumably for ransom—and the ferryman is more than content with this gift. He is of knightly descent and, with his daughter Bene, does all he can to show his gratitude. Indeed, Bene remains in Gawan's room until he falls asleep, and the narrator leaves no doubt that neither father nor daughter would have minded had Gawan taken advantage of the situation (552, 27 f.; 555, 17–30). But the same man who had made so free with Antikonie shows no interest in Bene. The reason seems to lie not so much in any distinction between the two ladies, as in Gawan's new preoccupation with Orgeluse. He laments to Plippalinot that he cannot see any prospect of consolation for the pangs of love Orgeluse causes him (547, 25–27); and later, at Schastel Marveile, he is similarly prevented by his longing for her from feeling any interest in the many ladies there:

> vil manec frouwe vor im stuont.
> im wart nie werder dienst kuont:
> ir dienst mit zühten wart getân.
> dô prüevete mîn hêr Gâwân
> Dise, die, und aber jene:
> er was et in der alten sene
> nâch Orgelûse der clâren,
> wande im in sînen jâren
> kein wîp sô nâhe nie gegienc
> etswâ dâ er minne enpfienc
> ode dâ im minne was versagt.   (581, 27–582, 7)

Once Gawan has met Orgeluse, he remains as faithful to her as does Parzival to Condwiramurs; neither is capable of being distracted by lesser beauties.

The ensuing episode of Schastel Marveile will be considered in detail later. Orgeluse does not witness it, and although, as will be shown, it plays a part in his suit for her hand, its ramifications are so considerable that it will only distract if pursued further here. That Gawan triumphs at Schastel Marveile may be taken for granted; after his triumph, he sees Orgeluse ride past with another knight, and, behaving at this stage of his suit somewhat more aggressively than usual, he insists on donning his armour and riding to meet her. He is of course impelled by his longing for her; compared with her fairness, that of the ladies of Schastel Marveile reminds him of a foggy day (591, 11–20).

Florant of Itolac, who now faces Gawan, lance ready for combat, is, like Lischoys, a suitor for Orgeluse's hand, and is

dignified by a unique title (*turkoyte*) the meaning of which is
not known; he has never been defeated and, relying on his lance
for victory, carries no sword. Gawan, weak as he is from his
struggle at Schastel Marveile—

> doch was er sô sêre wuont,
> den schilt er kûme dar getruoc   (595, 26 f.)

—unseats his opponent at once, but wins no praise from his lady.
In a speech of some length, Orgeluse pours scorn upon his
performance at Schastel Marveile and mockingly concludes
that, after his success with the ladies there, he will no longer
want to serve her:

> an disen zîten ungemach
> muget ir gerne vliehen:
> lât iu den vinger ziehen.
> rîtet wider ûf zen frouwen.
> wie getörstet ir geschouwen
> strît, den ich werben solde,
> ob iwer herze wolde
> mir dienen nâch minne.   (599, 6–13)

On this occasion it is clear that Orgeluse's ridicule is calculated
to spur her suitor on to further efforts; there is also a hint of the
possible success of his suit—a hint which recurs a few lines later
(600, 24), and which indicates a change in her attitude: Gawan's
persistence, and his many victories, have begun to impress her.

Orgeluse tells Gawan he must now break a branch from a
particular tree in Clinschor's wood, if he wishes to win her love.
The tree is in the charge of King Gramoflanz and, by breaking
it, Gawan throws down a challenge to its guardian. This, as
Gramoflanz informs him in the event, is Orgeluse's objective in
spurring him on:

> ich weiz wol dazs iu minne bôt,
> sît ir hie werbet mînen tôt.   (606, 15 f.)

No explanation of why Orgeluse hates Gramoflanz is, however,
yet given. To reach the tree indicated, Gawan has to jump his
horse across a wide river into which horse and rider fall. The
prospect of failure at this stage moves the rapidly softening

Orgeluse to tears (602, 18), but after some trouble—Gawan has
to swim for it and then help his horse out of the water—the
further bank is gained and the branch broken. Gramoflanz at
once appears, dressed for hunting, but rejects the challenge since
it is beneath his dignity to engage less than two opponents at a
time. Gawan, who does not yet know the identity of the other,
agrees that a combat is unnecessary, especially as for his part he
does not wish to take advantage of an unarmed man.

Success thus appears about to slip through Orgeluse's fingers
at the last minute, when Gawan asks who the other is.
Gramoflanz proudly gives his name and that of his father,
claims that the latter was treacherously killed by King Lot, and
says that Lot's son Gawan is the only knight worthy to fight
him in single combat (608, 14–24). Gawan now declares himself and denies the charge; and a meeting is arranged to take
place two weeks later before a noble company of knights and
ladies. Orgeluse's objective is thus accomplished: she has at
last found the one man who is willing and able to enter the lists
with her enemy. On Gawan's return she is overwhelmed with
gratitude:

> ze sîner antwurte
> erbeizte snellîche
> diu herzoginne rîche.
> gein sînen fuozen si sich bôt:
> dô sprach si 'hêrre, solher nôt
> als ich hân an iuch gegert,
> der wart nie mîn wirde wert.
> für wâr mir iwer arbeit
> füeget sölich herzeleit,
> diu enpfâhen sol getriwez wîp
> umb ir lieben friundes lîp.'   (611, 20–30)

From this moment on Orgeluse behaves as a perfect courtly lady,
anxious only to reward her servant's *arbeit*. Moreover, upon
Gawan now criticising her former discourtesy, she furnishes the
explanation. Her first lover, Cidegast, to whose memory she is
utterly devoted, was slain by King Gramoflanz; since when she
has known no other desire than to avenge him (615, 27–616, 10).

The light cast by this revelation on Orgeluse's character is considerable. Where, as in her case, there is no suggestion of foul play, vengeance for death in battle is not imposed by the ethic of chivalry: Parzival for instance is soon forgiven by Artus's queen, Ginover, for killing Ither. Neither, however, does vengeance conflict with this ethic, as Gurnemanz demonstrates when he makes provision for the slaughter of a defeated opponent who has caused his victor *herzen kumber* (171, 29). It all depends on the depth of feeling of the individual: Orgeluse's sustained attempt to assuage her grief by avenging her lover is proof of an exceptional *triuwe* which, like her beauty, distinguishes her from the average courtly lady.

Orgeluse goes on to say that only a knight capable of avenging Cidegast could earn her love, and that all her mockery of Gawan was intended to spur him on to brave this final test. This sounds to some extent like a rationalisation of her ill-temper, but the truth underlying her claim is that only when she had found, and tested, a suitable champion could this ill-temper disappear. Only now can Orgeluse begin to forget the grief that has hitherto inspired her every act, and can permit the likely avenger of Cidegast to be his successor in her affections. In explicit contrast to the earlier occasion, she now allows Gawan to press her to him as he lifts her to her horse, and promises him in the near future the fulfilment of all his desires (615, 1–20). When they picnic together in a boat near the ferryman's house, she lets him drink from the goblet her own lips have touched, and the following night, after a joyous feast in Schastel Marveile, the two are bedded by Artus's mother, Arnive. Gawan's wounds, which his longing for Orgeluse had kept open, are now healed by *minne*:

> âne wîplîch geselleschaft
> sô müeser sîne schärpfe nôt
> hân brâht unz an den sûren tôt.
>   ich wil iuz mære machen kurz.
> er vant die rehten hirzwurz,
> diu im half daz er genas

> sô daz im arges niht enwas:
> Diu wurz was bî dem blanken brûn.
> muoterhalp der Bertûn,
> Gâwân fil li roy Lôt,
> süezer senft für sûre nôt
> er mit werder helfe pflac
> helfeclîch unz an den tac. (643, 24–644, 6)

Gawan's long-suffering optimism is thus proved after all to have been well suited to the situation.

At this point the Gawan plot is practically at an end; yet there remains the combat with Gramoflanz. Arrangements made by Gawan for Artus and his court to witness the duel take up much of Book XIII, and incidents connected with it fill Book XIV. But twice postponed and eventually cancelled, this combat also, like the one with Kingrimursel, proves rather an anti-climax—though one can admire the elaborate and patient ceremony with which the entangled problems of the Arthurian world are here sorted out. Diplomacy and goodwill can clearly be as effective in settling outstanding disputes as battle and sudden death—but they certainly take longer.

The cancellation of the duel with Gramoflanz is arranged by Artus on behalf of Itonje, a sister of Gawan with whom Gramoflanz is in love. For her sake Gramoflanz agrees to abandon his attempt to avenge the alleged murder of his father. Similarly Orgeluse is persuaded by her love for Gawan to forgive her enemy—and in this way *minne*, by triumphing over the destructive demands of *râche*, plays a positive role in stabilising society and furthering happiness. Orgeluse's change of heart is explained psychologically:

> der was ergetzens gewin
> komen nâch Cidegaste,
> den si ê klaget sô vaste.
> ir zorn was nâch verdecket:
> wan si het erwecket
> von Gâwân etslîch umbevanc:
> dâ von ir zürnen was sô kranc. (723, 4–10)

Orgeluse appears here as a medieval version of the 'mixed-up kid', who is unable to cope on her own with her personal problems and has been engaged in a disorganised search for someone to take them over; when she finds such a person, she can relax in his arms. Indeed she attains with him such equilibrium that she finally abandons her hostility to Gramoflanz. Gramoflanz, having once injured her, had been fashioned by her into a symbol of her discontent; when this vanishes, he ceases to matter one way or the other.

This then is the sort of problem Gawan is able to deal with. His lineage, particularly on his mother's side—she is sister to Artus—destines him to find fulfilment in love, and in his union with Orgeluse this destiny is accomplished; no higher goal calls him, for he inherits no futher potentialities. Accordingly, before the next *aventiure*, Parzival reappears on the scene, and at the end of Book XIII the narrator indicates that he is from now on to have pride of place: 'an den rehten stam diz mære ist komn' (678, 30). The combat between Parzival and Gawan which opens Book XIV is primarily of interest because of Parzival's reaction to it. The outcome, however (Parzival's victory is only prevented by the sudden termination of the fight), does also reveal their respective merits: as Parzival's quest is more difficult than Gawan's, so is his strength the greater.

The episode of Schastel Marveile has been reserved for separate treatment, but should nevertheless not be dissociated from Gawan's love for Orgeluse. She leads him to the castle and draws his attention to the watching ladies, and he returns to it with her after gaining her love; and that the interlocking affairs are in fact integrally welded together is later revealed by the pact made by Orgeluse with Clinschor. Sure that Gramoflanz could not survive the ordeal of Schastel Marveile, Orgeluse once promised to marry whoever should do so; thus she hoped to lure her enemy to his death (617, 19–30). So in triumphing in the adventure at Schastel Marveile, Gawan is in fact guaranteeing the success of his suit for his lady's hand.

In general it may be said that Schastel Marveile presents the noblest knight of the Round Table with his supreme test. Like Parzival at Munsalvæsche, so Gawan is quite unaware beforehand of the opportunity for doing good that his victory over Lischoys has given him: ignorant of his whereabouts, he comes upon his destiny unawares. But where Parzival had failed to respond wholeheartedly to the mystery and the sorrow of the Grail (in spite of the hint given him by Anfortas), Gawan from the first shows a lively curiosity in the ladies who watch from the battlements of Schastel Marveile, and later puts aside all thought of self in his concern for their sorrow. The morning after his combat with Lischoys he wakes early and looks out of the window of the ferryman's house:

> er kôs ein burc, diers âbents sach,
> dô im diu âventiure geschach;
> vil frouwen ûf dem palas:
> mangiu under in vil schœne was.
> ez dûht in ein wunder grôz,
> daz die frouwen niht verdrôz
> ir wachens, daz si sliefen nieht.
> dennoch der tac was niht ze lieht.　　(553, 11–18)

Gawan is astonished that the ladies are watching so early, and takes the first opportunity of asking who they are. Bene is frightened by his question and tries to stifle his curiosity, but nothing can deter him from his inquiry. Getting no answer from her, Gawan turns to her father, who begs him for God's sake to desist:

> der wirt want sîne hende:
> dô sprach er 'vrâgets niht durch got:
> hêr, dâ ist nôt ob aller nôt.'　　(556, 14–16)

Plippalinot's remark makes it clear that the *wunder grôz* of the watching ladies does have a special significance, and that Gawan's curiosity in them is justified: they are in terrible distress. The question Gawan insists on asking, like the one Parzival failed to ask, is a test of true compassion. Gawan's reaction to their need is immediate: 'sô muoz ich doch ir

kumber klagen' (556, 17).[1] He asks why the ferryman and Bene
are loath to answer his question and is told they fear that, if he
persists in inquiring, he will not refrain from acting when he
knows the answer. However, by threatening to find out from
someone else if they refuse to tell him, Gawan at last discovers
what castle it is:

> ze Terre marveile ir sît:
> Lît marveile ist hie.
> hêrre, ez wart versuochet nie
> ûf Schastel marveil diu nôt.
> iwer leben wil in den tôt.
> ist iu âventiure bekant,
> swaz ie gestreit iwer hant,
> daz was noch gar ein kindes spil:
> nu næhent iu riubæriu zil.   (557, 6–14)

In this famous castle, which Plippalinot announces so por-
tentously, are imprisoned many heathens and Christians, including the mother, sister and two nieces of Artus—who are
respectively Gawan's grandmother, mother and sisters—
together with two hundred other ladies. Clearly their liberation
should be the goal of every Arthurian knight, and indeed
Cundrie called upon the members of the Round Table to
attempt it at the same time as she denounced Parzival, adding:

> al âventiure ist ein wint,
> wan die man dâ bezalen mac,
> hôher minne wert bejac.   (318, 20–22)

Success has, however, hitherto eluded everyone: Artus himself
had tried to redeem his mother when a young man (66, 1–8),
but apparently in vain; Clias admits that, defeated by one of
Orgeluse's suitors, he failed even to reach the castle (334, 11–22);
and the narrator summarily dismisses the fruitless attempts of
the rest of the Round Table (334, 23–25). With Parzival it is
different: since his prowess in arms excels even Gawan's, he too
overcomes all the preliminary obstacles, but is not moved to in-
quire who the ladies are; nor does the ferryman inform anyone

[1] See Wolfgang Mohr, 'Hilfe und Rat in Wolframs *Parzival*', *Festschrift
für Jost Trier* (Meisenheim am Glan, 1954).

who does not ask (599, 19–30). Parzival's lack of interest is explained later, when Orgeluse tells how, after defeating her knights, he yet refused her love; as his own wife is more beautiful and dearer to him than Orgeluse, so also his goal is higher than Schastel Marveile (619, 1–12). This adventure, the most difficult that a purely Arthurian knight can encounter successfully, is reserved for Gawan, the best Round Table knight and the closest relative of the chief ladies involved.

The ladies' captor and present lord of the castle is Clinschor, a knight who, having been discovered in the act of adultery, as Arnive later informs Gawan, was castrated. His goodwill turned to evil by shame, he renders unhappy all noble-hearted people with whom he comes in contact:

> Durch die scham an sîme lîbe
> wart er man noch wîbe
> guotes willen nimmer mêr bereit;
> ich mein die tragent werdekeit.
> swaz er den freuden mac genemn,
> des kan von herzen in gezemn. (658, 3–8)

In particular, since he is unable to bring happiness to any woman, he begrudges others that particular joy which is the basis of courtly society: the joy of *minne*. Accordingly those knights and ladies whom he keeps shut up in Schastel Marveile are separated into two communities which never meet (637, 20–23).

The source of Clinschor's power is magic, to which he turned after his disgrace—thus fulfilling his inherited destiny, for he is a descendant of Virgil (who in the Middle Ages was popularly thought of as a magician). In him is embodied that aspect of diabolic activity which presents a direct threat to Arthurian society. Without the aid of God, neither man nor spirit can prevail against him:

> er hât ouch aller der gewalt,
> mal unde bêâ schent,
> die zwischen dem firmament
> wonent und der erden zil;
> niht wan die got beschermen wil. (658, 26–30)

This crucial passage provides the ultimate explanation of the fear which all feel for Gawan from the moment he enters Orgeluse's service until he finally triumphs in Schastel Marveile; not only is he engaging in a series of adventures, every one of which is exceedingly difficult, but the culminating one, hitherto unattempted, involves a combat with a supernatural adversary against whom even the noblest knight is impotent without the help of God.

More than anything else the *aventiure* of Schastel Marveile demonstrates the dependence of Arthurian society on God. In the other episodes in which Gawan is involved, the references to God are few and, were it not for this final test, might perhaps be dismissed as superficial; nothing would actually prove that this apparent unconcern testifies to an utter trust and confidence in the creator and sustainer of all life. That proof is provided by Schastel Marveile. It has been suggested that the attitude adopted by young Parzival to God represents the general attitude of Arthurian chivalry, that the typical Arthurian knight conceives of his relation to God in feudal terms, considers that his own chivalrous merit puts God under an obligation to him. It has even been stated that the Arthurian ethic is essentially worldly and unconcerned with religion. There is, however, no certain evidence in *Parzival* to support either of these statements, and in connection with Gawan's final exploits positive proof is provided to the contrary. It seems worth while setting forth this proof at some length.

None of the other characters expects Gawan to win glory from his service of Orgeluse or his attack on Schastel Marveile. His obedience to his lady's first request, that he fetch her palfrey so that she can ride away with him, is greeted with dismay by all onlookers. One old knight warns Gawan that the adventure may well cost him his life and then, when Gawan is not deterred thereby, commends him to God thus:

> des hant dez mer gesalzen hât,
> der geb iu für kumber rât.   (514, 15 f.)

The creator who salted the sea is no mere feudal overlord to be put under obligation by his servants, but a God transcending human limits, whose unforced will is law to his creation. Gawan's reply, 'nu waltes got' (514, 21), indicates his complete acceptance of the will of this God; and even if this acceptance is expressed only in a formula, it is yet significant that such formulae occur far more frequently in the course of Gawan's final, supremely dangerous adventure than ever before. Moreover, the episode ends, as it began, with special reference to the creator; but this time the prayer is that Gawan, to whom God has granted the victory, should further be moved by him to restore joy to Clinschor's captives. Arnive addresses her unrecognised grandson with these words:

> der die sterne hât gezalt,
> der müeze iuch helfe lêren
> und uns gein freuden kêren. (659, 20–22)

The faith of the old knight who commends Gawan to 'des hant dez mer gesalzen hât', and of Arnive who begs 'der die sterne hât gezalt' to inspire Gawan to do good, is neither arrogant nor superficial.

The chivalric conception of God is further illustrated by the words addressed to Gawan by the ferryman, who appears to know more than anyone else outside about the secrets of Schastel Marveile:

> op daz got erzeige
> daz ir niht sît veige,
> sô wert ir hêr diss landes:
> swaz frouwen hie stêt pfandes,
> die starkez wunder her betwanc,
> daz noch nie rîters prîs erranc,
> manc sarjant, edeliu rîterschaft,
> op die hie'rlœset iwer kraft,
> sô sît ir prîss gehêret
> und hât iuch got wol gêret . . . (558, 15–24)

Plippalinot's opinion is quite clear: the success or failure of Gawan's attempt to free the captives depends entirely on the will of God. Nor, as is apparent from the ferryman's later remarks about the fabulous bed on which Gawan will be put to the test, can anyone foresee God's pleasure—though one can pray for a happy issue:

> sô waldes diu gotes gebe,
> so ir in die kemenâten gêt
> dâ Lît marveile stêt...
>
> dar an ze lîden iu geschiht
> swaz got an iu wil meinen:
> nâch freude erz müeze erscheinen.
>
> (561, 20–22, and 28–30)

Such utter dependence on God does not, however, excuse Gawan from exerting himself to the uttermost; rather must he do everything within his power to bring about a victory—and then confide the issue to God. So his eventual triumph is also due to the stout shield which the ferryman lends him, 'dâ von doch Gâwân sît genas' (560, 22), and can be stated by the rich pedlar by the castle gate to depend on Gawan's manliness:

> ob iwer herze manheit pfligt,
> sô sît irs alles hêrre.   (563, 24 f.)

But this same pedlar adds 'lâtes walten got' (564, 3)—which is precisely what Gawan does do after his great spring has landed him on the bed:

> Er lac, unde liez es walten
> den der helfe hât behalten,
> und den der helfe nie verdrôz,
> swer in sînem kumber grôz
> helfe an in versuochen kan.
> der wîse herzehafte man,
> swâ dem kumber wirt bekant,
> der rüefet an die hôhsten hant:
> wan diu treit helfe rîche
> und hilft im helfeclîche.
> daz selbe ouch Gâwân dâ geschach.
> dem er ie sîns prîses jach,
> sînen kreftclîchen güeten,
> den bat er sich behüeten.   (568, 1–14)

145

Gawan, having for the moment done his part, lies on the bed and leaves the issue to the God who has treasured up help and is never loath to distribute it, whose highest hand is rich in help and extends help willingly, the God to whose powerful help Gawan has always ascribed his own honour. Whatever wise and courageous man calls upon God in his distress, says the narrator, will surely receive his help—as happened to Gawan on this occasion.

Thus does Wolfram at this critical juncture portray the relationship of Gawan to God: the knight, brave yet humble, does his best, and leaves the issue to God's will; God, almighty yet loving, helps the brave knight who shows such trust in him. This is the essence of that relationship with God to which Parzival has to be educated, and it is the same relationship with God which characterises the Christianity of Willehalm and Arabel-Gyburc in Wolfram's second epic; because it is un-problematic for Gawan, it may attract less attention, but it is no different, no less important. Nor, since Gawan represents the ideal of the Round Table, can there be any doubt that this same relationship with God underlies and sustains the Arthurian ethical code and indeed the whole manner of life of courtly society. Arthurian chivalry, as portrayed by Wolfram von Eschenbach, rests upon that very form of Christianity which Parzival, as the sinful heir of a sinful king of the Grail, is called upon to explore so profoundly.

So Gawan survives the shaking about and the noise, the hail-stones and the arrows which beset him while he is lying on *Lît Marveile*; and undaunted he kills the lion who attacks him. When all is over, he faints, only to be revived by the happy ladies he has freed:

> si jâhn 'ir lâget unde liget
> als der des hôhsten prîses pfliget.
> ir habt den prîs alhie bezalt,
> des ir mit freuden werdet alt:
> Der sig ist iwer hiute.'   (576, 27–577, 1)

Thanks for the victory are given to God. Gawan, however, as

has been seen, leaves the castle again next morning on seeing Orgeluse and does not return until after his arrangement of a duel with Gramoflanz has won him her love. Then, as Lord of Schastel Marveile, he reunites the knights and ladies who have so long been imprisoned there and so takes the first step to restore them to the joyful world of chivalry from which Clinschor's malice had cut them off (637, 15–30). He does not yet reveal to his grandmother, mother and sisters his own identity, but postpones the reunion of the Arthurian family till Artus himself should be present; that occasion completes the joy of all concerned (672, 15–21). On it Artus, having reconciled Gawan and Gramoflanz, betrothes Itonje to the latter, and Orgeluse makes public her marriage to Gawan; in addition Gawan's second sister Cundrie and his widowed mother Sangive are given to Orgeluse's two unsuccessful suitors, Lischoys and Florant (729, 27–730, 22). 'Artûs was frouwen milte' (730, 11) comments the narrator, somewhat maliciously[1]; but the happy ending thus granted to all does at least reflect the peace and happiness restored to the world of chivalry by Gawan.

Looking back on Gawan's story, one may notice that at many points already mentioned it runs parallel to Parzival's—and closer comparison would reveal many further points of resemblance and contrast. For instance, it is not only Parzival who rides a Grail horse but Gawan too; but whereas Parzival wins his horse off a Grail knight himself, Gawan is given by Orilus one Lähelin had won (339, 26–340, 5); and whereas Parzival gives his horse his head and is led to Trevrizent, Gawan nowhere lets go of his horse's reins. Whether such points help to explain why Gawan's horse leads him not to Munsalvæsche (which he is supposed to be seeking for Parzival) but to Schastel Marveile, must perhaps remain a matter of opinion, but what can be said is that they are a weakness if they do not, a strength

---

[1] W. T. H. Jackson finds the sort of mockery I suspect here widespread throughout the whole episode of Schastel Marveile, see *The Literature of the Middle Ages* (New York, 1960), p. 123.

if they do—and this sort of argument applies to all the common features of the two men's lives. It should not, however, be expected that all comparisons will show Parzival as 'better' than Gawan: which of them responds more appropriately to a given situation will partly depend on the sphere of operation. Parzival for instance, fights with the same distinction as Gawan in Book VII but, perhaps because he remains incognito, a lone and solitary figure cut off from normal social life, he does not make the same contribution to the happy conclusion of the quarrel between Obie and Meljanz. And of course Parzival avoids the challenge of Schastel Marveile altogether. Clearly any particular task is either better suited to Parzival or to Gawan, seldom or never to both, and the man less well suited will either ignore it in the first place or pursue it half-heartedly and fail.

There are also a number of instances where the two do not encounter one and the same challenge, but different though similar ones. Examples occur when they are both upbraided at the Round Table but for different reasons, or when they both have the chance to ask compassionate questions but under different circumstances. Here it will in general be found that Gawan, 'der reht gemuote' (339, 1), is the simpler and solider character. Where Parzival's dual heritage and solitary upbringing lead him to raise a problem in its most intense form, and then to pursue it to its ultimate conclusion, Gawan will take it in his stride and make it appear that there was nothing to worry about in the first place. Thus both of the duels to which he is challenged are first postponed and finally cancelled, without his ever having been unduly disturbed by them. As Wolfgang Mohr has pointed out, Parzival and Gawan each provide perspective for the other: if from Parzival's point of view Gawan appears superficial, from Gawan's Parzival appears unnecessarily serious.[1] The work is more satisfying for containing both.

A comparison is also possible between Gawan and Gahmuret. These two, who come of different generations, do not meet in the work, and so cannot be compared in personal encounter;

[1] 'Parzival und Gawan', *Euphorion*, vol. 52 (1958), p. 15.

both belong exclusively to the Arthurian family, not also to the Grail one, both are outstanding in love and war. They are, however, contrasted in character and achievement: Gahmuret is more impetuous and extravagant, Gawan more cautious and modest; Gahmuret brings great grief to both his wives, Gawan, as is seen not only from Obie and Orgeluse but also from the ladies of Schastel Marveile, restores happiness to women in trouble. Perhaps it needs the fire of a Gahmuret, as well as the depth of a Herzeloyde, to beget a Parzival; but Gawan's quiet achievement is more humane than Gahmuret's.

The essential harmony of the religious attitudes of the Grail and the Round Table societies is in accord with the close and friendly relationship uniting them. Their territories are adjacent. Intercommunication is admittedly limited; but if Cundrie alone is permitted to move freely between Munsalvæsche and the outside world, her role is nevertheless crucial. That the special position occupied by Artus in courtly society is recognised at Munsalvæsche appears from the two occasions when she announces, first Parzival's disgrace and, later, his nomination as Grail King to full meetings of the *tavelrunder*. Moreover, from her declaration that his failure at Munsalvæsche has disgraced the Arthurian company, it may be inferred that the ethic of chivalry embodied in this society depends ultimately on Grail values. Then it is Cundrie who calls upon the Round Table knights to liberate Clinschor's captives—their fate is of concern to the Grail company, but can only be resolved by an Arthurian knight—and her desire to see these ladies after their release testifies to her deep attachment to them (784, 12–22). As Cundrie is the only regular visitor to Sigune's cell, so she alone appears regularly to have visited Arnive in Schastel Marveile (579, 24 f.). Her numerous activities thus reveal the concern of the Grail in all affairs of the courtly world.

The two societies are, moreover, interdependent. As was seen in the preceding chapter, the knights and ladies serving the

Grail are not allowed to marry so long as they remain at Munsalvæsche, and so the Grail company must rely on the outside world for new recruits: children of knightly descent are therefore called to the Grail. On the other hand members of the Grail do not necessarily remain all their lives at Munsalvæsche, but sometimes leave there to marry outside: in particular they may be called upon to rule over lands where the royal line becomes extinct. Even the daughters of the Grail King himself, the only member of the Grail company allowed a wife, frequently leave Munsalvæsche to marry; while the sons and heirs to the Grail kingdom may, like Parzival, bring in wives from outside. Neither society could survive without the other.

This exchange of knights and ladies between Munsalvæsche and courtly society does not mean that the individual can choose to which he will belong. On the contrary, no one can pass into the Grail company from outside unless he or she has been specifically named in a special message to appear on the Grail itself. Parzival's first visit provides the only (partial) exception to this rule—an exception which has been allowed for by the Grail's unusual announcement that one knight would arrive unnamed. Before Parzival's second visit both he and his wife are specifically named. The primary duty of the Grail knights is to prevent undesired adventurers from reaching the Grail, and they never fail. Arthurian knights such as Vergulaht and even Gawan may be compelled by Parzival to help in his search for Munsalvæsche, but so long as they are not named on the Grail, they have no prospect of success: in fact the efforts of both fade into oblivion. On the other hand it is equally impossible for the son of a Grail King to forsake his high calling and become an ordinary Arthurian knight; the attempt to do so is sinful and leads to catastrophe. The implication of Anfortas's disastrous attachment to Orgeluse is that the best and highest goal of a knight of the Round Table is yet sin and shame for a Grail King. Arthurian chivalry is not hereby disparaged, but the vocation of the Grail is higher, and for a Grail King to prefer a lower way of life is sinful. The two societies exist side by side and are interdependent; each in its own way is wholly admirable, and the members of each please God by obeying the laws and attending to the problems of their own society; nevertheless—as is for instance confirmed by the delight with which parents send their predestined children to the Grail (471, 5-9)— the calling of the one is 'higher' than that of the other.

The relationship of the two societies may be described in terms of Gradualism. As Günther Müller demonstrated in his fundamental article on this subject,[1] there was a school of medieval thought, at least in the thirteenth century, which did not think in categorical alternatives, but relative to God. For the whole of creation to appear as a perfect likeness of its creator, not one uniform, but many divergent grades of existence must be found therein; in the words of St Thomas Aquinas: 'Oportuit ad hoc, quod in creaturis esset perfecta Dei imitatio, quod diversi gradus in creaturis invenirentur.' Moreover, each grade of existence should seek perfection after its own manner, for perfection in any grade is imitation of God: 'Omnia appetendo proprias perfectiones appetunt ipsum Deum, in quantum perfectiones omnium rerum sunt quædam similitudines divini esse.' What is allowed, indeed demanded, in one grade may be forbidden and sinful in another. Were the lower grades to merge into the higher, the imitation of God would not be more but less perfect: 'Non enim esset perfectum universum, si tantum unus gradus bonitatis inveniretur in rebus.'

Clearly this Thomist conception of a creation which can only perfectly imitate God by seeking perfection in many divergent ways, may be considered as the theological equivalent to Wolfram's interpretation of human life: if the author of *Parzival* is to be set in a context of medieval thought, it is probably here that he belongs. The fact that he lived and wrote

---

[1] 'Gradualismus, Eine Vorstudie zur altdeutschen Literaturgeschichte', *Deutsche Vierteljahrsschrift für Literaturwissenschaft und Geistesgeschichte*, vol. 2 (1924). The quotations from Aquinas are taken from this article. I have not seen J. F. Poag, '*Minne' and 'Gradualismus' in the Works of Wolfram von Eschenbach* (Dissertation, University of Illinois, 1961).

over half a century before St Thomas Aquinas does not matter: what is under discussion is not an influence of one on the other, but parallel ways of thought; moreover, there is much evidence that lay artists can anticipate in their work the theoretical formulations of later thinkers.

What St Thomas describes as a *gradus* is very similar to what Wolfram calls an *orden* and, partly to demonstrate this point, and partly to call attention to the great diversity in *Parzival*—which the need to abstract a coherent picture of the work may have obscured—I propose to conclude this chapter with a brief study of this word. It is used most generally by Gurnemanz in 'gebt rehter mâze ir orden' (171, 13): give true moderation its 'due'. Elsewhere it refers regularly to the particular qualities or code of some group of human beings. Least significant is perhaps the *orden* of squires, which gives them the right to their lords' used standards (81, 14), deeper *wîbes orden* in which man and woman are united (172, 30); and when the narrator alludes to the feminine *orden*—

> wîpheit, dîn ordenlîcher site,
> dem vert und fuor ie triwe mite   (116, 13 f.)

—he says that *triuwe* is especially characteristic and especially required of women. Even heathendom has its own *orden*, which of course is distinguished by mistaken religious worship (13, 28; 107 17). Whether Wolfram considered even this category of mankind to have a proper place in God's creation is not sure; but if he did, then Gahmuret's desertion of Belakane suggests that its place is lower than that of Christian chivalry, for he writes:

> frouwe, in mac dich niht verheln,
> wær dîn ordn in mîner ê,
> sô wær mir immer nâch dir wê.   (55, 24–26)

Moreover, it is always possible to exchange the *orden* of heathendom for that of Christianity, as the second marriage of Feirefiz in *Parzival* and of Arabel-Gyburc in *Willehalm* demonstrate.

Like the peasantry and the merchant class, though at the other end of the scale, the order of priesthood plays no great part in *Parzival*, and (consequently ?) the word *orden* is nowhere used of it—but Trevrizent directs attention to its uniquely venerable quality:

> swaz dîn ouge ûf erden siht,
> daz glîchet sich dem priester niht.
> sîn munt die marter sprichet,
> diu unser flust zebrichet:
> ouch grîfet sîn gewîhtiu hant
> an daz hœheste pfant
> daz ie für schult gesetzet wart:
> swelch priester sich hât sô bewart
> daz er dem kiusche kan gegebn,
> wie möht der heileclîcher lebn ?   (502, 13–22)

After the priests perhaps come the hermits: those laymen who sacrifice the active for the contemplative life. Sigune's father wishes no more share in the world's joy after his wife's death (477, 2–6) and, together with his brother, becomes a hermit. Wolfram narrates this event more fully in *Titurel* (especially stanzas 22 and 23), but in *Parzival* too appears the definite statement:

> durch die gotes minne
> heten se ûf gegebn ir swert.   (186, 26 f.)

The heritage of sorrow is visited upon the child too, for Sigune's lover is killed in her service, whereupon she follows her father and uncle into retreat and becomes:

> . . . ein klôsnærinne,
> diu durch die gotes minne
> ir magetuom unt ir freude gap.
>   (435, 13–15)

Finally there is Trevrizent, specifically described as a holy man (448, 23), of whose fasting the narrator says:

> sus stuont sîn heileclîchez lebn.
> got het im den muot gegebn:
> der hêrre sich bereite gar

> gein der himelischen schar.
> mit vaste er grôzen kumber leit:
> sîn kiusche gein den tievel streit.   (452, 23–28)

Trevrizent is forbidden by his *orden* to eat before the canonical hour of None:

> der wirt sînr orden niht vergaz:
> swie vil er gruop, decheine er az
> der würze vor der nône . . .   (485, 23–25)

The fact that the adjective *heilec* is used throughout the work only of priests and hermits may imply that the *orden* of both is 'higher' than that of either Arthurian or Grail knights.

Herzeloyde refers to chivalry as *ritters orden* when Parzival first tells her he wants to be a knight (126, 7), and the boy's reply includes the synonym *schildes ambet* (126, 14): the office, or profession, of the shield. Knighthood appears on this occasion to be conferred by Artus alone (123, 7), and probably to be hereditary (123, 11); Gahmuret, however, derives his chivalry from his first lady, Queen Amphlise (above, p. 19). Both father and son consider that the *orden* of knighthood puts them under certain obligations: Gahmuret is obliged by it to accept the judge's decision that, having won Herzeloyde in a tournament, he must marry her (97, 25–98, 2); Parzival refers to the high honour of chivalry when swearing that Jeschute did not misbehave with him (269, 4–11). No clear distinction is made in this respect between the *orden* of knighthood in general and that of the Round Table in particular: Kingrimursel charges Gawan to fight with him so as not to disgrace either:

> kan sîn lîp des niht verzagen,
> ern welle dâ schildes ambet tragen,
> sô man i'n dennoch mêre
> bî des helmes êre
> unt durch ritter ordenlîchez lebn:
> dem sint zwuo rîche urbor gegebn,
> rehtiu scham und werdiu triwe
> gebent prîs alt unde niwe.
> Hêr Gâwân sol sich niht verschemn,

ob er geselleschaft wil nemn
ob der tavelrunder,
diu dort stêt besunder.
der reht wære gebrochen sân,
sæze drob ein triwenlôser man.   (321, 23–322, 6)

It is the distinguishing quality (*reht*) of the Round Table that its
knights should be irreproachable; they are, however, not necessarily different from other knights except in their ritual feasting
(as on the occasion of Gawan's reunion):

der tavelrunder orden
wart dâ begangen âne haz.
der künec ob tavelrunder az,
unt die dâ sitzen solten,
die prîs mit arbeit holten.   (652, 8–12)

The *orden* of the Round Table might therefore be considered
as a model sub-division of the general order of (Arthurian)
chivalry, as the knights of the Round Table are a model sub-
division of the general lineage of Mazadan.

Anfortas in his sickness seems to regard the Grail *orden* as
similarly subject to the general laws of chivalry, in the name of
which he pleads to be allowed to die:

sît ir vor untriwen bewart,
sô lœst mich durch des helmes art
unt durch des schildes orden.   (787, 19–21)

But the Grail knights do not listen to his arguments which,
indeed, are particularly suspect as he supports them by reference
to his past life: he is now, as then, in a state of ungrace. Later,
when he is cured, he makes a clear statement of the difference
between the Grail and the Arthurian orders of chivalry:

mîn orden wirt hie niht vermiten:
ich wil vil tjoste rîten,
ins grâles dienste strîten.
durch wîp gestrîte ich niemer mêr ... (819, 26–29)

This distinction Anfortas finally perceives between fighting for the Grail and fighting for women is endorsed by the narrator in his last comment on the man who sinned by confusing the two:

> der werde clâre Anfortas
> manlîch bî kiuschem herzen was.
> ordenlîche er manege tjoste reit,
> durch den grâl, niht durch diu wîp er streit.

(823, 23–26)

The Grail *orden*, which we learn in the sixth stanza of *Titurel* was presented in writing to its first king—'dâ vant ich geschriben al mîn orden'—is an order of chivalry, but has different rules from the Arthurian order. To it we must now return as we investigate the final stages of Parzival's progress.

THE GRAIL KING

daz slôz dirre âventiure.[1]

Parzival re-enters the story at the very end of Book XIII; is reinstated as a member of the Round Table in XIV; meets his half-brother Feirefiz and introduces him to the Round Table in XV; at the end of XV is called by Cundrie to the Grail, and in XVI takes his place there as king. During Books XIV and XV he is accordingly to be found in the neighbourhood of Schastel Marveile, together with Artus, Gawan and Gramoflanz: some of his adventures have therefore been touched on in the preceding chapter, though a fuller discussion is given here. By contrast in Book XVI he leaves the Arthurian world behind; he does, however, take Feirefiz with him, is joined at the Grail by his wife Condwiramurs, and visits Trevrizent and Sigune; his relationship with these four will thus need further comment. Yet in this matter, as in others, little remains to be said—partly because the poet himself is primarily engaged in rounding his story off at this stage, not in raising issues that are new, partly because even what is new in the work has to some extent had to be anticipated in this study.

The chapter is organised as follows. First Parzival's last meeting with Gawan and Artus, and his encounter with Feirefiz is reviewed. Then follows a brief mention of what is said in the work about Parzival's descendants. Next, and most important, comes a somewhat longer discussion of the main features of Parzival's election as Grail King, and of his meeting with his wife and Grail relatives. Lastly there is a short note on the narrator's final comments.

In the matter treated in this chapter Wolfram is once more independent of his source. Indeed, as Chrestien's original

[1] 734, 7.

breaks off in Wolfram's Book XIII, that is in the middle of the Gawan story, and as it is uncertain that Wolfram knew even the first of Chrestien's various continuators, even some of the matter treated in the preceding chapter must be regarded as independent.

As was stated at the beginning of chapter V, even after he has left Trevrizent, Parzival spends all his time fighting; and it is in order to pick a fight with Gramoflanz that he has come to the neighbourhood of Schastel Marveile and plucked a branch from Gramoflanz's special tree (701, 2–6). Instead of meeting Gramoflanz, he meets Gawan, who is trying out his armour in preparation for the forthcoming duel; each takes the other for Gramoflanz, and a mighty battle follows. It is the first of three battles in which Parzival engages in the course of a few days, and when each has been discussed separately, it will be necessary to raise the question of their common function.

This first battle is between relatives and friends, who do not recognise each other; the victor will therefore derive little joy from it (680, 13–17). The details of the battle are not given, the narrator breaking off to describe an embassy which Artus sends to Gawan. On the return journey this embassy passes the scene of the conflict; some of its members recognise Gawan, who is by this time clearly losing, and lament him by name. Hearing who his opponent is, Parzival throws away his sword and curses himself:

> 'unsælec unde unwert
> bin ich,' sprach der weinde gast.
> 'aller sælden mir gebrast,
> daz mîner gunêrten hant
> dirre strît ie wart bekant.
> des was mit unfuoge ir ze vil.
> schuldec ich mich geben wil.
> hie trat mîn ungelücke für
> unt schiet mich von der sælden kür . . .'
>
> (688, 22–30)

If, however, Parzival regards it as a sign of his ill-fortune (*ungelücke, unsælde*) that he should have fought Gawan, a limit is presumably set to this ill-fortune by the happy issue: the battle is not fought to a finish, but serves in the event to re-introduce Parzival to Arthurian society. It also brings about the first postponement of Gawan's duel with Gramoflanz, who has no wish to fight an exhausted opponent.

Gawan leads Parzival to his own tent, where he entertains his *geselle* and where Artus later comes to meet the stranger. Before this meeting Gawan insists on introducing Parzival to Orgeluse and to the ladies he has freed from Schastel Marveile. Parzival is reluctant to meet them, because he still feels the shame of Cundrie's denunciation of him to the whole Round Table nearly five years before (695, 25–696, 4); but Gawan stands firm, all the ladies greet Parzival with a kiss, and Parzival's shame—which, it will be remembered, was represented as a saving grace at the time (above, p. 61)—now leaves him:

> Parzivâl der clâre
> wart des âne vâre
> überparlieret,
> daz wart gecondwieret
> elliu scham ûz sîme herzen dô:
> âne blûkeit wart er vrô.   (696, 15–20)

Parzival's evident superiority to Gawan, who faints when the battle is over, confirms to all the Round Table his outstanding prowess in arms (*prîs*), of which much is now made as he rejoins the company:

> Artûs bôt im êre
> unt dancte im des sêre,
> daz sîn hôhiu werdekeit
> wær sô lanc und ouch sô breit,
> daz er den prîs für alle man
> von rehten schulden solte hân.   (698, 25–30)

To this greeting Parzival, who during this scene is several times referred to as the son of Gahmuret, replies that the last time he and Artus met, his honour had been attacked and nearly destroyed; now Artus's words give him hope that it is at least partially restored. A few lines later he claims rights (*reht*) as a comrade of Gawan; and altogether it seems for the moment as if Parzival's solitary exile has come to an end. So far as the others are concerned, this is certainly so: as the Round Table company had from the first been reluctant to accept Cundrie's denunciation of him, so now they see no further reason why he should not be fully accepted as one of them. They even promise to help in his search for 'what he still sadly lacks' (700, 18).

The duel between Gawan and Gramoflanz is now arranged for the following morning; Parzival has begged to be allowed to take Gawan's place, but has been refused. When the morning comes, however, while Gawan, who is never over-anxious to fight, is at Mass, the two impatient combatants Parzival and Gramoflanz rush on to the field and set to. By the time the main company arrive, Parzival is winning, and Gramoflanz is not sorry to terminate the fight. The duel with Gawan is once more postponed—this time to allow Gramoflanz to recuperate.

For the second time Parzival's indiscriminate lust for battle appears as slightly futile: his fight with Gramoflanz is unnecessary and achieves little. Moreover, there is an objection to it not altogether dissimilar to the objection to his fighting Gawan: for while Gramoflanz is traditionally, through Orgeluse, an enemy of Gawan (and therefore of Parzival), he is due to become a friend and close relative, for he is in love with Gawan's sister Itonje, and she with him. In fighting for Gawan, Parzival is thus fighting against Gawan's sister; and similarly Gramoflanz, in fighting for Itonje, is fighting against Itonje's brother. Nor is this distressing complex passed over in silence by the narrator (cf. 706, 15–20). Fortunately the combatants are separated in time, and little harm done. From one point of view indeed good may have resulted, for Gawan's duel with Gramoflanz has been again postponed—and will now never take place, since Artus takes advantage of the new delay to reconcile the two.

There follows the general betrothal of all the couples, and a season of Arthurian rejoicing is ushered in. Only Parzival finds

he can after all take no part—and in the closing sections of
Book XIV steals away.

What Parzival lacks is what so many others have just found,
the joy of *minne*:

> er dâhte 'sît ich minnen kan,
> wie hât diu minne an mir getân ?
> nu bin ich doch ûz minne erborn:
> wie hân ich minne alsus verlorn ? . . .'
>
> (732, 15–18)

Were there any uncertainty (*zwîvel*) in the love which unites
him and Condwiramurs, Parzival could perhaps look for solace
elsewhere; but her love makes it impossible for him to think of
other women:

> diu mich twinget minnen gir,
> stüend unser minne, mîn unt ir,
> daz scheiden dar zuo hôrte
> sô daz uns zwîvel stôrte,
> ich möht wol zanderr minne komn:
> nu hât ir minne mir benomn
> ander minne und freudebæren trôst.   (733, 9–15)

It may be noted in passing that it is not the legal nor the sacramental bond which keeps Parzival faithful, but the depth of
personal affection. And similarly the reason why he does not
return to Condwiramurs even though he can find no happiness
apart from her lies in no external, but in an inner compulsion:
he has sworn to dispense with all happiness until he has found
the Grail (cf. above, p. 62). Nor has he given up this resolve
since leaving Trevrizent; on the contrary, he again expresses
his twin desires at this point:

> sol ich nâch dem grâle ringen,
> sô muoz mich immer twingen
> ir kiuschlîcher umbevanc,
> von der ich schiet, des ist ze lanc.   (732, 19–22)

This inflexible determination to fulfil his highest potentialities, no matter what suffering is involved, is one of Parzival's most constant and positive characteristics; perhaps the

161

unverzaget mannes muot of the Prologue, it makes it impossible for him to accept defeat. But in the midst of the general rejoicing, he feels his continuing sorrow particularly acutely: 'ich pin trûrens unerlôst', he complains (733, 16), and ascribes his fate to the will of God: 'got wil mîner freude niht' (733, 8). It is as 'der freudenflühtec man' that he leaves the Round Table (733, 25): the man who, seeking a higher happiness, will not be content with that of Arthurian society.

Parzival rides off and quickly encounters his half-brother Feirefiz; both are looking for a fight, and they fall on one another without delay. This is the most difficult of all Parzival's battles and, because of their relationship, also the most unhappy; it is therefore fortunate for him that he is now at peace with God:

> der getoufte wol getrûwet gote
> sît er von Trevrizende schiet,
> der im sô herzenlîchen riet,
> er solte helfe an den gern,
> der in sorge freude kunde wern.   (741, 26–30)

The crisis comes when Parzival begins to lose: calling on Condwiramurs, he deals his opponent a mighty blow, but the sword, instead of killing Feirefiz, breaks:

> von Gaheviez daz starke swert
> mit slage ûfs heidens helme brast,
> sô daz der küene rîche gast
> mit strûche venje suochte.
> got des niht langer ruochte
> daz Parzivâl daz rê nemen
> in sîner hende solde zemen:
> daz swert er Ithêre nam,
> als sîner tumpheit dô wol zam.   (744, 10–18)

Parzival is using the very sword he took from Ither; but God saves him this time from killing a relative. The 'accident' of the breaking sword reveals, like all other accidents in *Parzival*, the hidden working of the hand of God: now that Parzival has found favour with God, he is protected from sin.

Feirefiz is now in a winning position; however, his chivalry prevents him from taking advantage of it, and in the resultant pause in the fighting, they discover each other's identity. Had Parzival killed Feirefiz, his sin would presumably have been particularly grave since they are half-brothers.

Once more Parzival's eagerness for battle has led him to fight not an enemy but a relative, and a potential friend; once more the battle has been broken off before the end; once more there is a positive issue to the affair, in that Parzival and Feirefiz become firm friends (cf. 748, 8–12). Clearly all three combats have common features, but their function is not easy to assess. They show that Parzival can outfight Gawan for all his caution, and also Gramoflanz for all his pride—but that as a fighter he is no better than Feirefiz. His recklessness, moreover, seems rather foolish by comparison with Gawan, who is always willing to do what is required of him, but never seeks trouble for its own sake. On the other hand his aspirations are unmistakably higher than those of all his opponents, and what leads him into such wild behaviour is prolonged frustration of a sort they know nothing of. Finally, God now wishes him well, and so his rashness does not result in disaster.

Before the final stages of Parzival's progress are discussed, a little will be said about Feirefiz, and about the descendants of both him and Parzival.

Feirefiz, who was born of a white, Christian father and a black, heathen mother, and who changes his own faith in the course of Book XVI, is striped black and white like the page of a book (747, 19–29). This comic touch corresponds to the role allotted him: to a considerable extent he provides light relief to offset the more serious matter in the final book. From the moment of his meeting with Parzival, the two are almost inseparable, and it is Feirefiz whom Parzival, permitted to take one person with him to Munsalvæsche, chooses as companion. But Feirefiz is the son of Gahmuret and Belakane, not of Gahmuret and Herzeloyde. While his strength, courtesy, wealth and heathen domains are fabulous, while women find him most attractive (he has won the favour of two queens even before he met his present lady Secundille, 771, 15–18), while he pays constant, if somewhat nominal, tribute to his gods, of whom Jupiter and Juno are mentioned by name (cf. 768, 29 f.) and while, like Belakane, he can demonstrate an almost Christian emotion in his tears (752, 23–30), he nevertheless remains essentially shallow, forgetting Secundille easily when he meets Repanse de Schoye (811, 4–16), and changing his religion without scruple solely so as to marry his new lady:

> Feirefîz zem priester sprach
> 'ist ez mir guot für ungemach,
> ich gloub swes ir gebietet.
> op mich ir minne mietet,
> sô leist ich gerne sîn gebot.
> bruoder, hât dîn muome got,
> an den geloube ich unt an sie
> (sô grôze nôt enpfieng ich nie):
> al mîne gote sint verkorn.   (818, 1–9)

But this superficiality, however similar to that which once proved disastrous to Parzival, is acceptable in Feirefiz. Whereas before his baptism he cannot see the Grail, after it he can (818, 20–23); moreover, Secundille's convenient death in his absence saves him and Repanse from any unpleasantness on his return (822, 18–22); and finally his conversion leads to the spreading of Christianity in the East, and indeed the famous Prester John is, according to this story, his son. Feirefiz's life is thus glorious and unproblematic; it is told with a light touch, and provides a gay counterpart to that of Parzival.

Parzival has two sons, Kardeiz and Loherangrin: they had been conceived before Parzival left Condwiramurs, and she brings them with her to see their father at the final reunion. Kardeiz is not called to the Grail: he inherits Parzival's and Condwiramur's non-Grail territories, and rules them well (803, 2–23); that ties up one loose end. Loherangrin on the other hand has been named on the Grail along with his parents.

Thus Parzival's Arthurian and Grail heritages are both accounted for at the end of the work (cf. 803, 11–13).

Precisely why Wolfram includes a résumé of Loherangrin's story in his final paragraphs is not clear: perhaps it shows nothing more than that the future will bring its own (partly inherited) problems. Loherangrin is the Grail knight whom a swan takes to marry a non-Grail queen on condition that she never inquires who he is. After some time, and the birth of several children, her curiosity overcomes her, and the swan takes Loherangrin away again (824, 1–826, 30). This story is made to depend on Parzival's by the explanation that the sorrow Anfortas suffered in waiting for a question led Grail knights to dislike questions altogether; the Grail accordingly instituted this condition (818, 24–819, 8), which incidentally is a development of the previous statement that men leave the Grail secretly (495, 1 f.). It is, however, difficult to see any more in this explanation than a whimsy of the author. But at least Wolfram is seen providing through Prester John, Kardeiz and Loherangrin the same continuity in the future of which he made such good use in the past. Many people in Brabant are stated by the narrator to know Loherangrin's story well to this day (826, 10–14), and kings of India are still called Prester John (822, 26 f.). Wolfram's narrative thus gives the impression of linking up with the whole course of history, with the whole race of mankind.

After their battle Parzival returns with Feirefiz to Artus, who arranges a full assembly of the Round Table to greet the stranger. This is only the second such assembly mentioned in the work; at the first Parzival was cursed by Cundrie, at this she arrives, begs his forgiveness and announces that a new message has appeared on the Grail:

> zuo Parzivâle sprach si dô
> 'nu wis kiusche unt dâ bî vrô.
> wol dich des hôhen teiles,
> du krône menschen heiles!
> daz epitafjum ist gelesen:

> du solt des grâles hêrre wesen.
> Condwîr âmûrs daz wîp dîn
> und dîn sun Loherangrîn
> sint beidiu mit dir dar benant . . .' (781, 11–19)

No longer is it an unknown knight who is expected, no longer is there any uncertainty as to whether, when he comes, he will prove worthy; Parzival, Condwiramurs and Loherangrin have found favour with God, and are called by name. Moreover, Parzival is now told to ask the question, told that his question will cure Anfortas:

> wær dir niht mêr sælden kunt,
> wan daz dîn wârhafter munt
> den werden unt den süezen
> mit rede nu sol grüezen:
> den künec Anfortas nu nert
> dîns mundes vrâge, diu im wert
> siufzebæren jâmer grôz:
> wâ wart an sælde ie dîn genôz? (781, 23–30)

Far from being ill-fated, Parzival is the luckiest, the most blessed of men. He has, Cundrie goes on to say, won for himself peace of soul, has waited in sorrow for bodily joy:

> du hâst der sêle ruowe erstriten
> und des lîbes freude in sorge erbiten. (782, 29 f.)

He himself, however, now sees his success, not as a reward his chivalry has earned, but as a grace granted by God to a sinner:

> dô sprach er 'frouwe, solhiu dinc
> als ir hie habt genennet,
> bin ich vor gote erkennet
> sô daz mîn sündehafter lîp,
> und hân ich kint, dar zuo mîn wîp,
> daz diu des pflihte sulen hân,
> sô hât got wol zuo mir getân . . .' (783, 4–10)

This exchange introduces us to the chief problem seen by scholars in the final sections of the work: what is the relationship between grace and free will in Parzival's story? Is there a sense in which Parzival wins the Grail in defiance of its conditions?

Does his persistence force God's hand, and so alter the appearance of providence? Or is he simply rewarded, in a thoroughly traditional way, when he has submitted completely to the divine will? These questions, to which attention has been directed above all by Gottfried Weber,[1] seem forced on the reader not only by the sequence of events in the work, but also by direct and to some extent conflicting statements of both narrator and characters. It is not, however, certain that we should expect to be able to give a definite and universally agreed answer: that Wolfram's work raises such problems does not necessarily mean that it answers them. They may possibly have to be regarded as mysteries which can be illuminated and discussed, but not finally resolved; and any proffered resolution may reflect more the preferences of the individual reader than the complexity of the problem itself.

Cundrie says Parzival has fought for and won peace of soul, using the verb *erstrîten*. Shortly afterwards, using the same verb, Parzival publicly pronounces that no one can win the Grail—unless he is called to it by God:

> Parzivâl sîn rede alsus huop an.
> en franzoys er zin allen sprach
> als Trevrizent dort vorne jach,
> daz den grâl ze keinen zîten
> niemen möht erstrîten,
> wan der von gote ist dar benant. (786, 2–7)

The narrator's statement that Parzival is here quoting Trevrizent can be corroborated, for in Book IX Trevrizent told Parzival:

> jane mac den grâl nieman bejagn,
> wan der ze himel ist sô bekant
> daz er zem grâle sî benant. (468, 12–14)

The verb here is *bejagen* and not *erstrîten*, but both imply conscious effort, and it is doubtful whether in such a (metaphorical) context there is any material difference between 'hunting' and

---

[1] *Parzival: Ringen und Vollendung* (Oberursel, 1948), p. 80 *et passim*.

'fighting'. Trevrizent has to all intents and purposes anticipated Parzival's pronouncement; both are agreed that the Grail cannot be won by anyone who is not called—and presumably that it can be won by anyone who is.

The difficulty comes in Book XVI, when Parzival visits Trevrizent a second time. Then, without any reference to the possibility of being called, Trevrizent, now using the verb *erstrîten*, states that it is most unusual for anyone to 'win' the Grail:

> ez was ie ungewonheit,
> daz den grâl ze keinen zîten
> iemen möhte erstrîten:
> ich het iuch gern dâ von genomn.
> nu ist ez anders umb iuch komn:
> sich hât gehœhet iwer gewin. (798, 24–29)

Parzival's success surprises Trevrizent, and indeed now seems to him to be contrary to Grail tradition. Moreover, he appears to think that Parzival has forced God to change the conditions on which the Grail can be won:

> Trevrizent ze Parzivâle sprach
> 'grœzer wunder selten ie geschach,
> sît ir ab got erzürnet hât
> daz sîn endelôsiu Trinitât
> iwers willen werhaft worden ist . . .' (798, 1–5)

The construction of this passage is unusual, but its import has traditionally been taken as: 'nothing was ever more miraculous than that your anger should have forced God to grant your will through his endless Trinity.'[1] The supposition here is that it was not God's will that Parzival should be called to the Grail, at least not after his initial failure, and that if he has been called,

---

[1] Heino Gehrts in '*abe erzürnen*. Das Bindewort *ob*—zwei Wolfram-Fragen', *Zeitschrift für deutsche Philologie*, vol. 79 (1960), suggests *abe erzürnen* means 'to part from God in anger'. This suggestion, which seems to me to be forced on Gehrts by his views on theology and his interpretation of Parzival's story, is even less well founded linguistically than the traditional version. One can, however, agree that too much importance should not be attached to an isolated passage of doubtful meaning.

this is because he has persisted and forced recognition of his claim. Much depends on whether this supposition is an illusion of Trevrizent's, or whether it can be substantiated.

The issue is not resolved by any categorical statement of the narrator, or of any character, about God's intentions for Parzival (though throughout one should remember that Parzival is heir to the Grail and therefore presumably in some sense predestined). In a tale of such complexity God's workings are, as Trevrizent realises, mysterious, and it may be that God intended to have his hand forced, intended that the laws he had laid down, the aspect revealed to men of his providence, should be changed by Parzival. The issue would then turn on whether the laws for attaining the Grail have in fact been changed by Parzival, or whether this is an illusion of Trevrizent's.

The most categorical statement is that of Sigune in Book v: she says that Munsalvæsche can only be found accidentally, and not by searching:

> swer die suochet flizeclîche,
> leider der envint ir niht.
> vil liute manz doch werben siht.
> ez muoz unwizzende geschehen,
> swer immer sol die burc gesehen.   (250, 26–30)

The implication of this is that those alone are called to the Grail who do not seek it; it is an implication which perfectly accords with Parzival's first visit, but not at all with his second. In this development Weber sees the source of Trevrizent's astonishment at Parzival's success: he has won the Grail in spite of its conditions, has forced God to recognise him, has thereby changed the appearance of providence; from now on election will not appear purely as a matter of grace (*unwizzende*), but can in part be achieved by conscious endeavour (*erstrîten*).

Two points may be made about this. One is that it is not absolutely certain that Trevrizent's surprise should be related to Sigune's statement; at both ends there is room for doubt. Sigune admittedly expresses herself very generally, but she may possibly be thinking primarily of the special Grail message referring to Parzival's first visit, which stipulates the chance arrival of a stranger; otherwise it is difficult to explain her encouragement of Parzival at the beginning of Book IX. Trevrizent for his part expresses himself very vaguely in Book XVI, and seems to forget that he has himself earlier said that under certain conditions the Grail can be 'won'; nor does he anywhere repeat Sigune's general statement that it must be found *unwizzende*. Moreover, it is clear in Book IX that Trevrizent (like the Grail company in Book XVI, cf. 788, 13–20) never gives up hope of Anfortas's being cured, and therefore must anticipate a new dispensation—but who is this to involve if not the only available heir ?

Even if Weber's thesis is not absolutely provable, so far as this point is concerned it is certainly very attractive. Its limitation is, I think, revealed by a second point: it accounts too little for Parzival's uniqueness. The general aspect of providence does not so much appear changed by Parzival's success, as confirmed. Trevrizent had said that only those who were called could win the Grail; and Parzival, as king, repeats this— with the consequence that the many people whom Sigune mentions as seeking the Grail (in vain) now give up. If therefore Parzival has broken the rules, he has not changed them; for most people indeed their validity is greater than before. He himself is a special case for, as he specifically says, he has inherited the Grail: 'mit sælde ich gerbet hân den grâl', (803, 13).

In conclusion then one may say that pre-destination (*erben*), free-will (*erstrîten*) and grace (*benennen*) all play a part in Parzival's success.[1] The story at different times emphasises the necessity of being the right person in the first place, the impossibility of succeeding in spite of God, and the glory of persisting no matter what the cost. Apparent conditions, and the opinion of others, are inadequate as guidance for the chosen

---

[1] See Georg Misch, 'Wolfram's Parzival. Eine Studie zur Geschichte der Autobiographie', *Deutsche Vierteljahrsschrift für Literaturwissenschaft und Geistesgeschichte*, vol. 5 (1927), p. 291.

individual; if he is right, and if he persists, there is no limit to
the wonders of God: who—as Trevrizent asks in a manner
reminiscent of Old and New Testament alike—who ever sat in
his council, or knows the extent of his power (797, 23–25)?
Those who are not chosen, however, need not waste their
efforts.

Trevrizent links up his astonishment at Parzival's success
with his revocation of a former statement. In Book IX he told
Parzival that the neutral angels might well have been pardoned
by God (471, 23–25); now he states this to have been a lie, and
pronounces them eternally damned (798, 6–22). The reason
for his lie, he seems to say, was to dissuade Parzival from
seeking the Grail (798, 24–27). Earlier scholars mostly regarded
this revocation as extraneous to the work: Wolfram, who almost
certainly published *Parzival* in instalments, gave unorthodox
information about the neutral angels and was persuaded by the
Church to revoke it. More recent scholars have tried to integrate
it into the work, to my mind with little success. I do not think
there can be any doubt that the earlier passage to which
Trevrizent refers is 471, 15–29, and not 489, 13–21 as Weber
maintains; but 471, 15–29 has the effect not of discouraging
Parzival from seeking the Grail, but of calling forth his defiant
outburst that he deserves to be appointed to it (472, 1–11); nor is
it obvious how it could have been intended to discourage him.
Bodo Mergell has suggested that the neutral angels' progress is
antithetical to Parzival's: their fate first appears hopeful (454,
24–26), then uncertain (471, 23–25), is finally resolved ad-
versely.[1] But for the antithesis to be effective the first (hopeful)
stage would need both to be more clearly distinguished from
the second and to be mentioned earlier (before God takes pity
on Parzival, 435, 12). Neither of these explanations of
Trevrizent's famous lie thus seems to me acceptable—and
reluctantly I suggest that we admit the possibility of the earlier

[1] *Der Gral in Wolframs Parzival* (reprinted from *Beiträge zur Geschichte
der deutschen Sprache und Literatur*, vol. 73, Halle, 1951), pp. 63–74. Mergell's
suggestion is sharply criticised by Hermann J. Weigand, 'Wolfram's Grail
and the Neutral Angels', *Germanic Review*, vol. 29 (1954).

scholars being right, and of it having no internal function in the work and therefore constituting a minor fault.

The remaining points can be treated in summary fashion. Book XV closes with Cundrie leading Parzival and Feirefiz away from the Round Table assembly towards Munsalvæsche, and Book XVI opens at Munsalvæsche before their arrival. Anfortas, weary of suffering, is begging to be allowed to die; but the Grail knights, hopeful that Parzival will return and ask the question successfully, keep him alive by the power of the Grail (788, 13–29). On arrival Parzival faces the Grail and bows three times in honour of the Trinity, praying that Anfortas may be cured. He then asks his uncle: 'œheim, waz wirret dier?' (795, 29), and the God of miracles restores Anfortas to health and beauty. Parzival is then acclaimed as Grail King, and Anfortas takes his place as one of his knights, fighting no longer for women, but only for the Grail: Feirefiz's attempt to persuade him to visit heathen lands fails (819, 9–820, 8).

Parzival now rides out to meet Condwiramurs, and on the way calls on Trevrizent who, as already stated, expresses great wonder at his nephew's success. Husband and wife meet appropriately just within the bounds of Terre de Salvæsche, at the very spot where Parzival's senses had been rapt away in thought of Condwiramurs by the sight of drops of blood on snow (797, 4–12). Although she, like him, has suffered much from their separation, Condwiramurs is now so happy that she cannot be cross with her husband (801, 8–14); the two are quickly bedded, and Condwiramurs's embrace rewards Parzival's long continence (802, 1–10). The love of these two is thus represented as simple, and perfect: both endure indefinitely without wavering, neither feels any resentment at the eventual reunion. Parzival's ability to endure the prolonged agony of his quest for the Grail may be considered as largely due to the support of such a love.

On the way back to Munsalvæsche, Parzival seeks out Sigune. She is found dead in her cell, and is laid in the coffin beside

Schionatulander (804, 21–805, 2). Her function in the work is not simple. Obviously she gives Parzival certain information, and calls forth certain responses from him; but is there not more to her than this? It was stated in chapter IV that her grief is reminiscent of the sorrowing women of the opening books. In the main story the women around Artus are led, with Gawan's help, not to sorrow, but to joy; and Parzival not only finds happiness for himself but also restores it to Anfortas and the whole Grail company. There thus appears, in a sense, to be a new dispensation operating in the later books of the work; only Sigune is excepted from it. She provides the one counter-figure to the main procession, and she eventually disappears. Perhaps now, so long as Parzival and Gawan set the tone, joy will be possible on earth?

On the return of Parzival, with Condwiramurs and Loheran-grin, to Munsalvæsche, there follows the Grail feast, the baptism of Feirefiz, his marriage to Repanse, and their departure. With the sketch of Loherangrin's future history, the story comes to an end. The narrator says he has told the true tale—

> wie Herzeloyden kint den grâl
> erwarp, als im daz gordent was   (827, 6 f.)

—as he received it from Kyot. And he draws a moral:

> swes lebn sich sô verendet,
> daz got niht wirt gepfendet
> der sêle durch des lîbes schulde,
> und der doch der werlde hulde
> behalten kan mit werdekeit,
> daz ist ein nütziu arbeit.   (827, 19–24)

This is, of course, like similar morals, a very flat comment on a story of great depth and complexity; and it has perhaps been made too much of by scholars. Yet it does confirm that the dual purpose of Parzival's life is to please both God and the world, and is for this reason of some value.

X

STYLE AND STRUCTURE
OF THE POEM

mîn tiutsch ist etswâ doch sô krump.[1]

Most of this book has been devoted to the subject-matter of
Parzival. Admittedly this could not be studied without some
attention to structure: to the relation for instance of Gahmuret,
Parzival and Gawan; to the interaction of the two families of
Mazadan and Titurel, and of the two societies of the Round
Table and the Grail; to the positioning of Parzival's encounter
with Trevrizent in Book IX between two long stretches in which
Gawan occupies the foreground. Nevertheless such large
structural issues have been subordinated to a consideration of
content, and detailed problems of style have been almost totally
ignored. In all this the scholarship of the last fifty years is
reflected. Towards the end of the last century positivistic
studies of stylistic problems were fashionable,[2] but the conclusions reached had little or no significance for the meaning of
the whole, and were neatly listed and put into cold storage by
Ehrismann and others. Schwietering then sketched out a
grandiose parallel between the form of medieval literary art and
that of Romanesque and Gothic architecture,[3] a parallel which
certainly related form to content, but in a way which was both
far too sweeping and far too dependent on historical abstractions to gain general acceptance—and, with the decline of
'Geistesgeschichte', his scheme has virtually been forgotten.

---

[1] *Willehalm,* 237, 11.
[2] E.g. P. T. Förster, *Zur Sprache und Poesie Wolframs von Eschenbach*
(dissertation, Leipzig, 1874); Karl Kinzel, 'Zur Charakteristik des Wolfram-
schen Stils', *Zeitschrift für deutsche Philologie,* vol 5 (1874); Gotthold
Bötticher, Über die Eigenthümlichkeiten der Sprache Wolframs', *Germania,*
Vierteljahrsschrift für deutsche Alterthumskunde, vol. 21 (1876).
[3] *Die deutsche Dichtung des Mittelalters* (Potsdam, 1932 ff).

Style and Structure of the Poem

Only in the last decade have structural studies of individual works begun to show how, in medieval German too, the study of form may be meaningfully related to the study of content—and even so most of the attempts which have appeared to date are in my opinion either misguided or trivial. Nevertheless, this latter method is I think the one which now needs developing, is the necessary and promising path by which future scholarship can progress beyond the stage of understanding of *Parzival* represented by this present book—and in introducing students briefly to past and present ideas on the style and (still more briefly) on the structure of the work, I will try to indicate in very general terms what sort of work seems to me to need doing next.

The stylistic studies of half a century ago set out to characterise such things as the vocabulary and grammar, the phraseology and imagery, the narrative technique and the metre of *Parzival* by (explicit or implicit) contrast with other works of the same period or the same genre. They looked for the peculiarities of Wolfram's style, tabulated and documented them, without asking how they interact, how they are related to the other more conventional features in his works, or what purpose they serve in the poet's overall scheme. Among the unusual features to which attention was thus drawn are the following (not all of which are of course unique to Wolfram; but their combination is widely, and probably correctly, felt to distinguish his work from that of his fellows).[1]

Wolfram's vocabulary, though small by the standards of many modern novelists, is larger than that of some of his contemporaries. While its centre is high-toned, courtly, ethical (as is theirs), he extends the fringes to include both archaic

---

[1] For further references see Ernst Martin, *Wolframs von Eschenbach Parzival und Titurel*, vol. 2, pp. lxiv-lxxiv; Samuel Singer, *Wolframs Stil und der Stoff des Parzival* (*Sitzungsberichte der kaiserlichen Akademie der Wissenschaften in Wien. Philosophisch-historische Klasse*, vol. 180, no. 4, Vienna, 1916); Gustav Ehrismann, *Geschichte der deutschen Literatur*, vol. 2, 2, 1, pp. 264–70.

heroic words, such as *recke, wîgant, marc, urliuge, gemeit* and *veige* (usually confined to heroic epics such as the *Nibelungenlied* and not permitted in the Arthurian romance), and, at the other extreme, ultra-fashionable French borrowings like *klâr* and *kurtoys*, and a spattering of actual French phrases (*fil li roy, bêâ curs*).

Wolfram's grammar is more often than not straightforward, similar to that of his contemporaries; like his vocabulary, it too, however, has its unusual and characteristic moments. For instance his syntax tends to be imprecise, to flout grammatical conventions, and to leave the reader to choose between various possible constructions. Thus he is fond of the so-called ἀπὸ κοινοῦ construction, in which a single element has to serve different functions in separate clauses; cf. *den helm* in:

> gein strîter wolde füeren
> den helm er mit den snüeren
> eben ze sehne ructe. (260, 13–15)

And he also makes use of almost every type and degree of anacoluthon (broken construction). On a simple level this is illustrated by his more than customary willingness to construe plural verbs with singular subjects:

> dâ liefen unde giengen
> manc werder man. (75, 4 f.)

And vice versa:

> dar nâch gienc dô zer tür dar în
> vier clâre juncfrouwen. (243, 20 f.)

Then there are instances of subordinate-clause word order being used in main clauses (cf. 719, 24 f.), of unmediated changes from indirect to direct speech (29, 30–30, 3), of the so-called 'nominativus pendens' being taken up in the following sentence in some case other than the nominative:

> ein ander ors, sus hœre ich sagen,
> dar ûf saz der werde. (40, 28 f.)

And this inconsequence occasionally reaches an extreme, as in the sentence:

> entwâpent wart der tôte man
> aldâ vor Nantes ûf dem plân,
> und an den lebenden geleget, (156, 21–23)

where the presumed subject of the last sentence ('the dead man's armour') is nowhere grammatically expressed.

Wolfram's phraseology is remarkable for the relative frequency with which he replaces simple direct words by periphrastic sequences often of a rather abstract nature. The most obvious instance is his oblique way of referring to people: to Parzival for instance as 'aller manne schœne ein bluomen kranz' (122, 13) or as 'des site man gein prîse maz' (145, 3); to God as 'dem elliu wunder sint bekant' (454, 8); or to Christ as:

> den man noch mâlet für daz lamp,
> und ouchz kriuze in sîne klân. (105, 22 f.)

Such circumlocutions usually only occur once each and so may not be immediately intelligible. Similarly, proper names (or personal pronouns) can be replaced as agents by abstract properties attributed to them: not *er* but *sîn ellen*, not *ir* but *iwer jugent* appear as the subjects of verbs of action (108, 25; 372, 9).

Even abstract nouns themselves often have personal properties attributed to them in a not dissimilar way: not *mit zorn* but *mit zornes gir* (48, 11), not *ir hôchvart* but *ir hôchverte vlîz* (353, 20). And there are parallel adjectival and verbal constructions: *valsches laz, freuden lam* (128, 20; 125, 14), or 'ein tjost im sterben niht erlouc' (27, 30). Abstract phrases of this kind are striking (and difficult) if used once, banal and rather like padding if repeated. Wolfram uses them with both effects. Indeed in phraseology as elsewhere, he includes both the archaic, formulistic, simple on the one hand, and the unique, abstract, involved on the other; both the flat and the dramatic—and most of the time he is just direct, interesting, middle-of-the-road. When, however, he does combine loose syntax and abstract periphrasis, he can be very obscure indeed—as in the Prologue. His

12

contemporary, Gottfried von Strassburg, was almost certainly aiming at *Parzival* when he attacked a colleague's work which needed interpreters and glosses for its understanding (*Tristan*, 4638–90), and Wolfram himself admits in *Willehalm*:

> mîn tiutsch ist etswâ doch sô krump,
> er mac mir lîhte sîn ze tump,
> den ichs niht gâhs bescheide:
> dâ sûme wir uns beide.   (*Willehalm*, 237, 11–14)

Wolfram's liking for periphrasis is not to be separated from his use of imagery: phrases like *freuden lam* are not simply a circumlocution for 'sad', but also a metaphor ('lame in joy'); compare too the reference to Parzival as 'aller manne schœne ein bluomen kranz'. Such imagery often employs terms of chivalrous warfare, as for instance when the narrator says that Gahmuret's death snapped the blade of Herzeloyde's joy:

> dô brast ir freuden klinge
> mitten ime hefte enzwei.   (103, 18 f.)

One other sphere much drawn upon is that of nature—see several of the examples already given, or for instance 'er was ein quecprunne der tugent' (613, 9).

The chief aspects of Wolfram's narrative technique[1] to have aroused comment are his 'realism', and the frequency and peculiarity of the interpolations addressed by the narrator (usually referred to by earlier scholars as 'the poet') to his audience. What is meant by Wolfram's 'realism' is probably only an extreme version of that 'realism of presentation' which C. S. Lewis regards as characteristic of medieval writers in general.[2] It consists, I think, in giving details of a scene or action in such a way as to make it unusually vivid, to make it stand out with unusual clarity from its background. Providing the scene or action is one commonly met with in everyday life

---

[1] See further Max Wehrli, 'Wolfram von Eschenbach, Erzählstil und Sinn seines *Parzival*', *Der Deutschunterricht*, vol. 6 (1954).
[2] *An Experiment in Criticism* (Cambridge, 1961), p. 57 f.

or, if not, is compared with something everyday or illustrated with detail from everyday, then the effect may be described as 'realistic'. A famous example in *Parzival* is the extended description of the starving inhabitants of Pelrapeire:

> ouch was diu jæmerlîche schar
> elliu nâch aschen var,
> oder alse valwer leim.
> mîn hêrre der grâf von Wertheim
> wær ungern soldier dâ gewesn:
> er möht ir soldes niht genesn.
>   der zadel fuogte in hungers nôt.
> sine heten kæse, vleisch noch prôt,
> si liezen zenstüren sîn,
> und smalzten ouch deheinen wîn
> mit ir munde, sô si trunken.
> die wambe in nider sunken:
> ir hüffe hôch unde mager,
> gerumphen als ein Ungers zager
> was in diu hût zuo den riben:
> der hunger het inz fleisch vertriben.
> den muosen si durch zadel dolen.
> in trouf vil wênic in die kolen.
> des twanc si ein werder man,
> der stolze künec von Brandigân:
> si arnden Clâmidês bete.
> sich vergôz dâ selten mit dem mete
> der zuber oder diu kanne:
> ein Trühendingær phanne
> mit kraphen selten dâ erschrei:
> in was der selbe dôn enzwei.   (184, 1–26)

This passage consists largely of a series of detailed statements about the inhabitants, either describing them (they were pale as ashes or as white clay; their bellies had fallen in, their hips stuck out and the flesh clung to their ribs), or contrasting them with normality (they lacked cheese, meat and bread, and did not pick their teeth or wash the wine round their mouths; no fat dripped into their fire, nor did mead spill from their glasses). Three times in twenty-six lines, the contrast with normality involves a reference to the everyday life and immediate environment of Wolfram's contemporary audience—references which may have had a special savour for those who knew all about the Count of Wertheim or the pancakes of Wassertrudingen, but whose general function is still clear to those of us who do not: they enhance the 'realism'. This is the sort of description which is not uncommon in medieval writers; Wolfram, however, often takes it to extremes, as on this occasion, and seems even to play with the technique, to use it with comic rather than purely dramatic effect. (But this is to anticipate a point which will be made below in connection with the narrator.)

The narrator is virtually omnipresent: not only do we find literally hundreds of minor traditional formulae both flatly stating ('ich sage iu wie,' 'des sît gewîs,' 'ir habt gehœret ê'), and rhetorically exhorting ('niemen sol des lachen', 584, 22, 'waz möhte in liebers sîn geschehn?' 565, 28, 'nu jehts im niht ze schanden', 445, 2); there are also more important and more individualistic interruptions. Some of these mark major divisions of the story, as when the narrator says that his main hero is now born and the father's story completed (112, 9–15), or that the story is reverting to this main hero once again after spending some time on Gawan (678, 28–30); the longest, and most affected, is the dialogue the narrator holds with his muse, 'frou aventiure', at the beginning of Book IX. Other unusual interruptions simply relate passages in the story to contemporary people, places and events, as for instance when Antikonie is compared with the Margravine of Heitstein (above, p. 80), or when the fires in the Grail castle are stated to have been larger than any ever seen 'hie ze Wildenberc' (p. 115). And a third group comprises those passages where the narrator, ostensibly speaking as though he were the author, as though he were outside not inside the work, discusses the function of this work in his life: note especially the long excursus 114, 5–116, 4 (or 116, 14) where 'Wolfram von Eschenbach' denies he is writing in the hope of pleasing a lady (for his 'real' vocation is the sword)—and the last six lines of all, where by contrast he hopes that, if he has told his story for a lady, she will thank him pleasantly.

Wolfram's celebrated humour[1] is frequently connected with his use of a narrator. For if it is true that he can create engagingly amusing episodes and characters—as particularly can be seen from Books III, VII and VIII—yet the wilful, absurd, irreverent but gentle mockery which is most peculiarly his is most frequently and characteristically found in comments of the narrator. Sometimes these take the form of mocking some convention, either by pushing it to an extreme length, as when the narrator personifies and apostrophises not Love or his Muse, but 'hêr minnen druc' (533, 1), 'Sir Pressure of Love'; or by turning it upside down, as when instead of himself swearing the truth of his story to his audience, he calls on them to swear it for him:

> . . . diz sag ouch ich
> ûf iwer ieslîches eit. (238, 8 f.)

The fantastic and metre-breaking lists of names recited by Feirefiz and Parzival as those of their vanquished opponents in sections 770 and 772 might be considered as a parallel extravagance put in the mouth of characters. Nor is it entirely dissimilar when on another occasion the narrator plays both with a common device of the epic in his day, the interpolated tribute to past or present writers of distinction, and with the interrelationship of much of the literature of the time. In first introducing his hero to the Arthurian court, the *Parzival* narrator begs Hartmann von Aue to take care of Parzival when he appears before 'Hartmann's' King Artus and 'Hartmann's' Queen Ginover—a request he follows up with a threat: if Parzival is badly treated, then Hartmann had better look out for his own heroine Enide and her mother (143, 21–144, 4)! Similarly there occurs gentle mockery of the usual Arthurian literature on the occasion of Parzival's second visit to Artus, when the snow which lies on the ground leads the narrator to

---

[1] See further Max Wehrli, 'Wolframs Humor' in *Überlieferung und Gestaltung. Festschrift für Theophil Spoerri* (Zurich, 1950).

comment that that 'May-like' king is usually associated with Whitsun festivals and fair weather:

> Artûs der meienbære man,
> swaz man ie von dem gesprach,
> zeinen pfinxten daz geschach,
> odr in des meien bluomenzît.
> waz man im süezes luftes gît!
> diz mære ist hie vast undersniten,
> ez parriert sich mit snêwes siten.　　(281, 16–22)

Elsewhere the narrator disturbs the atmosphere of compassionate solemnity he has built up—in the starvation scene when Condwiramurs is besieged, or in Trevrizent's cell where the fasting is a holy choice—by contrasting it with a supposed normality, by intruding, that is, his own supposed real life and his practical needs and attitudes. (Even if the besieged are starving) he too eats so poorly that not much is left over for the mice (184, 27–185, 11); (even if Trevrizent's fasting is holy) he would fly away were he a falcon and only offered such miserable morsels (487, 1–22). (This latter example contains a 'characteristic' extra twist: the narrator does not simply say that he would dislike such food or that a falcon would, but *if he were a falcon* he would!)

Such is the sort of detailed point which had been made about Wolfram's style by the early part of this century. From these points scholars went on directly to make generalisations and comparisons: they found more or less appropriate general terms with which to characterise his whole manner of writing, and they suggested more or less appropriate biographical or historical explanations of this manner.

At one time the most favoured generalisation was that the style was 'oral'.[1] Wolfram's syntax was loose because he was illiterate—or at the very least because he had not received a

---

[1] This belief is renewed in a manner reminiscent of long ago by Blanka Horacek, 'Ichne kan deheinen buochstap' in *Festschrift für Dietrich Kralik* (Horn, 1954).

school training in medieval Latin grammar and logic. It was close to the syntax of conversation; possibly the poet made up his tale as he went along, night by night before his audience. Such an explanation was also taken to account for the conspicuous role of the narrator, and his assumption of a close relationship with his audience. Moreover, the various affinities with the style of the heroic epic could be fitted in, for the heroic epic too was considered a native 'popular' genre, by contrast with the foreign bookish genre of the Arthurian epic—had not the ballads on which the *Nibelungenlied* depended survived orally for nearly three-quarters of a millennium amongst the German 'Volk'?

Nor was it simply Wolfram's education and impromptu delivery which could be supposed to account for his style, but also his personal character. He was undoubtedly aristocratic, idiosyncratic, even wilful; he liked to go his own way and could not be bothered with those who were too slow to follow. This independence, coupled with the deep religiosity of his nature, largely explained the difficulties in his work; he tended both to deliberate perversity and to mystical profundity.

Now it is not possible to deny that considerations of this kind may well be correct, and are certainly worth voicing. The trouble is that they can never be checked so long as the evidence on which they rely is exclusively derived from the works themselves, so long as there is no independent witness to the character, education or method of work of the author. When Ehrismann says 'Wolframs Character findet seinen zutreffenden Ausdruck in seiner Sprache',[1] he seems not to be aware that he is using a circular argument—for since virtually all we surmise about Wolfram's character is deduced from his work, how could this not confirm our deductions? My point is not that speculation of this sort is necessarily wrong, but that from a scholarly point of view it is valueless: it is unsatisfactory to investigate the relationship between two things when only one of them is known.

[1] *Geschichte der deutschen Literatur*, vol. 2, 2, 1, p. 264.

On the other hand the slightly later scholarly fashion for comparing Wolfram's style with that of other poets and seeing it as one variant in a long chain of 'mannered' literature, even if it has not so far proved very illuminating for Wolfram's particular work, is nevertheless methodologically unobjectionable. Scholars of this persuasion usually doubt that Wolfram was illiterate or that he composed impromptu, they stress that long sections of his narrative are relatively conventional, and they suggest that his deviations from convention are a deliberate literary affectation. They may agree that this affectation perhaps suited his 'oral' style and his independent character, but in general they are concerned not with his personality so much as with his place in literary tradition. Thus for instance Ehrismann summarises the research of himself and others by pointing to the introduction (from Asia) in late Classical times of a flowery, obscure, 'unclassical' style called 'Asianism' which continued into the Middle Ages, was related both to the esoteric Provençal 'trobar clus' of the twelfth and to the German 'geblümte Rede' of the thirteenth century, and never again entirely disappeared.[1] And from this point of view Wolfram's style has sometimes been described as and likened to Baroque.

It seems to me, however, that unless an intermediate stage is inserted between the detailed positivistic assertions about Wolfram's style and the large historical comparisons which are always only too readily available to anyone widely read, very little more is gained than by the evidently sterile biographical approach. For the simple fact remains that neither one nor all of the various idiosyncrasies found in Wolfram's work constitute his style as a whole. They are merely features of it, and until one has discovered how these features are used, what

---

[1] *Loc. cit.* See also Gustav Ehrismann, 'Wolframprobleme', *Germanisch-Romanische Monatsschrift*, vol. I (1909). The similarity to 'trobar clus' is denied by Hans J. Bayer, *Untersuchungen zum Sprachstil weltlicher Epen des deutschen Früh- und Hochmittelalters* (*Philologische Studien und Quellen*, vol. 10, Berlin, 1962), p. 214, a book which contains an interesting but undisciplined last chapter on Wolfram's narrator and general style.

purpose they severally and jointly serve, with what normality they are contrasted and under what conditions, one has not the slightest idea of how Wolfram's style works, of what all the bits add up to and how they function, and so one has no sufficient basis for comparison.

Moreover, one should not be too naïve about these comparisons. For even if it is true that Wolfram's 'normal' style and idiosyncrasies resemble those of X, yet a sophisticated comparison may reveal more the contrast than the similarity. This will, for instance, be so if Wolfram's idiosyncrasies function differently from those of X, if he, say, uses obscurity or humour on one sort of occasion and with one sort of effect and X uses obscurity or humour on another sort of occasion and with another effect. To this extent the functioning of Wolfram's work may be compared more profitably with the functioning of that of Y, a writer whose normal style and idiosyncrasies are completely different in themselves, but who manipulates them according to a comparable pattern.

Adequate preliminary studies on the functioning of the various stylistic elements in Wolfram's work have not yet been made[1] —the need for them offers present-day students one of their more obvious and more promising challenges. Yet I will venture one or two suggestions to show both the sort of thing I have in mind and the discipline with which one might attempt it.

To begin with a lead from someone else. Wolfgang Mohr, whose various studies show a sensitive concern for the structure and style of *Parzival*, believes that the Gawan episodes should be read (aloud) in a different tone of voice ('Tonfall') from those concerning Parzival—and suggests they would have been so read when Wolfram originally recited them. Such suggestions, Mohr admits, can no longer be proven, but he finds the distinction of tone reflected in the syntax, which in a characteristic Gawan passage is 'perhaps a little more transparent, cooler and

---

[1] The various short studies by Wolfgang Mohr and Max Wehrli, referred to at appropriate points throughout this book, show how a satisfactory start can be made.

clearer' than in a corresponding passage for Parzival.[1] Now this supposed distinction in tone is an intuitive conclusion, and derives no support from speculation about the character and quality of Wolfram's delivery, for which of course we have no evidence. But let us reverse Mohr's order of priority, and remember that, whatever may have been the case when Wolfram first invented his story, if Mohr's intuition is valid and not simply conditioned by the subject-matter, it must depend upon and reflect a primary distinction in the metre, vocabulary and syntax of the written word. Now here is a point which needs systematic investigation. Wolfram's 'normal' narrative style, which has been referred to above by contrast with certain specified idiosyncrasies, will of course itself not be homogeneous. Is there in general a distinction between the 'normal' style used for Parzival and that for Gawan ? In what does it consist ? Does it sometimes break down ? When and under what circumstances ? These are surely the sort of verifiable realities which scholars should investigate, instead of indulging in unverifiable speculation.[2]

I must admit that the 'normal' narrative style for Parzival does not seem to *me* to differ from that for Gawan. But there do occur other indisputable variations in style throughout the work, all of which need to have their nature and function investigated. For instance, in the middle of the 'realistic' description of the famine scene quoted above, p. 179, come three 'idealistic' lines (184, 19–21), explaining what caused this famine. In these we find, not vivid, everyday, but impersonal, stock phraseology— reflecting perhaps the attitudes responsible for the war. How then are these two styles contrasted elsewhere in the work ? And to what extent does this contrast illuminate the meaning ?

My next point concerns the function of the narrator and his humour, and here I want, not simply to suggest that they need investigation, but to make tentative suggestions about their

[1] 'Parzival und Gawan', *Euphorion*, vol. 52 (1958), p. 2.

[2] A beginning has been made by Blanka Horacek, 'Zur Wortstellung in Wolframs Parzival', in *Österreichische Akademie der Wissenschaften, Philosophisch-historische Klasse, Anzeiger*, Jahrgang 89 (1952), pp. 270-299.

function—or perhaps functions, for any element can of course serve several purposes. Obviously the principal functions of the narrator in *Parzival* are to tell the tale and comment on it, to offer the audience both a story and an interpretation. The audience is free to accept, reject or modify the narrator's comments and interpretation, but it cannot ignore them. They are part of the work, and they must be reacted to along with the story. Now in other works of the time, especially in Hartmann's Arthurian romances and in the *Nibelungenlied*, the comments of the narrator seem to me misleading, and I have suggested elsewhere that this need not be a weakness but may be a source of strength and enjoyment.[1] But when Wolfram's narrator calls Gawan 'ein manlîch höfsch man' (above, p. 71), or says of Parzival early in Book ix 'sîn wolte got dô ruochen' (above, p. 87), or draws a moral at the end of the story (above, p. 173), he is in my opinion making appropriate, even if inadequate, comments on his story. Yet if the public is to take the narrator's comments as a guide for their interpretation of the tale, what of the 'necessary inadequacy' of any interpretation? What are readers to do when the story suggests something which does not accord with the narrator's comments? What are they to make of the inevitable tension which must exist between the two? Of course they must interpret for themselves, draw their own conclusions—and much more remains to be done in this direction than this Introduction indicates—but some of these tensions have, I think, given occasion for and to some extent been neutralised by the narrator's humour.

For instance in *Parzival*, as in other Arthurian epics, Artus is a rather weak king, regularly persuaded by his advisers to take the easiest way out, to do what brings himself credit and others pleasure at the moment, but what has or may have unpleasant consequences in the long run. This is apparent during Parzival's first visit, when Artus yields to Keie's foolish pressure

---

[1] 'An interpretation of Hartmann's *Iwein*', *Germanic Review*, vol. 36 (1961); 'On Irony and Symbolism in the *Nibelungenlied*: Two Preliminary Notes', *German Life and Letters*, vol. 14 (1961).

to let the boy fight Ither (149, 27–150, 28)—which results in Ither's death. Any reader of this episode is likely to react critically to Artus's weakness, and this reaction could well be supported by a knowledge of similar episodes in other Arthurian romances—but in interpreting in the relevant chapters the implications of Parzival's killing of Ither and the general role of Artus, I have not elaborated on this point because I cannot see that any positive function is given to this weakness of Artus in this particular work.

Nevertheless this weakness is present, and could be disturbing. There exists a latent tension between it and the generally constructive picture of Arthurian society presented both by the narrator and by Gawan's exploits. It is perhaps out of this tension, heightened as it could be by a knowledge of other Arthurian epics, that Wolfram's joke about the 'May-like' king is born. And the effect of this joke is surely to neutralise this tension. By bringing into the open, by revealing his own consciousness of the rather fatuous role usually attributed to Artus, Wolfram's narrator implies that his story takes account of this aspect of the king, but is not dominated by it. *His* story mingles snow with sun, *his* Artus is no Utopian figure, but lives in the world of reality. (Of course a Utopian figure can either be sublime or ridiculous, whereas Wolfram's Artus, rendered innocuous by the story and the narrator's joke, is worthy, but a little dull. That is perhaps the price of harmonising the world, of releasing the tension.)

On how many other occasions the narrator's humour could be considered as neutralising a latent tension between the implications of a particular incident and its suggested interpretation and general function in the work I do not know. But presumably there is some similar point to the joke about the fasting of Trevrizent and Parzival in Book IX—for having had his laugh at them, the narrator then specifically enjoins his audience to take them seriously (above, p. 107):

> wes spotte ich der getriwen diet ?
> mîn alt unfuoge mir daz riet.   (487, 11 f.)

Anyone who might have thought Book IX a little over-serious is forced here to realise that the narrator sees how it could be thought so—but does not agree that it is!

In those other cases where literary conventions are exposed, the humour seems to derive more from a tension between matter and form, than from one between matter and interpretation. Even here, however, the effect may well be parallel, may be to make the conventions in general more acceptable, by showing that they are used self-consciously—but it would take too long to follow this up here.

The third and last stylistic element on whose functioning I propose to comment is the metre. This is one of the many stylistic features which was left out of consideration earlier in this chapter, partly because the positivists do not seem to have established very much of interest in this field—the great advance in the study of medieval German metre came with Andreas Heusler's *Deutsche Versgeschichte*[1]—partly because it has seemed fitter to leave its fuller treatment till now. Up to Ehrismann's time Wolfram's metre was widely considered rough and careless—it was noted, for instance, that he allows more 'bad' rhymes (such as *gâben: lâgen*, 17, 29 f.) than his best contemporaries. This roughness could of course be admired, as it was by Heusler—though it seems rather simple to use the statistically proven high proportion of 'masculine' rhymes in his work as evidence of his virility.[2] Great admiration was, and still is, often expressed for Wolfram's one really dramatic—or melodramatic?—effect: when he extends the four syllables of *Cundwîr âmûrs* over a whole line (283, 7), to emphasise that it is she who has rapt Parzival's thoughts away in a famous scene (above, p. 43 f.). But much more needs to be said about Wolfram's metre than this, more about how it functions both in general and from one occasion to the next.

One general statement which seems to me true is that Wolfram's metre usually supports his sense and seldom runs

---

[1] For Wolfram see especially vol. 2 (Berlin and Leipzig, 1927).
[2] See for example Edward Hartl in *Die deutsche Literatur des Mittelalters, Verfasserlexikon*, vol. 4 (Berlin, 1953), column 1089.

counter to it. Some people may think this true of all verse, but it is not—for instance Gottfried von Strassburg frequently balances metre against sense in *Tristan*, putting important words in unstressed positions and vice versa, so that a subtle ambiguity and fluidity results, and the melody is often at first more apparent than the meaning. But just as Wolfram's narrator usually makes comments which are appropriate to his story, so his metrical emphasis usually coincides with the sense: each element supports the others in what might be described as a rhetorical way, 'rhetorical' being used in the dictionary sense of 'expressed with a view to persuasive or impressive effect'.

I hope that the following three examples will all illustrate this general point, but I intend to concentrate primarily upon two specific ways in which they are to some extent contrasted. The basis of Wolfram's metre, as of that of other medieval German poets, is the roughly regular alternation of more and less strongly stressed syllables. I am going to check the two variants here, the degree of regularity of alternation and the degree of distinction in stress, in three obviously different couplets, each of which begins a paragraph and forms a complete sentence. Clearly the conclusions from so small a sample will prove nothing; they may, however, be suggestive and, more important, the method may be worth developing.

> Ist zwível hérzen náchgebúr,
> daz múoz der séle wérden súr. (i, i f.)

In the opening couplet there is strict alternation (as indicated by the accents), and the difference in weight between the stressed and the unstressed syllables is throughout maximal. (The stressed syllables are all grammatically long, are virtually all root syllables of strongly contrasting shape and sense, and are laden with emotive force; the unstressed syllables mostly contain weak e's, and are inflectional affixes, or form-words merely conveying the grammatical relationship linking the others.) The basic metrical pattern is thus emphasised as greatly as possible in this sententious couplet: regularity and maximal distinction between stress and unstress operate like a steam hammer to drive home the meaning.

Gawan's second series of adventures is introduced by a very different couplet:

eins mórgens kóm her Gáwán
geríten uf éinen grǘenen plán.   (504, 7 f.)

Here the regularity of alternation is twice broken (*Gáwán*; *ríten uf*), and the distinction in stress is not so great (the form-word *éinen* is stressed, so is the short open syllable in *geríten*; and not one of the stressed syllables is very emphatic). An incidental piece of narrative like this, then, is characterised by gentle breaks in the metrical pattern, and by a relatively small distinction between stress and unstress; the metre is as unobtrusive as the sense.

Compare lastly the couplet which introduces Cundrie's announcement of Parzival's final election as Grail King to the Round Table:

si stúont mit zühten únde sprách
des mán für hóhiu mǽre jách.   (780, 29 f.)

Here there is once again absolutely regular alternation of stress and unstress, but the distinction between the two is not very great. The effect of the regularity is I think to suggest a certain solemnity, the effect of the unemphatic stresses to indicate that the meaning of this sentence is not very important (it just points to the ones that follow).

There are of course other factors besides those mentioned which determine the metrical effect of the couplets quoted—for instance the relationship of syntax to metrical line. Further, the factors I have mentioned can be analysed with more subtlety and at greater length. And, as already mentioned, many more instances need to be taken into account before generalisations about the function of the metre in *Parzival* can be accepted. What I wish to suggest nevertheless is that this function does need investigating, and that such investigation can be both methodical and meaningful.

The functioning of stylistic units, as discussed here, can be considered as a question of structure—to which these last few paragraphs are devoted.[1] The structure (composition or design) of *Parzival* did not interest scholars very much until recently, and as stated above, recent studies of it do not seem to me very satisfactory. Admittedly a number of interesting observations have been made, but the underlying principles are so seldom understood that no generally agreed progress has been possible. Some scholars have tried to reveal numerical patterns consciously created by the author ('Zahlenkomposition'); the weakness here is that the patterns found usually both depend on arbitrary decisions of the particular scholar as to where the divisions fall (and so were not indubitably intended by the poet) and also have very little significance for the meaning of the finished work.[2] Other scholars have seen the structure of *Parzival* as exemplifying either some medieval artistic style, such as 'Gothic',[3] or some medieval pattern of thought, such as the various stages in the salvation of man.[4] The weakness here is the tendency to consider the style or pattern of thought as primary, the individual work as secondary. No matter how appropriate

[1] See further Jean Fourquet, 'La structure du Parzival', *Colloques internationaux du centre national de la recherche scientifique*, vol. 3, *Les romans du Graal* (Paris, 1956). Of the two recent theses on the structure of *Parzival*, Theo Velten, *Der 'Plan' von Wolframs Parzival* (Heidelberg, 1956), endeavours to show that the work was conceived in stages, and mistakenly assumes that if it was it would be wrong to treat the finished product as a unified whole; while Werner Jäger, *Strukturprobleme im 'Parzival' Wolframs von Eschenbach* (Tübingen, 1959), carefully investigates how various scenes in Book III and elsewhere are built up, but spoils the investigation by an *a priori* attachment to the strange concept of *Formgradualismus*.

[2] See for example Hans Eggers, 'Strukturprobleme mittelalterlicher Epik, dargestellt am Parzival Wolframs von Eschenbach', *Euphorion*, vol. 47 (1953).

[3] See Bodo Mergell, *Der Gral in Wolframs Parzival* (Halle, 1952; reprinted from *Beiträge zur Geschichte der deutschen Sprache und Literatur*, vols. 73 and 74).

[4] See Walter Johannes Schröder, *Der dichterische Plan des Parzivalromans* (Halle, 1953; reprinted from *Beiträge zur Geschichte der deutschen Sprache und Literatur*, vol. 74).

to the times a theory about style or thought is, it can never do more than illuminate particular aspects of a given work of art.

What has so seldom been realised, at least in practice, is that it is only through its structure that a work is unique. Virtually every unit which one can pick out for analysis—Arthurian society, God, heathendom, the Grail, Parzival, the interpretation of the narrator, the concept of sin or love, the short rhyming couplet, the word *helfe*, and all the others—these units are found elsewhere too. But even if there is some similarity, they do not 'mean' just the same anywhere else—for the simple reason that nowhere but in *Parzival* are they arranged in the same pattern. Let me take one final example.

So long as scholars were not much concerned with structure they showed little interest in Gawan's role in Wolfram's work. Those interested in 'Quellengeschichte' assembled such facts about him as were common to various stories in which he figured, and speculated about the original conception from which all were supposed to be derived. Those interested in 'Geistesgeschichte' concentrated on the main hero, Parzival, who was clearly a more profound thinker than Gawan and could be considered without reference to his friend. But whatever scholars may say, it is in practice difficult for a reader not to wonder why Parzival's adventures alternate with Gawan's, and certain scholars concerned with structure have in fact recently taken this question seriously. Unfortunately, however, there has been a tendency to go too far, to make extreme, impressionistic statements rather than balanced, disciplined analyses. Noting that most of the time only one or other hero is on the stage, and that when they fight one another at the end of the work they hyperbolically regret that each has been fighting himself, both W. J. Schröder and Peter Wapnewski have decided that Parzival and Gawan are really only one person! And for Wapnewski at least, Feirefiz too is but another aspect of Parzival.[1]

---

[1] See W. J. Schröder, *op. cit.* pp. 30–3; and Peter Wapnewski, *Wolframs Parzival, Studien zur Religiosität und Form* (Heidelberg, 1955), pp. 123–39.

But to claim that these three are identical is surely as arbitrary as not to notice that they are closely related. It is just as bad to ignore the distinctions between the various elements in a work of art, as to ignore their interrelationship. One wonders when a majority of scholars will realise with Wolfgang Mohr that the work is the ultimate reality, and not the generalisations they make about it.[1]

All criticism distorts. It is perhaps possible to react to the complex pattern of *Parzival* in its entirety, but it is not possible to think adequately about this pattern. Any abstractions made by thought, no matter in what terms they are expressed, no matter how carefully their limitations are emphasised, must direct attention at certain features or aspects of the work at the expense of others. But surely we can be aware of this? Surely we can guard against idolising our own constructs? Surely we can aim at seeing more each time we read a work, and seeing what we do see in its right proportion—even if this means repeatedly modifying or abandoning previously held positions? If not, should we study literature at all?

To conclude, then. I think that new progress will be made in the investigation of *Parzival* when interpretations are accepted in any terms which illuminate the work (and not just in 'authentic' medieval ones), when attention is concentrated on form and function (and not just on content and thought), when precise and verifiable statements about the work replace impressionistic generalisations, and, lastly, when it is fully realised that an interpretation is at best only a partial illumination from a particular point of view and needs to be put aside almost as soon as made—to leave room for its successor.

[1] See 'Parzival und Gawan', *Euphorion*, vol. 52 (1958), p. 16.

A GUIDE TO FURTHER READING

A. REFERENCE WORKS

(1) Gustav Ehrismann, *Geschichte der deutschen Literatur*, Part 2, Section 2, 1st Half, pp. 212–70 (Munich, 1927).

(2) *Die deutsche Literatur des Mittelalters, Verfasserlexikon*, vol. 4, edited by Karl Langosch (Berlin, 1953). (The article on Wolfram is by Eduard Hartl.)

(3) Helmut de Boor, *Geschichte der deutschen Literatur*, vol. 2, *Die höfische Literatur*, pp. 90–114 (Munich, 1953).

(4) W. T. H. Jackson, *The Literature of the Middle Ages* (New York, 1960).

(5) M. O'C. Walshe, *Medieval German Literature* (London, 1962).

B. SELECTED BOOKS

(1) Margaret Fitzgerald Richey, *Gahmuret Anschevin* (Oxford, 1923).

(2) Julius Schwietering, *Die deutsche Dichtung des Mittelalters* (Potsdam, 1932 ff.).

(3) Georg Keferstein, *Parzivals ethischer Weg* (Weimar, 1937).

(4) Benedikt Mockenhaupt, *Die Frömmigkeit im Parzival Wolframs von Eschenbach* (Bonn, 1942).

(5) Gottfried Weber, *Parzival: Ringen und Vollendung* (Oberursel, 1948).

(6) Bodo Mergell, *Der Gral in Wolframs Parzival* (Halle, 1942) (reprinted from *Beiträge zur Geschichte der deutschen Sprache und Literatur*, vols. 73 and 74).

(7) Walter Johannes Schröder, *Der Ritter zwischen Welt und Gott* (Weimar, 1952).

(8) Peter Wapnewski, *Wolframs Parzival: Studien zur Religiosität und Form* (Heidelberg, 1955).

(9) Ralph Lowet, *Wolframs von Eschenbach Parzival im Wandel der Zeiten* (Munich, 1955).

(10) Margaret Fitzgerald Richey, *Studies of Wolfram von Eschenbach* (Edinburgh and London, 1957).

(11) Hans-Joachim Koppitz, *Wolframs Religiosität* (Bonn, 1959) (a published thesis with extensive bibliography).

C. ARTICLES REVIEWING THE LITERATURE ON WOLFRAM

(1) Hans Eggers, 'Wolframforschung in der Krise?', *Wirkendes Wort*, vol. 4 (1953–4).

(2) Bodo Mergell, 'Wolfram und der Gral in neuem Licht', *Euphorion*, vol. 47 (1953).

A Guide to Further Reading

(3) Hugo Kuhn, 'Parzival. Ein Versuch über Mythos, Glaube und Dichtung im Mittelalter', *Deutsche Vierteljahrsschrift für Literaturwissenshaft und Geistesgeschichte*, vol. 30 (1956; reprinted in H. Kuhn, *Dichtung und Welt im Mittelalter*, Stuttgart, 1959).

(4) Otto Springer, 'Wolfram's Parzival' in *Arthurian Literature in the Middle Ages*, edited by R. S. Loomis (Oxford, 1959).

D. ANNUAL BIBLIOGRAPHIES INCLUDING 'PARZIVAL' STUDIES

(1) *The Year's Work in Modern Language Studies* (Cambridge, 1931 ff.).

(2) 'Bibliography of Critical Arthurian Literature', *Modern Language Quarterly* (1940 ff.).

(3) *Bulletin bibliographique de la Société Internationale Arthurienne* (Paris, 1949 ff.).

(4) *PMLA* (*Publications of the Modern Language Association of America*: international bibliography 1957 ff.)

(5) *Germanistik, Internationales Referatenorgan mit bibliographischen Hinweisen* (Tübingen, 1960 ff.).

E. EDITIONS AND TRANSLATIONS

(1) Edited by Karl Lachmann, 7th edition revised by Eduard Hartl (Berlin, 1952). Quotations in this book are from the 5th edition as reprinted Hamburg, 1947.

(2) Edited by Albert Leitzmann, 7th edition being revised by Wilhelm Deinert (Tübingen, 1961 ff.).

(3) Edited with separate commentary by Ernst Martin (Halle, 1900–3).

(4) Edited with footnotes by Karl Bartsch, 4th edition revised by Marta Marti (Leipzig, 1927–9).

(5) Translated into modern German by Wilhelm Stapel (Heidelberg, 1937; reprinted Munich, 1955).

(6) Translated into modern German by Friedrich Knorr and Reinhard Fink (Jena, 1940).

(7) Translated into English by H. M. Mustard and C. E. Passage (Vintage Books, New York, 1961).

F. WORD INDEX

Alfred Senn and Winfred Lehmann, *Word-Index to Wolfram's Parzival* (University of Wisconsin, 1938). Republished in *Collected Indexes to the works of Wolfram von Eschenbach*, edited by R-M. S. Heffner (University of Wisconsin, 1961).

INDEX

The use of bold type denotes a main entry

Index

Index

Mohr, W., 35 n., 66 n., 74 n., 141 n., 148, 185 f., 194
moral of *Parzival*, 173
Müller, G., 151
Munsalvæsche, 115
see also Grail

narrative technique of *Parzival*, 178, 185 f.
narrator, **xvi**, 7, 14, 16, 40 f., 87, 106 f., 125, 133, 139, 147, 152, 167, 169, 173, **180–2**, **186–9**
neutral angels, 113 f., 171
Nibelungenlied, xvi, 176, 183, 187
Norman, F., 2 n.

Obie, 74–9, 132
Obilot, 76–9
oral style of *Parzival*, 182 f.
orden, 152–6
Orgeluse, 57, 76, 117, **130–9**
original sin, 46 f., 49, 57, 61 f., 97 f., 102
Orilus, 34, 38, 43, 50

Panzer, F., 7 n., 9 n.
Parzival
  absolution, 111
  atonement, 58, 107 f., 110 f.
  beauty, 32, 59 f.
  chivalry, early lack of, 7 f., 31–7
  compared with Gahmuret, xi f., 8, 22, 33, 39 f.
  compared with Gawan, xi, 66, 72, 77 f., 128, 130, 134, 139–42, **146–8**, 159, 163
  compassion, 49, 51, 54, 56, 60
  Condwiramurs, marriage to, 38–44, 52, 55, 142, 161, 172
  —, reminded of by blood on snow, 43 f., 172
  —, reunion with, 172
  contrition, 89, 92, 94 f., 99, 105–9
  Cundrie's denunciation, 46, 58–60, 63
  Feirefiz, fight with, 125, 162 f.
  Gawan, fight with, 158 f.
  God, conception of, 31, 47 f., 62, 72, 90, 92, 97, 100, 108
  —, reliance on guidance of, 53, 93 f.
  God's pity for, 87 f., 162

Parzival—(*cont.*)
  'Gotteshass', 5, 61 f., 72, 90, 92 f., 95, 98 f.
  Grail, desire to win, 62 f., 102, 110, 161 f.
  —, first visit to, 53–8
  —, second visit to, 165 f., 172
  Grail horse, riding of, 93, 103, 147
  Grail knight, fight with, 89
  Gramoflanz, fight with, 65, 160
  Gurnemanz, visit to, 36 f.
  heritage, see maternal, paternal
  Ither, killing of, 34 f., 52, 103
  joylessness, 64–6, 87 f., 111, 160–2, 166
  knighthood, urge towards, 31 f., 34–6, 48 f.
  knights, mistaken for God, 31
  marriage, see Condwiramurs
  maternal heritage, 8, 22, **46**, **53**, 59, 63, 93, 170
  minne, 37–44, 142, 161, 172
  mother's death, responsibility for, 48 f., 105 f.
  name, 47, 49 f.
  Orgeluse, lack of interest in, 141 f.
  paternal heritage, 7 f., **22** f., 36 f., 45, 59, 63, 159
  pride, 92, 94, 102 f., 108
  question, failure to ask, 52–4
  red knight, appearance as, 65
  religious education, 37, 47 f., 89–102
  Round Table, admission to, 45, 159 f.
  Schastel Marveile, lack of interest in, 141 f.
  selfishness, 49
  sense of shame, 61, 108, 159
  sinfulness, 47, 49, 52–63, 94, 103–9
  society, withdrawal from, 60, 65 f., 161 f.
  swords, 53 f., 162
  tumpheit, 29 f., 32, 35–7, 47, 52, 103
  Trevrizent, fasting with, 106 f.
  vocation, dual, 24, **29** f., 46 f., 66, 148, 164 f., 173
  zuht, 33–6, 51, 55–7
phraseology of *Parzival*, 177 f.
Pietà, 50

200

Index

Index